A Handbook for

Constructive Living

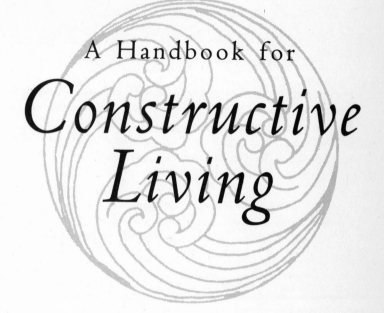

A Handbook for
Constructive Living

David K. Reynolds, Ph.D.

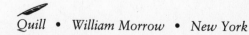

Quill • *William Morrow* • *New York*

It is the policy of William Morrow and Company, Inc., and its imprints and affiliates, recognizing the importance of preserving what has been written, to print the books we publish on acid-free paper, and we exert our best efforts to that end.

LIBRARY OF CONGRESS CATALOGING-IN-PUBLICATION DATA

Reynolds, David K.
    A handbook for Constructive Living / David K. Reynolds.—1st ed.
      p.   cm.
    Includes bibliographical references.
    ISBN 0-688-15130-2
    1. Morita psychotherapy.   2. Naikan psychotherapy.   3. Conduct of life.   I. Title.
    RC489.M65R438   1995
    158'.1—dc20   95-2360
                                                               CIP

Printed in the United States of America

First Quill Edition

3   4   5   6   7   8   9   10

BOOK DESIGN BY CYNTHIA DUNNE

To the readers who buy these books and then kindly loan me your eyes and time and thoughts while reading about Constructive Living. I am in your debt.

Preface

THIS IS NOT the authoritative single reference work on Constructive Living. Constructive Living doesn't fit in any single book or any series of books. Your life doesn't fit in a photograph or a videotape. Images are deceptive.

The way to find out about Constructive Living is to do the assignments and exercises attentively. You will encounter the depth and breadth of this practical orientation to life. You will see yourself with your possibilities and limitations from a new, and changing, perspective. You will earn this achievement through your own effort, or you won't get it at all.

Perhaps you have already learned the lesson that nothing works for you . . . except you. It is also true that everything has been working for you right along, but you may not have noticed it. I'm not interested in writing just another book about another life philosophy. I write about the way reality operates. Perhaps you expect me to insert here "—or so it seems to me." Of course. And not quite. Check out Constructive Living with your own experience. Don't believe a word in this book without verification from your familiarity with life. If you lack years or life experience to make a judgment about aspects of this lifeway, give yourself some time. But don't wait too long.

I would like you to try a little experiment. In this book you may read statements that sound a bit strange to you at first. It doesn't matter whether you believe what I write or accept it as truth. What does matter is that you consider the possibility that I'm not completely out of my mind and that my mind works pretty much as yours does. I don't think I write anything either foolish or enlightened. I write about how our minds work and how reality works; just ordinary, everyday experience. Please consider what you read here in the light of your own experience and don't dismiss it immediately on the basis of what you have read or been taught somewhere else. You might gain some useful insights and a new perspective on how your mind functions.

The Opportunity for Real Success

There are a lot of pop self-help psychology books in our bookstores. Readers of such books want tips, tricks, special knowledge that will make pain avoidable and life a series of fulfilling highs. The bottom line, however, is that no one lives on a perpetual high and everyone has to live through some pain. Our time is better spent getting done what is important for us to do in life than staying on our guard to bypass suffering. Playing life by the tactics in pop-psychology books can actually distract us from more important purposes and goals.

I am not writing of spartan endurance here. In these pages you will find the strategy that will pay off in greatest life satisfaction. That strategy does not involve minimal misery. It involves maximal accomplishment. Again, don't get me wrong. I'm not suggesting that accumulating money or power or fame or such superficial accomplishments are worth the sacrifice of our lives. I am asserting that when major life goals are built around keeping emotional distress at a minimum and feeling good or confident or joyful or loved or any other delightful mental state, then the real-life payoff won't meet expectations in the long run. Disappointment results, and dissatisfaction.

On the other hand, when we set ourselves behavioral objectives, and do something to achieve them, we run a better chance of both accomplishing our aspirations and also (as a sort of side effect) of keeping unnecessary misery to acceptable limits.

Nevertheless we sometimes feel insecure. The human need for security these days may manifest itself in sleepless nights over the decision to invest in treasury notes or gold, in thoughtful voting for elected governmental representatives, in neighborliness and concern for the institution of marriage and the proper use of cosmetics. What will happen to me tomorrow? What will happen to me in old age?

How can I increase the likelihood that I will be safe and prosperous and well and comfortable and cherished? Of course there are no guarantees, whatever our course of action. But every culture is designed to increase the odds of attaining future goals for at least some culture members.

We live in a time and culture with its own characteristic forms of insecurity. When the basics of food, water, and air become dangerous with the potential to kill, we become insecure. Understandably. There can be no perpetual high. However, there can be reasonable living and a flexible, responsive disposition toward life. Constructive Living offers such a possibility.

Just as we now recognize that physical health is a matter of lifestyle (smoking, dieting, exercise, etc.) and not merely a matter of what goes on in a doctor's office, so mental health is not something one achieves merely through psychotherapy. Mental health depends on how one lives every day. Unfortunately in some psychotherapists' offices the clients are hearing worn and outmoded advice about how to live constructively.

Constructive Living developed fundamentally from the thought of Masatake (or Shoma) Morita (1874–1938) and Ishin Yoshimoto (1916–1988). One of the goals of Constructive Living is to shake the foundations of clinical psychology and psychiatry in the West. This goal is accomplished by challenging the assumptions and models that underlie traditional Western psychotherapies. The assumptions we seriously question include the following: feelings need to be and can be repaired, expressing feelings "gets them out" somehow, unfelt feelings exist, "getting in touch with" hidden feelings is possible and useful, professional training confers the ability to understand a client's thoughts and feelings better than the client does, a brief weekly session has more impact on a client's life than the rest of the week, improper parenting is the primary cause of client difficulties, neurosis and alcoholism and obesity are diseases, self-esteem and self-confidence are necessary and useful for a constructive lifestyle, shyness is a disorder, clients can be debilitated by anxiety and other feelings, anyone knows why anyone does anything. Watch any daytime talk show on television and you will see that the above assumptions have trickled down into popular culture. They are taken-for-granted truths.

And they are wrong. Simply wrong. Maybe nobody told you that before. I'm telling you now.

Letters from CL Readers

Check out the contents of this book, evaluate it in terms of your own experience, and you will understand why we get thousands of letters like the following:

My husband and I are reading *Playing Ball on Running Water* for the second time. We are convinced that the Morita lifeway is *the* way to go about living. . . . I can readily recognize the benefits of doing what needs to be done since I spent so long not doing it.   K.W.

I recently read your book. I truly believe that Morita therapy is a pragmatic approach to helping people achieve what they want in their lives. Thank you.   P.G.

I have read *Playing Ball on Running Water* with great interest and find in many ways my counseling practice incorporates the ideas of Morita therapy you outline.   F.H.

I bought your book through a book club. I have been in therapy for about three years. . . . I have made more progress on the whole in the last month than in the prior years. . . . Thank you for this book. . . . This therapy may be particularly appropriate for the times we confront today.   A.N.

I was introduced to David Reynolds's Morita therapy in 1986 through his book *Playing Ball on Running Water*. The book helped me a great deal since then to follow through on making significant personal changes in my life. . . . My research indicates that many of the ideas and techniques used in Morita therapy's Western adaptation might be very helpful to my clients.   K.D.

I find all this information very useful to my personal life and in my job. Thanks again.   M.D.

Your article on Morita therapy has greatly inspired me.   I.C.

I am intrigued and interested in Morita therapy . . . it appears the perfect answer for me. . . . Taking this step to write for more [information] is in itself doing what needs to be done.   N.H.

Please send more information about this new therapy (actually an old philosophy). It seems these days people are a lot more willing to talk about their problems than do anything about them.   S.J.

We are a church with a little more than eight thousand members. . . . I have just read about your type of treatment and am intrigued. It fits my thinking better than most anything I have heard about in the field.   H.R.

A friend recently gave me an issue of *Cosmopolitan* magazine containing the article "Getting It Together, Far-East Style," and I have not been so affected by anything in a very long time. I have never heard of Morita therapy before now—though I have been in and out of therapy since my twenties (and I am now fifty-five). I have suffered (and that's a very descriptive word) from depression for most of my life. . . . I have tried nearly everything—self-help books, psychologists, psychiatrists, group therapy, etc.—for help. Morita therapy is the most direct, honest, simple and intelligent approach to helping people that I could have ever imagined. It's wonderful. . . . I want to know more, more, more! Morita has stirred in me the most enthusiasm I have experienced over anything in my life.   J.R.

I'm intrigued by your approach . . . the first that seems possibly useful to me.   R.W.

I work for the public schools and am interested in its application to the school-age population.   D.W.

I have just read the article in *Cosmopolitan,* and it sounds like just what I need. My life is a shambles right now, and I've got to do something to change it. . . . At least I've roused myself out of my inertia to the point of writing you. But I need further help.   S.C.

Constructive Living sounds like exactly what I've been looking for.   M.K.

After reading the article I was moved to write this letter. . . . I, too, am tired of trying to dig up old feelings which must be the root of my problems. I would definitely be interested in the active approach. D.M.

After seventeen years in the mental health field I am thrilled to find there is a name for the type of therapy I have come to believe in over the years. V.E.

I'm twenty-four years old and my feelings *rule* my life. I'm sick of it!! I understand fully what your therapy is about. . . . It sounds wonderful and *true*! L.M.

I received more insight in that brief article than five years of therapy. R.J.

I read the article, used the information, and *it works*! I'm telling my friends about it. V.C.

This is it! This is *life*! I photocopied the article and passed it out to all my staff. P.W.

I'm so excited! I got up this morning, made a list of things to do, and did everything on it! I want to learn more. S.A.

I've been interested in metaphysical/religious stuff for fifteen years. . . . This sounds *practical*. J.H.

I've been in therapy—why didn't I know of this before? V.F.

In conventional, Western, psychological terms, I have experienced lots of "depression" and lots of "anxiety" ever since I was very little. I can hardly remember a time when I didn't struggle with these in one way or another. Virtually every therapy I can think of has taken the position that these conditions can be "cured." My experience does not bear this out. With such an experience, the principles of Morita's therapy and Yoshimoto's Naikan come as a breath of fresh air. They have validity not just because they make sense (which they do) but because they work in my own life. I still get depressed from time to time and I still get very anxious from time to time. But I find it liberating to remind myself (or to be reminded by you) that I don't need to "fix" these feelings; I don't need to indulge them; I don't need to apologize for them; and I don't need to understand them. I just need to do what needs to be done. N.Y.

For Mental Health Professionals

For mental health professionals I offer some special advice: There are at least two ways you can dismiss what you are about to read. You may actually *need* techniques to dismiss this information, because it may be disturbing, challenging your assumptions and perhaps your professional practice and long investment in training or treatment. One way to dismiss these words is to consider Constructive Living merely an Oriental psychotherapy that probably operates just fine in Japan and must be considered in cultural context—that is, the context in which it originated. The second way to dismiss it is to see Constructive Living as merely an Oriental version of behavior therapy or cognitive behavior modification or Gestalt therapy or some such existing Western therapy.

In my opinion if you take either of these routes of dismissal, you will be doing yourself a grave disfavor. You will be missing the chance to make your life and your professional practice more congruent, more realistic, and more helpful to your clients. Please don't forget that Sony televisions and Toyota automobiles work quite well in the West.

I recommend that you try the Constructive Living exercises on yourself before assigning them to your clients. You will have a better understanding of the benefits and limitations of this method. It's possible to use Constructive Living techniques piecemeal in your practice, but there is the possibility of misusing them if you haven't grasped the lifeway from which they spring. Formal CL training is helpful.

What you have here is (at last!) a brand-new paradigm for investigating drug abuse and crime and violence and phobias and obsessions and homelessness and the whole gamut of human problems. We are no longer limited to simpleminded economic or psychoanalytic or political models. Take a look at the Constructive Living approach for a breath of fresh air and a clear perspective that is understandable to professional and layperson alike.

For the New Age Reader

For those readers who waltz on the fringes of psycho-healing, you might be interested to know that in this book we *won't* explore your biomagnetic, crystal-centered past life, thus producing ultimate organic enlightenment, emancipation, liberation, and awakening to your oneness. You *won't* find here an approach to your inner child self, inner wisdom, awareness of your intentionality, self-empowerment, balanced wholeness and transformative sacred space, psychic harmony, and release of blocked mystical energy that will permit self-mastery, wellness, whole consciousness, effortless joy, and illumination of the beingness within, thus channeling an affirmation of the cleansing path of profound peace. If you are enamored of such satiny words, you may find this book gritty going.

Not Just Talk

Words—how fond we are of them! How we wish they could save us! Occasionally in this book I'll play word games with you. Perhaps some of you want words, more or better words that will give you peace, make your life richer, make your work with others better. We'll see. When your crystals are all worn out, let's talk about the real world. The capacity of people to hear and read about reality shouldn't amaze me, but it does. People kindly read books about Constructive Living and attend lectures about Constructive Living because of their eagerness for straight information about the way things are. Even when the information is presented in my inexact, repetitious, irritating style, people read and listen. Constructive Living seems to fill a vacuum. I don't sell dreams; I sell reality. Why, then, do people wish to buy? It's free for the noticing.

Here is the natural way to mental health. When the outside temperature is hot, you are hot; when it is cold, you are cold. You will find little that suggests interference with the natural functioning of the mind in the pages that follow. Why do you need to fix that which isn't broken? And what can I tell you that's not already in the Constructive Living books?

Constructive Living (CL) is an interpretation and extension of ideas found in two Japanese therapies, Morita and Naikan. I have been studying these therapies since the 1960s. I spend at least a few months in Japan each year and lecture to Japanese in Japanese about Japanese psychotherapies. I have lived there in temples and homes and inns and hotels, in cities and villages and spas and aboard ships, and one night on the top of Mount Fuji. My doctorate is in anthropology (the dissertation was on Morita psychotherapy), but my colleagues and research and writing have been primarily in the fields of psychology and psychiatry. I taught at the UCLA School of Public Health, the USC School of Medicine, the University of Houston, and elsewhere before devoting full time to Constructive Living. In 1988 the World Health Organization sent me to China to train psychiatrists there in Constructive Living. There are more than one hundred CL instructors in seven countries, and seventeen books on the subject with well over a hundred thousand readers in the East and in the West.

I don't care whether people remember Constructive Living as an interesting philosophy, or remember it at all. I want you to assay living it, thoughtfully.

When you get tired of juggling words, come to CL.

Acknowledgments

I WISH TO thank the Mental Health Okamoto Memorial Foundation for support during my research in Japan over many years. Will Schwalbe of William Morrow and Company has been an exemplary editor, encouraging without pushing, grasping the importance of Constructive Living. Because Lynn answers phones, handles correspondence, and runs an efficient office while I'm at home or away, there is time for me to study and write. Finally, my CL colleagues provide inspiration and materials for my writing. Who ever did anything on his or her own?

Contents

PREFACE .... *vii*

ACKNOWLEDGMENTS .... *xvii*

AN INTRODUCTION TO CONSTRUCTIVE LIVING

First Things *3*

The Action Aspect of Constructive Living *9*

The Reciprocity Aspect of Constructive Living *35*

CONSTRUCTIVE LIVING THEORY

Action and Reflection *51*

Misconceptions *56*

Beginnings *74*

Acceptance *76*

Feelings Observed *79*

Appraised Value *86*

Making Sense of Reality *91*

The Extension of Morita's Thought *94*

Psychotherapy *99*

Leveling *109*

Shink Shock *111*

Constructive Action *119*

Constructive Living Observations *123*

Keeping Pace *125*

Wanting, Wanted, Wanton 126
Everyday Wonders 128
Comments from Constructive Living 130
Simplification 132
Inadequacies of Words 134

CONSTRUCTIVE LIVING ARTS
Constructive Living Maxims 139
Constructive Living Poetry 143
Constructive Living Tales 148
Constructive Living Koans 166
If I Were the Devil 172
The Bird Feeders 174

CONSTRUCTIVE LIVING PRACTICE
Life's Predicaments 179
Assignments 206
Remote World 219
The Practice of Constructive Living 221
Constructive Living Communications 232
Taking In Life 242
Quality Time 245
Principles of Constructive Living—
    An Examination 251
A Brief History of Constructive Living 262

CONCLUSION
Endings 271

APPENDIX: INTENSIVE NAIKAN GUIDANCE 273
BIBLIOGRAPHY 281
CONTACT INFORMATION 285

INDEX 287

If I insist that my work be rewarding, that it mustn't be tedious or monotonous, I'm in trouble. . . . It's ridiculous to demand that work always be pleasurable, because work is not necessarily pleasing; sometimes it is, sometimes it isn't. If we're detached and simply pick up the job we have to do and go ahead and do it, it's usually fairly satisfying. Even jobs that are repugnant or dull or tedious tend to be quite satisfying, once we get right down to doing them. . . . This happens when we just do what we have to do.
— THOMAS MERTON (quoted in *Inc.,* July 1992, p. 11)

A Handbook for

Constructive Living

—

*An
Introduction to
Constructive
Living*

—

First Things

I's ABOUT TIME for a sensible, practical approach to mental health, an approach that is not childishly magical with unbelievable promises, yet not ascetic or dryly academic either. I think we are ready for an approach to living sensibly that allows us to stand on our own two feet without depending on expensive professionals with arcane skills.

We are ready to taste the ripened fruits of life. It's important to realize that it takes time and effort to ripen the fruits of life. A worthwhile life doesn't fly in on fairy wings with a magic wand to produce a fantastic prize. I think you know that truth already. So if you are ready to consider an investment of some exertion and perseverance in order to achieve a satisfying life, you might want to give Constructive Living (CL) a try.

In this book you will find a wide range of life situations and problems along with realistic Constructive Living advice and information. Whenever a problem involves the possibility of illness, including mental illness, we recommend you consult with a physician or other health professional. Constructive Living is not psychotherapy. It is simply sound, practical advice about daily living.

What you will read in the pages below may sound outrageous at first, but check these ideas and recommendations against your own experience; no faith or belief or trust is necessary. You might discover that CL makes good common sense after you have given this lifeway some thought. What may sound radical at first—for example statements such as there is no need to fix feelings, cure shyness, fight fear, or that there is no need to generate self-esteem or self-confidence—

may turn out to be perfectly down-to-earth. For instance haven't you found that the feeling of confidence came *after* you were successful at a task or a job and not before? Then why are so many current approaches to life and therapy aiming to produce confidence *first* so that the clients can succeed at something? They have it backward. We all start with doubts and effort, and then we go on to gain confidence after succeeding. The whole business of "working on feelings" merely distracts people from doing what needs doing to get their lives in shape.

There are dangers to a feeling-centered life. Aim for a constantly happy, anxiety-free life and you won't get it. Focus your attention on your feelings a lot and you end up miserable. Think of the people you know with the most satisfying, enviable lives. Do they ruminate about their emotions all day long? My guess is that they don't. Now consider the people you know who appear to be most miserable. Do they spend long periods of time dwelling on their feelings? I'll bet they do. One of the problems with an emotion-centered lifestyle is that no one is good at fixing feelings. No one is capable of directly turning off feelings in themselves. No one knows how to repair feelings in anyone else either. No one. So if you build your life on uncontrollable feelings, if you center your life on your emotional state, you are in for a roller-coaster ride. You are in for frustration and despair, and perhaps expensive therapy bills.

Constructive Living offers a way to get off that roller coaster. The advice is simple: Accept or acknowledge whatever feelings (or any other reality) that comes your way, and then get on about doing what you need to do in your life. Although the advice is simple, the practice is quite difficult. It isn't easy to say to oneself, *I don't feel like getting up on this cold morning, but I promised to meet Lee at six-thirty, so I'll get up,* and then do it. But that is the way to get back in control of your life. If you allow your feelings to push you around, you are in trouble. If you lie in bed trying to psych yourself into *wanting* to get up, you are inviting unnecessary frustration and a real-time delay in actually getting up. *I ought to be able to get up without any trouble. Why am I different from others? If I could only take a positive attitude toward the day, getting up would be easy. I don't feel ready for the day. If I had gone to bed earlier last night, I wouldn't feel so tired now. I'm so angry at my parents for neglecting to teach me better sleep habits.* The fact of the matter is that feelings offer us information about reality; they don't dictate what we do.

Lamentably many so-called experts are recommending that you insert a number of steps to psych yourself up before taking action. You are advised to find your center and think affirming thoughts to empower yourself to produce esteem and confidence to get yourself together in order to make a commitment to claim your right to overcome your past and achieve insight that will enable you to do something. Constructive Living suggests that all those preliminary steps are useless. Moreover they may actually distract you from doing what needs doing. Just do it. The trap here is that it is often easier to complain and explore and excuse than it is to do what we know needs doing.

The alternative that Constructive Living recommends is to give up the ephemeral task of working on yourself and realign your life toward getting done what reality sends that needs doing. In other words we advise you to focus more on purposeful behavior. Let the feelings take care of themselves. What I think you will find is that when you get good at doing what needs doing in your life, the feelings stop giving you such trouble. And even if your feelings become troublesome, when you are involved in constructive activity, they remain in perspective. Feelings cease to be the whole show.

So Constructive Living advice suggests that you adopt a purposeful, behavior-oriented life. You may have difficulty understanding this option at first, especially if you have been a long-term patient in psychodynamically oriented therapy, or if you are a mental health professional with extensive psychodynamically oriented training, or if you watch a lot of television talk shows and dramas. Exposure to such stimuli fosters the notion that anyone who isn't self-focused and feeling-focused and digging for deep, hidden motives is missing out on life. It is time such assumptions be reconsidered. They are wrong.

Why Is Constructive Living Catching On Now?

There have always been people who were dissatisfied with their lives in some way. In modern times we can actually learn new ways to be dissatisfied by watching television and reading magazines and newspapers and listening to talk shows on the radio. Many dissatisfied people are looking for a simple, realistic method of dealing with their problems that provides relatively rapid results. We have had the resources in the past to try a variety of solutions to our problems. Most of the methods were expensive and time-consuming and moreover unsuccessful in satisfactorily handling our problems. Constructive Living offers a system in which the principles are easily understood and the personal applications easy to figure out. The doing of Constructive Living is not easy. But the effortless paths haven't produced the desired results with any consistency. People are ready to give this alternative path a try.

Who Is a Good Candidate for Constructive Living?

The forerunners of Constructive Living thought were concerned with problems of particular sorts of people. The characteristics of these people are shared by nearly all of us humans, so CL has broad applicability. Morita psychotherapy in Japan provides the base for the action orientation of Constructive Living. Morita psychotherapy was originally developed for treating *shinkeishitsu* (we call them "shinky") characteristics. In our shinky moments we are overly sensitive, introspective, ruminating, and worrying. We expect the worst, fear to try something new without the assurance that we can succeed at it. We prefer clear-cut categories and answers, finding the gray, ambiguous areas of life disturbing. We are idealistic, perfectionistic, too often preferring to think and talk about a situation than to act on it. We hold on to things long after we should have put them behind us. Changes in our lives produce bodily complaints—stomach troubles, headaches, stiff shoulders, and the like—and we focus on our somatic difficulties too much. We regret the past, dread the future, and as a result we miss much of the now. People with lots of shinky moments are usually bright, overconcerned with their health, obsessive, self-conscious, and rather self-centered. Some people seem to grow out of much of their shinkiness by late middle age.

The predecessors of Constructive Living thought were also concerned with our moral place in the world. What are we here for? Is life worth living? What does the world owe us and what do we owe the world in return? In our troubled moments we may consider ourselves lonely individuals struggling uphill against obstacles placed in our paths by those around us. We may perceive ourselves to be harried, overworked givers in a world of takers. We may see ourselves burning out in the service of others or merely busy ensuring that we get our fair share. Naikan psychotherapy in Japan, the foundation for the reflective aspect of Constructive Living, was designed to deal with such issues.

As you can see, both individual-personal and social-moral aspects of human life are covered by Constructive Living. There are people who cannot understand and apply CL principles because they have a very low IQ, because they are out of contact with reality due to some mental illness such as schizophrenia or psychotic depression (and they are not taking required medication for the illness), because they are high on drugs, and so forth. There are others who cannot benefit from Constructive Living because they may study the theory but they won't do the assignments. Once more, reality requires us to earn what is valuable.

About the Author

What are my qualifications for challenging some of the assumptions of Western psychotherapy? We could spin out my credentials—a Ph.D. from UCLA with a dissertation about Japanese psychotherapies; faculty member at the UCLA School of Public Health and the USC School of Medicine; Fulbright, NDEA, NSF, and other grants and fellowships; and World Health Organization sponsorship of my teaching Constructive Living to psychiatrists in China. I was the first foreigner to receive the Kora Prize, awarded to Morita therapists by Japanese Morita therapists. We could consider more than twenty books in print in the United States and Japan, lectures and workshops across both nations, more than a hundred certified CL instructors around the world. But my qualifications mean nothing compared with your experience trying out this method. Your experience will challenge many of the traditional Western assumptions about mental health. Even before your encounter with Constructive Living ideas, your experiences have already called into question common notions that expressing feelings always gets rid of them, that taking care of yourself first leads to life satisfaction, that going with your feelings produces consistently positive results, that your parents are at fault for all your current troubles. But you may not have realized there are alternative ways of considering mental health, ways that fit your everyday understandings more closely. After all, you were exposed to such a consistent (though erroneous) perspective on the soaps and television talk shows, psychology courses and lectures, novels and films.

The Action Aspect of Constructive Living

The Underlying Framework—Some Basics of Experience

LET'S CHECK OUT some basic elements of experience. It isn't sufficient simply to consider these elements intellectually; we'll run through some exercises that will help us appraise the validity of these principles.

Set an alarm clock to ring three minutes after you begin the first exercise. Your task is to focus your attention on some object (a painting, a floral bouquet, a ceramic piece, anything of the sort will do) for a mere three minutes. Focus your eyes on the object and think of nothing but that object for three minutes. If a stray thought comes into your mind before the alarm rings, simply notice that you have strayed from your task and return to thinking about the object of your attention. After completing the exercise we'll consider what happened from a Constructive Living perspective.

Were you able to focus your attention on a single object for the full three minutes? If so, you are a rare individual. Ordinarily all sorts of thoughts intrude. Sounds may interfere, or thoughts about what you'll eat for your next meal, or questions about the purpose of this exercise. You strayed from the task if thoughts came into your mind about whether the three minutes were up yet—it seemed such a long time was passing—or if you noticed that you were actually doing the exercise well. You see, *noticing* yourself observing and the observing itself are two different things.

My guess is that you were able to keep your eyes focused on the object of attention better than you were able to keep your mind focused on it. In other words you had more direct control over your eyes than you did over your mind. To put it another way, you had more direct control over your behavior than over your thoughts. This principle seems quite obvious. In general we have most control over our behavior, less over our thoughts, and even less over our feelings.

You can check out the validity of the uncontrollability of feelings by trying to will anxiety away before an examination or job interview or public speech. It is impossible to turn anger on and off at will (even actors can't do that—they must use indirect, behavioral means to generate feelings, as we shall see), or love, or joy, or any other feeling. Because both behavior and thinking are under greater control than feelings, we see such psychotherapies as behavior modification and cognitive behavior modification in use these days. Frankly no one has any idea how to control feelings directly. It is useless to "work on your feelings," whatever that might mean. Curious or bored, confident or anxious, refreshed or miserable, you feel what you feel.

If your thoughts and feelings aren't completely controllable by will, what is? The next exercise is to make a list of all the aspects of your life over which you have perfect or near-perfect control. Take out some writing materials and sit down for a few minutes to complete the list.

What did you come up with? My guess is that you found plenty of aspects of life that are not under your control: your spouse, your children, the weather, the stock market, the aging process, the results of your actions, even your health. A great deal of your experience is the result of events that happen to you, events over which you have no direct control. Perhaps as you contemplated your list, you came across the one thing over which you do have control nearly all the time—your behavior. The list falls within a single category—what you do. Even with behavior there are degrees of controllability, some behaviors are less controllable than others—for example, stuttering, impotence, tics, trembling, sneezing, and the like are members of a small subset of behaviors under relatively little or no control.

The point of this exercise is to remind you that if there is any freedom in your life, it lies in your behavior, in what you do. Remember, you could keep your eyes on an object for three minutes even while your thoughts wandered and your feelings hopped from curiosity to boredom to doubting to appreciation to whatever. It just seems sensible to build life on that area that offers you freedom and control—your actions—rather than trying to build life on elusive feelings.

Rather than trying to psych yourself up or motivate yourself or generate confidence or self-esteem, it is actually simpler and more feasible just to do what you need to do. Confidence, after all, is a feeling. It comes and goes outside of your control, like any other feeling. Doing what needs doing is behavior. Just do it.

Morality, Responsibility, and Control

So far we have made a clear distinction between controllable behavior and uncontrollable feelings. It seems reasonable to assess that we have no moral responsibility for what we cannot control directly. In other words good and bad have no moral meaning in the realm of feelings. We are not bad people for feeling lazy or angry or hatred or lust or disgust or any other emotion. Feelings are natural phenomena that happen to us, like storms and bugs on the windshield and sunny days and aging and beautiful scenery. How could we be held responsible for that which we cannot control?

Sounds pretty charitable so far, doesn't it? We have no responsibility for any feeling. The balance is righted, however, when we recognize that we are responsible for everything we do. In the area of the controllable—our behavior—we carry moral responsibility for every single act. Constructive Living theory holds us accountable for our sexual behavior and work habits of course, but also for such matters as how we brush our teeth and sit in a chair and scratch our shoulders and greet our neighbors and throw away trash.

In other words every act is a moral act. Every action carries moral implications because behavior lies within our control—no matter what we are feeling. Any kind of statement such as "I was so angry that I hit him" must be parsed into the amoral feeling for which no responsibility exists (anger in this case) and the action for which responsibility must be taken (hitting in this case). Feelings are no longer an excuse or explanation for behavior. It is fine to feel lazy, but get up out of bed if that is what needs doing. It is not wrong to feel rushed, but breaking speed limits carries moral implications.

You have been exposed daily to communications based on the incorrect assumption that feelings are reasons for behaving in certain ways. Get clear on this point: *No one has any idea why people do what they do.* We can't even explain our own behavior (much less the behavior of others), though we make a pretense of explaining it every day to someone or other. We learn as children to answer the question *Why did you do that?* with replies that usually satisfy those who ask. Then they stop asking about our motives in a particular situation. But such talk about motivation, such verbal explanations, are nothing more than expedient means for satisfying others' (and sometimes our own) curiosity.

For example, to say that a person drinks alcohol in excess because he or she is alcoholic or has an addictive personality is no explanation at all. To label it *alcoholism* is just another way of saying a person drinks alcohol in excess. *Addictive personality,* similarly, is just another way of describing the same set of behaviors that one is trying to explain. Professionals in the field of medicine and mental health are skillful at talking as if they understood the reasons why people do what they do. They use jargon and impressive words to appear as though they know what they don't. Trusting that someone knows the sources of behavior may be reassuring and calming to a patient, but no one knows such things. We are complex creatures. What we can usually agree on is the reality of what we do. But there is a myriad of conflicting theories to explain why we do what we do. Take a look at a compendium of theories of personality, for example. Notice how many psychological theories are offered to make sense of our actions. If any one of those theories were superior, you would find nearly all psychologists adopting it. The theory that had the most proponents for many years, Freudian psychodynamic theory, is in some disrepute these days. Fads come and go in psychology too. Constructive Living recommends that you not believe any of those theories; they are too limiting. Of course the theory that there are no worthy theories at all shouldn't be believed either, should it? Let's get back to some solid ground.

Haven't you had the experience of doing something and then later not being able to come up with a satisfying explanation of your behavior for yourself or someone else? "It isn't like me to do that. I wonder why I acted that way." Haven't you looked back on some behavior and then later interpreted the reasons for acting that way—"Oh, that must have been why I did it!" I insist that any kind of explanation about behavior is a sort of personal or social fiction aimed at stopping questions about "why" from others or yourself.

So what? Right or wrong, we shall all go on trying to make sense of what we do. We must all come up with replies that will cause others to stop asking about our reasons for doing what we do. Constructive Living merely suggests that we spend less time on elaborate explanations and more time on simply doing what needs doing, whether fully understanding what underlies the behavior or not. Too many people spend too much time evaluating why they aren't making those necessary phone calls instead of making the phone calls. We can immobilize ourselves by overinterpreting, overplanning, overevaluating. Remember, the locus of freedom and control in our lives remains in our behavior.

To believe that feelings *cause* behavior leads anyone to the dangerous belief that feelings must be "fixed" somehow before behavior can change. They don't need to be fixed, and no one knows how to fix them anyway. That whole theoretical pathway walks us away from our natural freedom of behavior. It restricts us where we need not be restricted. We may become unnecessarily sidetracked into feeling-focused self-analysis.

First Aid for Feelings

It is not that I think feelings are unimportant. Far from it. Feelings provide vital information and spice to our lives. When we are on top of the world, it is wonderful. When we suffer, it is terrible. Constructive Living is not about ignoring or dismissing or devaluing feelings. Constructive Living even offers some practical hints for relieving undesired, unpleasant feelings on a temporary basis. But the bottom line remains that a feeling-centered life is built on a shaky foundation, whereas a behavior-centered life offers a sturdier foundation for a satisfying life.

If I said to new students of CL, "All I intend to tell you in a variety of ways is that you really have no reasonable choice but to accept whatever feelings come your way and go on about doing what needs doing," do you think these new students would return for a second session of instruction? Probably not. There are therapists right down the hall who offer the students the promise of "working on feelings." New students want to work on their feelings; feelings are what brought them seeking help, they believe. Strange as it may sound, they are wrong. Their problems lie not in what they feel or what they don't feel; their problems lie in what they do or what they don't do.

Constructive Living instructors are not coldhearted. We don't enjoy suffering, and we don't enjoy seeing others' pain. As you will see as your study of CL deepens, there is a very real sense in which others' pain *is* our pain. So we have developed some tactics to bring immediate relief to some of the unnecessary misery in our own lives and in the lives of our students. Again, short-term relief has immediate benefits, but it must not be confused with the Constructive Living approach for dealing with underlying, long-term habits of thought and behavior. Let's examine some of the emergency relief we can offer:

Distraction

We cannot hold many things in mind at once. Attention is rather like a spotlight, illuminating some foreground topic while the rest fades into the background. Consider that your nose is in your visual field. Look to the left; it is there. Look to the right; it is there. Yet you rarely, if ever, found your nose to be a distraction as you looked about the world. It wasn't a problem for you until you began attending to it. Now for some readers the nose has become intrusive. While thinking about your visible nose, however, you may have forgotten about some of the problems that face you in everyday life. Now that I have reminded you of them, they reappear to haunt you. And perhaps your nose temporarily dropped from your attention. Oops, there it is again.

Be very clear that I am not suggesting that distracting yourself from your problems makes the problems disappear altogether. Bills that are unpaid remain unpaid, a dead battery remains without a charge.

Of course. Yet such an obvious observation needs to be made because there are some dreamers who believe that positive thinking will actually have some direct effect on the world. Redirecting your thoughts toward positive topics may provide you with temporary relief from your suffering, but it won't solve the underlying problems of unpaid debts, angry partners, failing health.

The kind of distraction you are likely to find most helpful involves physical activity, movement of your large muscles. Check out your experience. When you are upset, isn't it easier to wash the car or mow the lawn or clean the house than it is to calculate income tax or study for an exam? Constructive Living thought recommends activities that are distracting and constructive rather than activities that merely distract. Pounding pillows may divert your attention and work off some nervous energy, but when you are finished, all you have are pillows with dents in them. Why not get your shoes shined and clean the garage while distracting yourself?

One problem with distraction is what I call the hopscotch phenomenon. The name *hopscotch phenomenon* came from an event that occurred on the island of Maui. A little girl, Brookie, had just learned how to play hopscotch. I was visiting on the island. She wanted to show me her new ability. "Uncle David, are you watching?" "Yes, Brookie, I'm watching." She stopped her hopping to look at me. "Are you sure you're watching?" "Yes, I'm watching." Again she looked over her shoulder to check whether I was following her intricate maneuvers. Something very similar happens to people who use the temporary solace of distraction. They keep checking to see if it is working, if they are still escaping their misery. Each time they check to see whether the misery is still there, it wells up to fill their consciousness again. They hurt.

Distraction techniques are aimed at temporarily short-circuiting distressing patterns of thought and behavior. When you have doubts about yourself, we suggest that you doubt your doubts. When you have fears or other undesired feelings, we suggest that you look for the beautiful source from which they emerge (for example your fear of flying comes from your desire to stay alive, your shyness comes from your desire to be liked by others, your tendency to recheck that light switches and water are turned off comes from your desire to protect your home environment and avoid wasting money, and so forth).

Most of our students have spent so much time fighting against their tendencies that they are surprised to learn that they don't doubt enough (they don't doubt their doubts), that they can be even more careful (about a new set of more constructive thoughts and behaviors), that they don't compare enough (comparing themselves only with some ideal models), that they don't hurt enough (not enough to change what they are doing), and the like. New perspectives, even the new perspectives offered by the reflective (Naikan) side of Constructive Living, offer distraction from immediate suffering.

There is a stage in the development of many Constructive Living students in which they ask themselves *What would a Constructive Living person do in these circumstances to deal with these feelings?* or *What is the Constructive Living response to this situation so that I can get some relief?* or *What would my instructor (or David Reynolds or Morita) do now to feel better?* Such questions are better than wallowing in misery. They may lead to positive behaviors. But they are still merely productive distractions. When students go beyond the stage of considering Constructive Living measures for coping with feelings at all, when they simply respond naturally and constructively to what each situation presents, then they have graduated from the CL course.

Remember, all of these temporary methods for dealing with suffering are nothing more than first-aid bandages. The only long-term solution to unnecessary misery is to stop being feeling-centered. And the only proper response to any feeling is to feel it.

Waiting

The second piece of Constructive Living advice for handling misery is to wait. This technique may be more difficult in some circumstances than active diversion, but it works eventually. Feelings fade over time unless they are restimulated. Hasn't it been your experience that feelings don't continue on forever at the same intensity? The sharp grief you felt at the loss of a loved one diminishes to a dull ache and then is forgotten until memories of that person resurface. The embarrassment and chagrin over past blunders recede and are forgotten. The intense anxiety of a panic attack withers and dissolves as time passes.

An active life makes this natural diminishing of unpleasant feelings easier. In contrast some people actually behave in ways to keep restimulating unpleasant feelings. They go through old photo albums and reread old love letters to regenerate feelings of anger and abandonment. They dress themselves in ways to remind themselves of feelings of worthlessness. They maintain the rooms of dead relatives and celebrate their birthdays.

However, unless events or behaviors occur to revive emotions, the feelings will lessen with the passage of time. Unfortunately for those of us who desire an even greater measure of pleasant feelings, the same principle applies to joy as to misery. Joy and other gratifying feelings fade over time, too, unless something restimulates them. We can't hold on to the highs.

While waiting for disagreeable feelings to pass it is best to be about constructive action. Then, while distracting yourself with washing dishes or whatever, the time is passing and feelings are fading. After a period of time the feelings have diminished and the dishes are clean, or the garage is orderly, or the bathtub sparkles or the car's oil is clean, or you have worked off the calories from that large piece of cherry pie.

Indirect Influence of Feelings Through Behavior

Actors don't simply will feelings to appear. In the famous Stanislavsky method, for example, actors are taught to use sharp observation and appropriate behavior to prompt the emergence of genuine feelings on stage. Stage scenery and stage props are used effectively to provoke feelings. A good actor is not so much skillful at faking portrayal of feelings as skillful at calling up real feelings through memories of personal experiences and activating behavior.

Bill and Bob went on job interviews the same day for the same job opening. Both of them blew the interview miserably. Each returned home knowing he had done poorly, feeling dejected. Bill ate lunch, then sat down to rework his resume for another potential employer. He called to make an appointment for the next interview. After that, though he wasn't in the mood and he knew it, he went to dinner and a movie with friends.

Bob, on the other hand, kept going over and over the interview. He pulled out a bottle of dry gin and drank into the afternoon. Then he curled up in bed and slept until morning. The next day he dragged himself around the house recounting his faults to himself. Increasingly he felt hopeless, helpless. The telephone rang, but he didn't answer it. He ripped the page with the offending interview date from his schedule organizer and tore it into little pieces, flinging the pieces around his living room. He sat for three hours in a reading chair staring and ruminating about his failure.

Whose gloom lasted longer, Bill's or Bob's? When I ask this question during a lecture, I can expect to get two kinds of answers. Laypeople tend to give the correct answer. They see clearly that Bill's positive action is likely to get him past this setback relatively quickly. Bob's negative action simply prolongs the agony.

The response I get from some professionals, however, is that Bill's gloom will last longer because he isn't properly expressing his anguish. It will continue to persist in his psyche causing all sorts of mental difficulty until it is allowed to reveal itself. These professionals believe that feelings must be expressed or they will be suppressed. They see only two possibilities.

Over and over I remind them that Constructive Living is not about ignoring or suppressing or belittling feelings. But there is a third possibility in addition to expressing and suppressing. That possibility is the one Bill demonstrated. He recognized that he didn't feel much like going out with friends, but he went out anyway. He recognized what he was feeling, and then he did what he considered best. The feeling provided information about what he was feeling. The feeling didn't determine what he did. I daresay that is how we all live most of the time.

It isn't necessary to let feelings run our lives. It is important to feel them and acknowledge them. Furthermore it is possible to use our behaviors to give us some influence over what we feel. There is no way to control feelings perfectly, and there is no need to do so. But behavior can give us some handle on reducing unnecessary suffering.

Again the warning I must proffer is that sometimes behaviors are quite effective at influencing emotions. Why should you be warned about such a pleasant proposition? The danger is that as you gain some temporary influence over feelings, you run the risk of becoming more feeling-centered. Building a life around feelings is quicksand country. The more stable foundation recommended by Constructive Living is purposeful, behavior-centered, realistic living. You will never gain complete control over feelings—pleasant or unpleasant. They will continue to happen to you. The long-term payoff will come from accepting them and getting on with life. If you invest too much time and effort trying to groom your feelings, you are distracted from more important concerns that need doing before you die.

When I prepared myself for the difficult role of suicidal, depressed David Kent in a research project funded by the National Institute of Mental Health in the early 1970s, I was of course unable to turn on depressed feelings at will. It was necessary to behave myself into the new identity. Then, when the research was over and I was discharged from the psychiatric hospital, it was necessary to use behavior to leave the David Kent role behind me. Even though David Kent didn't feel like living an active life, he was helped by physical activity, increasing stimulus input (by walking through shopping malls, for example), and changing the environment that reminded him of his depressed identity. For more details about the research, see David K. Reynolds and Norman L. Farberow, *Suicide: Inside and Out* and *Endangered Hope.*

Using Feelings Differently

It may be necessary to change your attitudes toward feelings. Responding from an emotion-centered stance to what reality brings may lead you into trouble. Evaluate the consequences of actions and act on information from a variety of information sources, including feelings. You have been misinformed about the role and importance of feelings in human life. Here are some modern myths about feelings. Very likely you are exposed to them every day, as though they were accepted, scientifically derived facts. How many of them do you still believe?

Myth 1. Feelings cause us to do what we do. Don't believe it. The same man who strikes his wife when angry doesn't strike his boss when angry. But he may tell you his blow came from the anger.

Myth 2. We must fix feelings somehow in order to get on with our lives. The proper order of things is first to get on with our lives, then feelings take care of themselves.

Myth 3. We have hidden feelings lurking in our psyches. An alternative, more productive, perspective is that feelings emerge anew each time they occur, just as fresh moments arise. The only evidence for the existence of unconscious feelings is that someone tells you they exist. If you were aware of them, they wouldn't be unconscious.

Myth 4. Getting in touch with hidden feelings and letting them out is possible and necessary. This myth may also be called the myth of modern exorcism. There is no essential difference between believing this myth and believing that we have evil spirits lurking within us that must be exorcised by some knowledgeable professional.

Myth 5. "How do you feel about that?" should be the basic query in psychotherapy. Therapists find this verbal ploy useful, at least in part because it tosses the responsibility for talking into the client's court. It is a harmful ploy because it keeps directing the client's attention toward feelings, an uncontrollable element in human life, as though feelings were the most important aspect of life to focus upon and talk about. Focusing on the uncontrollable makes clients feel increasingly helpless and dependent on therapists.

The Three Themes of CL Action

Constructive Living is not psychotherapy. It is education in the best, most useful sense. It is education about living sensibly. Sensible living begins with sensible perception; in other words it involves a realistic appraisal and appreciation of the world. Then sensible living invites us to put that realistic information to some use, to develop purposes or objectives for action. Finally, the sensible life must find expression in actual behavior. To only sit and ponder gets nothing done but pondering. We have a responsibility to act on reality. Without action we get no response from reality, we fail to grow (in fact we wither), and we cannot work on repaying the debt our very existence implies.

The three themes of Constructive Living action can be summarized as *accept reality, know your purpose (objective),* and *do what needs to be done.* Sometimes the first theme is given as *accept your feelings* because feelings are that part of reality that is likely to give us trouble, to be difficult to accept. Acceptance doesn't mean you have to like what reality presents to you. It doesn't mean that you must sit patiently and do nothing about your situation. "Accept reality" means you must acknowledge the actual circumstances in which you live. Don't dwell on how things might be or might have been; don't focus on what ought to be. This is the way things are. Now, is there something that needs to be done about the way things are?

Sometimes the second theme is given as *know your objective.* Purposes or objectives come in various time frames. You have short-term and long-term goals. Knowing your purpose means being clear on what you are aiming for right now. Your purpose/objective right now might be planning for some long-term future goal. That is fine. Beware of spending too much time, however, on making extensive distant future plans while neglecting what is immediately in front of your nose right now. Think seriously about what you can do today (or even, putting this book down, what you can do right now) to move a step closer to achieving some short-term or long-term goal.

Purposes or objectives are also useful means of keeping us directed. When I am frightened on an airplane, I remind myself of the purpose of my flight. When I am distracted from the tedious task of writing something I have written about before, I recall my objectives in producing words. Objectives help bring us back to our focus.

"Do what needs doing" is the recommendation to put our plans into action. If you find that your purposes and objectives don't direct you to constructive action, then you need to redefine your objectives. Perhaps the objectives you have set for yourself are uncontrollable directly by your will. You may have set yourself the goal of being always happy and worry-free. That's impossible (and undesirable, though it may sound pleasant). You may have a vague goal of losing weight this year or becoming a more likable person. More useful goals will lead you to specific, controllable actions—exercising forty-five minutes each day, riding a bike for one hour each day the sun is shining, spending a couple of hours each weekend doing volunteer work at the nursing home, writing a letter a week to someone in the hospital. The possibility of specific action is a good test of the reasonableness of your goals. Sensible goals give you the chance to act and thus to win life's game with some consistency. That part of the real world that is "outside of you" only responds to action, not to dreams or wishes or thoughts.

Based on these three themes, CL is a kind of reeducation aiming at long-term rehabilitation of a less-than-optimal life. One need not be "neurotic" to benefit from this CL education. One need not have great insight into one's motivations or past traumatic experiences. In fact CL theory denies that anyone at all has any real understanding of why anyone does what he or she does. No explanations exist to make your past or current behavior understandable. There is no definitive analysis possible for making sense of who you are now. There is no need to put your life on hold while you try to figure yourself out. You are who you are. You have done what you did. Now what needs to be done next?

In CL there is no attempt to remove "neurotic symptoms," whatever they might be. We are interested in building character, whatever that might be. More importantly we are interested in helping people accept reality as it is while purposefully working to change it. Can you see the three themes in the last sentence? The result is a kind of seamless life, a life of flexibility, meaning, accomplishment.

Stages of Development

The most pitiful person from a CL perspective is someone who is miserable, his room is messy, and he doesn't notice that the room is messy. This person is to be pitied because he doesn't notice that the room is messy. Everyone is miserable some of the time. Misery doesn't place one on the bottom rung of the ladder of life. Failing to notice what needs doing and then failing to do what needs doing is limiting, even losing, life.

On the next step up the ladder of life is someone who is miserable, his room is messy, he notices that the room is messy, and he feels even more miserable because he has to live in a messy room. This person wallows in the misery without doing anything about cleaning up the room. Nevertheless this is the second rung up on the ladder of life because at least the person notices the mess. This second stage of development is where we can find many people. They are aware of their situation, they are dissatisfied with it. Yet they don't do anything to change it.

The third step up is characterized by a person who is miserable, his room is messy, he notices the room is messy, and he begins to clean up the room. When asked why he is cleaning the room, he reports that he has learned from Constructive Living (or life experience) that he can distract himself from his misery by cleaning up the room. In other words he uses housecleaning to escape from unpleasant feelings.

The room gets cleaned up. The result is fine. However, the person at this stage of development is still feeling-centered. His life is built around trying to get rid of unpleasant feelings and trying to generate and sustain desirable ones. As we know, feelings are directly uncontrollable by the will, so the efforts of this person are doomed to failure in the long term. There may be temporary times of ecstasy, but there will be down times as well. Aiming to manage feelings is an unsatisfying basis for life.

On the next rung of life's ladder is a fellow who is miserable, his room is messy, he notices that the room is messy, he cleans up the room. Why does he do so? No one really knows, but if you ask him, he will tell you it is because the room is messy. Messy rooms deserve to be cleaned. The difference between this stage and the previous stage is quite important. We have entered a series of stages that are no longer feeling-centered. You may call them behavior-centered, or purpose-centered, or simply more realistic.

One danger at this stage is that of unrealistic pride. The fellow may believe that he is cleaning the room on his own, with his own strength. He may exhibit a "Zennier than thou" attitude: "I am the sort of fellow who has the ability to do a lot (clean my room, fly even when frightened, walk away from a fight, make a good living) even when life is difficult."

At the next stage we find a fellow who is miserable, his room is messy, he notices that the room is messy, he cleans up the room. If you ask him, he will tell you that he cleans the room because it is messy. He will also point out that his mother taught him how to use a vacuum cleaner, that there is someone at the electricity company who keeps the current flowing so that the vacuum cleaner works, that someone he never met invented brooms and cleansers and dust mops and detergent and so forth. He sees himself not as a heroic figure working alone on this task but as a member of a team cleaning up the room even though he is the only team member physically present at the moment. He might point out that the very energy he uses in the cleaning comes from food grown by others and prepared by others for his consumption.

His stage is advanced beyond the previous stage not because his perspective is nobler or more social, his perspective is simply more realistic. It cannot be denied that without electricity the vacuum cleaner doesn't run, without others' efforts to teach us to read we couldn't understand written operating instructions, without parents we wouldn't have bodies to clean our rooms. To fancy that we accomplish our goals on our own, that we can be self-made, is simply foolish, unrealistic, wrong.

On the subsequent level we find a fellow who is miserable, his room is messy, he notices that the room is messy, he cleans up the room. He recognizes that it is thanks to the efforts of others that he is able to clean the room. Here we begin to run into difficulties explaining in words (be they English or Japanese or perhaps any language) a difference in perception. This fellow can talk in terms of being a discrete member of a team cleaning the room, but he also sees himself as reality's way of getting reality's work done. The room is not his, strictly speaking, but reality's. Reality is just going about getting reality's room clean. Cleaning is going on.

If such a subtle distinction between these last two stages makes no sense to you, that's fine. I lack the skill to clarify them further. There may be even further stages, but those yield not at all to my ability to understand and describe in words.

If you hope to develop yourself to the point where you rise to one of the advanced stages of development and stay there the rest of your life, your goal is impossible. Everyone moves up and down on this ladder all the time. Zen masters and priests and psychoanalysts and scholars and anyone else I have known are sometimes sitting on the bottom rung. Remember, we are nothing if not changeable.

It is not that some people have extraordinary powers. The main difference (perhaps the only difference) between psychotherapists and patients is that psychotherapists show up for all the meetings. Feel like it or not, therapists appear at the office for their clients. Patients characteristically cancel or simply fail to show up for their sessions when the mood strikes them. No one enjoys his or her job all the time; no one is happy with life all the time. We need to recognize that on some level maturity means being there for others (and ourselves, the two are the same) whether we are in the mood or not.

Paying Attention to Reality

Feelings are real. Of course. But they are not the whole of reality. They are not even the most important part of reality, despite what you may have been led to believe. To give an exclusive focus or even a paramount focus to feelings will lead you into trouble. I don't need to tell you that. You have life experience that confirms my words. Let me give you five reasons why you need to pay attention to that larger reality that includes your feelings but is greater than feelings alone.

1. **Reality is inherently interesting.** Without going outside to check on them, describe to yourself the houses and yards of your nearby neighbors. Better yet, write out the description in detail. Then go outside and check on the reality. My bet is that you will find more detail and color than in your description from memory. Those people who are so focused on their internal states miss this varied and colorful reality. People who feel bored and emotionally flat aren't noticing the stimulating circumstances that surround them. Reality is waiting to flood you with stimuli, both pleasant and unpleasant. Give it a chance and something will grab your attention.

2. **Reality sends information about what needs to be done.** When I was a teenager, I would go body surfing at Santa Monica Beach. When I forgot to pay attention to the waves, I got knocked around by them. Reality kept sending waves. My responsibility included watching out for them. When I failed to do my job, the waves had a way of getting my attention anyway. You want to check for trains before crossing the railroad track. You could scan your living quarters or garage to see if cleaning is something that needs to be done and where to start. You will miss important goals and pursuits if you aren't attending to reality. Your feelings, too, give information about what needs doing. That information is not to be ignored. But make certain that feeling reports are not the only information you glean from the dispatches of reality. The waves keep coming.

3. **Reality deserves to be noticed.** Whether you recognize it or not, reality keeps supporting you. Attending to reality increases the likelihood that you will notice the detailed ways in which you are fed, allowed to do your work, assisted in moving about, nurtured psychologically and socially, educated, and sustained in every aspect of life. If you have spent years in psychotherapy exploring the ways in which you have been damaged by others, then you have had to use a lot of energy ignoring the overwhelming support that exists now and existed in the past. Look around you.

4. **Reality is truth.** This phrase is Morita's, in translation. His point is that you can count on reality, just as science counts on it. Ideas and interpretations and preferences and ideals and feelings may shift around from time to time. They are real and true this moment qua ideas and interpretations and preferences and ideals and feelings and the like. Whatever happens with them, you can be pretty sure that if you face a blank sheet of paper and don't write on it, your term paper won't get written. You can count on your car getting older year by year. You can trust the truth that you will die someday.

Whatever I write, whatever you hear your minister say, whatever your lover whispers in your ear, whatever your competitor brags, keep your eye on reality (the reality that includes all these words as words but isn't encompassed by them). Such openness to your situation will give you information about truth, is truth.

5. **Reality is you.** Reality is a way of talking about who you are. All you hear are sounds from reality. All you see are sights from reality. All you know are thoughts that spring from nowhere and appear as real thoughts in your mind. It isn't important whether this description of reality as you makes sense to you now or whether you believe it. This point is trivial when compared with how you live day by day. But for the record, Constructive Living theory holds that you are composed of reality, and reality is composed of you. One of the implications of such a perspective is that what you do to any part of you that you call your "surroundings" you are doing to yourself. Another implication is that the more you notice and learn about your "surroundings," the more you are learning about yourself. The task of psychoanalytic exploration, for example, is only one narrow method for studying only one tiny aspect of who you are. Physics and anthropology and history and religion are also among the many valid ways of studying yourself. So you certainly want to pay attention to reality so as not to miss too much of yourself.

On Dying

One aspect of inevitable reality is death. Someday life will send each of us a big wave called death. The wave of reality won't carry a placard spelling out the word *death*. It may come in the form of an oncoming car, or a failed aortic valve, or an invasion of bacteria. However it makes its appearance, Constructive Living offers preparation for it. However, the preparation for dying that is offered by CL may not be of the sort you expect or desire. Constructive Living won't help you face death peacefully or joyfully. However you feel at the time—terrified, anxious, relieved, hopeful, despairing, calm—you will have much practice at accepting your feelings and doing what reality sends you that needs doing.

As Morita was dying, he was explaining to his medical students the sensations and feelings going on at the moment. He used his dying to teach. He remarked that he came into the world screaming and frightened, he might just exit in the same fashion. In other words he was pointing out that there is no "proper" or "required" way to die. Another well-known author and Morita therapist in Japan, Hiroshi Iwai, continued writing manuscripts from his hospital bed until the cancer in his kidneys metastasized to his eyes. Then he dictated book manuscript material to an assistant at his bedside, who also used a tape recorder to preserve Dr. Iwai's words. Into the morning of the day of his death, Dr. Iwai continued to accomplish his purpose in writing the beloved books that would be published posthumously. With failing health and failing vision and failing hearing and death peering around the nightstand, Dr. Iwai kept on doing.

No one can keep you from failing sometimes. We all have moments of failure. And we can keep on doing nevertheless.

Living in the Now

There is no need to work on curing youself of neurotic difficulties in the future. Cure is possible now. More than that, cure can *only* be accomplished now. When you are involved in this book or any other constructive activity, you are not neurotic. When you lose yourself in some positive behavior, you forget your fears and worries; temporarily they cease to exist. When you give yourself fully to a project, your self-doubts and shyness and anger are gone for the moment. Your life is a string of moments, of nows. The process of living is momentary. String together a lot of constructive moments and you have a constructive life. A neurotic person never *becomes* a cured person. Can you see the meaning in the previous statement?

Morita held that "effort is good fortune." He did not argue that effort leads to good fortune. Sometimes it does; sometimes it doesn't. The effort itself *is* good fortune. Can you see how that is so? Dogen, the famous Zen master of the thirteenth century, said that one who sits in zazen meditation in order to achieve future enlightenment is wasting time. Zazen meditation is already enlightenment. The doing of zazen meditation is already the purpose achieved.

Certainly neither Morita nor Dogen was suggesting that we make no plans for the future. How, in fact, future circumstances turn out and how we shall have to revise our plans in the light of changing situations no one can predict with great accuracy. We shall go on planning anyway and working toward our goals. But the process of the doing now is crucial, is cure. We cannot control the ends, the results of our work. A flood or earthquake or car accident or destructive illness may create havoc with our projections. To win life's game with regularity, we must focus on doing well now what needs doing. This moment's victory is possible. In CL we say, "Run to the edge of the cliff and stop on a dime." How reality responds to our actions is not directly controllable, but running all the way to the edge of the cliff is possible.

Life isn't organized in scenes or chapters. All that really come are fresh moments, one after another. We conceptually divide our days and months and years into artificial categories as though we lived in movies or books. A lot of traditional Western psychotherapy is aimed at producing annotated scrapbooks of life with headings created in consultation with the therapist. Life doesn't happen that way.

One of my students told me of a terrible occurrence in school that day. The teacher asked if there were any questions, my student raised his hand, and then couldn't think of his question when called upon. He ended his tale of failure by remarking on how embarrassed he felt. I asked him what he did next. He replied that his story ended at that point. I insisted that he report on what he did next. It turned out that he continued taking notes as the teacher continued lecturing. Depending on where the story ends, it is a failure or a success. This student had learned to move along to the next objective even when abashed. Before he began studying Constructive Living, a public failure would result in long periods of mental wheel spinning and efforts to get the accompanying inferiority feelings under control. Now he's just embarrassed and taking notes.

Living Realistically

Some people live much of their lives in unreality. We call them neurotics, though more accurately they are ordinary people with many neurotic moments. We all have such moments. The kind of unreality we live in when neurotic is different from the unreality of the mentally ill—psychotics, for example. The unreality of neurosis is grounded in the following ways of thinking: What if they hadn't left, if only I had been born to different parents, I wish I were taller, my employer ought to appreciate me more, I'm always depressed, she never thinks of my needs, that's the worst/best thing that could possibly happen. The preceding statements are all statements about unreality. The fact of the matter is that they did leave, I was born to my parents, I am this height, my boss doesn't appreciate me as much as I would like, I'm sometimes depressed, and so forth. These latter statements are more tempered by realistic thinking. In our neurotic moments we emphasize *shoulds* and *if onlys* and extreme generalizations and abstractions and other mental processes that distance us from reality. In that sense we become unrealistic during our neurotic episodes.

During those neurotic periods we often become so focused on our internal state that we fail to notice external reality. We make mistakes then which further frustrate and disturb us. We may begin to worry if our minds are failing. And off we go into another round of absolutes, generalizations, and wishful thinking. We are caught in a vicious cycle. For those of us without a medical diagnosis of a genuine mental illness caused by trauma or schizophrenia or syphilis or some such malady, it is most effective just to accept the quirks of our neurotic thinking and get on about doing what needs doing in life. Such constructive action seems to be the fastest and surest way of getting the thoughts back to a realistic level. To fight with thinking and feeling simply focuses more attention on those problem areas and leads to more introspection and neurotic misery. Behavior offers the map to get out of the maze of self-centeredness. Behavior keeps leading us to responses from reality. Through behavior we get feedback from our surroundings that is unavailable through rumination and speculation. Constructive action directs us toward getting back on the realistic track.

It is important to be clear on what actually exists in substantive reality and what is conceptual. We talk of personality and society and relationships as if there were such things in the real world. We talk as though we could work on personality, society, and relationships. However, you have never actually seen a personality. You infer one from regularities in the behavior you observe. You even have phrases to use in case someone acts "out of character"; you might say, "That's not like her," for example. Personality (like ego, id, superego, and many other psychological terms) is just a concept, an idea that points toward what some real human is doing in the real world.

I would go so far as to say you have no personality. No one else has one either. You are changeable. Your behavior depends on the circumstances you are in, your past history, your physical condition, and many other variables. It is all so complicated that I despair of ever explaining why anyone does what is done. You are so changeable that no simple explanation using the concept "personality" can ever be of much value. At best the concept is a broad, generalized description of what you have been doing so far. It can't then be turned around to be the explanation for why you have been doing what you did so far. To do so would be rather like saying that a description of Van Gogh's paintings could be an explanation of why he painted them. Beware of anyone who offers simple explanations for your actions, whether they be based on your personality, your past, spirit beings, your diet, or your society. Motivation is an area of murky unknown. Skip the complex talk and change what you do.

Similarly you may talk as though society can make people do things. Beware of such unrealistic talk. You can see specific relatives, judges, police officers, merchants, teachers, politicians, and so forth. But you can never see a society. The concept may be useful or not. But beware of any suggestion that it actually exists in the real world. And be especially wary if someone tries to use society as an explanation (read excuse) for some behavior.

One of the reasons why Constructive Living instruction sessions are relatively brief is that we stick pretty much to talk about what actual people are doing in the actual world. One of the reasons why traditional Western psychotherapy sessions can go on and on for years is that much of the talk is about talk, words, concepts. Labeling people using static concepts, even diagnostic categories, will mask the reality of change that characterizes any human.

Feeling Better—Plus and Minus

The flight from Los Angeles International Airport should have been in the air and headed for San Francisco, but we were still waiting at the gate. The fellow sitting next to me used to be as afraid of flying as I am. He had gone to a behavior therapist and had eliminated some of his current fears through a technique called systematic desensitization. As we talked, I learned that he believed he could fly that day because he felt more "comfortable" about flying than before. Of course I believed that he could fly because he had bought a ticket. (If you doubt my explanation, try to fly somewhere without a ticket and see what happens.) The luggage was being loaded at last. We were already a couple of hours late for takeoff. I was, as usual, scared to death. The most dangerous part of the flight was upcoming.

At last we pulled away from the gate. Because of the initial delay we had to wait even longer for other planes to take off. At last our turn came. We taxied out to the active runway and began to pick up speed. My hands were clammy, my stomach tight. The fellow sitting next to me looked annoyingly relaxed. Partway down the runway the pilot hit the brakes, and the plane skidded to a stop. Very slowly we taxied off to a side runway. The pilot's voice came on the intercom, "Ladies and gentlemen, I've been flying for twenty years now and I've never had to abort a takeoff before. We've got a bit of a mechanical problem up here in the cockpit. So I think we'll just go around and try it again."

TRY IT AGAIN!? That's what he said. That's all he said. The cabin became very quiet. Even the flight attendants were silent. We peered around and saw worried looks on the other passengers' faces. The same people who were complaining vehemently about the delayed start of the flight were now thinking *I'm not really in any hurry to get to San Francisco. Take your time. Pull back to the gate, unload the passengers, unload the luggage. Put us on a plane that doesn't have any mechanical problems in the cockpit. No rush at all.*

The fellow sitting next to me was a basket case. He was feeling the same fear we all felt, but he thought it was a recurrence of his flying phobia. It was natural to be afraid in this situation. He was trying to feel comfortable. What was going on in his mind was something like *Dear God, if we ever get to San Francisco alive, I must find a therapist who can make me feel comfortable about flying again so I can return to Los Angeles.* What was going on in my mind was something like *Dear God, if we ever get to San Francisco alive, I must buy a return ticket so that I can return to Los Angeles.* Is the difference clear?

Just because the therapy was relatively successful in reducing fears, my seat mate is convinced that the increased level of comfort allowed him to fly. He is hooked on the notion that his feelings must be fixed before he can fly. By extension he may believe that mending his feelings is a necessary prerequisite for any difficult undertaking. Such an attitude is splendid for those who make a living trying to fix feelings. It is rather inconvenient for the fellow who is now dependent on seeking out a therapist whenever he feels fearful. It makes little difference whether we are talking here of behavior therapy or psychoanalysis or tranquilizers or alcohol. The mistaken belief that feelings must be fixed prior to action inevitably leads to being hooked into some sort of dependency relationship. Beware, a feeling-centered life shrinks in on itself with increasing self-imposed limitations.

By the way, the plane had a problem with a circuit breaker in the main computer. On the second time around we took off safely using the same computer. Flying scared, we made it to San Francisco.

Freedom and Responsibility

One of the features of Constructive Living that appeals to me is the solid principle that students get to decide for themselves what needs to be done. Instructors may give suggestions based on what students say they want to accomplish in their lives. But the students do the assignments or they don't. They select the direction they wish to take in life on the basis of their own individual values (insert here whatever explanatory basis you wish).

In the same way, when students do the reflective exercises in Constructive Living, they are the ones who select the people in their past to reflect upon and how to define what they received from others, gave to others, and the troubles they caused others. In other words they judge themselves in their past relationships on the basis of their own standards. No instructor listens to their reflection reports and says, "Oh, that was a terrible thing you did there. No, you can't count that as something you did for your father." The CL instructor's own standards apply only to the instructor himself or herself.

That freedom to define one's own past and chart one's own direction for the future sounds very appealing to me as an American. We like that sort of independence. We have worked hard throughout our national history to preserve our independence. Dictators and cult leaders and dominating parents are basically unacceptable to our way of thinking. Constructive Living principles value individual liberty.

However, what happens if some student comes for Constructive Living instruction with the goal of becoming a skilled presidential assassin or an alert drug pusher? Are such individual goals to be supported within CL? I suspect strongly that no Constructive Living instructor would offer individualized instruction to someone with such harmful goals. Instructors have valued principles and goals too.

Constructive Living study could actually assist a student in achieving any realistic goal. Furthermore the prospective student's goals may actually be redefined during CL study. But I doubt that students with clear, injurious objectives would find an instructor to work with them to achieve those goals.

Some people believe that the more you pay attention to reality, the less likely you are to engage in harmful behaviors. When you begin to see the interconnectedness (or identity) of yourself and your surroundings, you naturally begin to give up harmful behavior. Perhaps so.

The Reciprocity Aspect of Constructive Living

Introduction

CONSTRUCTIVE LIVING REFLECTION offers a unique way of look-ing at the world. It provides a practical, realistic view of our lives. The view is not always pleasant, but it is relentlessly accurate. It helps us discover and repair some of our recurring blind spots. Developed by a devout Shinshu Buddhist layman, Ishin Yoshi-moto, Naikan provides the basis for CL's reciprocity, or moral aspect. Naikan looks beneath Buddhism, beneath Japanese culture, to our fundamental human nature. We desire to look good to others and to ourselves. We desire to see ourselves as having struggled to earn our success through our own efforts. We want to believe we deserve what we have achieved. We think that such a perspective will give us self-esteem, confidence, pride. We want to view ourselves as "givers," "helpers," "contributors" to the world.

Yet we keep running into the indisputable fact that sometimes we act thoughtlessly, even hurtfully. We do cause trouble and worry and pain to others, whether we choose to look at that reality or not. Other people (and cars and phones and vitamins, for that matter) have con-tributed to our success while we called ourselves self-made. Naikan asks us to witness those aspects of our lives too. The clearer picture is worth the effort. We really do want to know the truth, the whole truth, not just some convenient part of it.

Although the practice of this perspective on life developed out of Shinshu Buddhist thought, Yoshimoto adapted it so that non-Buddhists could use the methods for psychological development. He also reduced some of the physical rigors of deprivation associated with *mishirabe,* Naikan in its earlier form. In the West we extended and adapted Yoshimoto's thought so that a broad spectrum of people could evaluate their lives from this perspective.

The Naikan-inspired reflection assignments of Constructive Living are based on the three Naikan reflection themes: (a) What have I received from others? (b) What have I returned to others? (c) What troubles have I caused others? Saying "thank you" at least ten times a day, for example, forces me to look for situations in which I am receiving some thing or some service (whether I am feeling grateful at the moment or not). Writing a letter of apology to my mother forces me to look at the way I have caused her trouble (whether I feel remorseful at the moment or not). The purpose of CL reflection assignments is not to promote feelings of gratitude or remorse, although a variety of feelings are likely to emerge as one applies the perspective to daily life. The purpose is to see the reality of our lives more clearly. The changes that occur in our lives from this clearer vision are up to us.

This reciprocity aspect of Constructive Living puts our lives in a more realistic perspective. Earlier on I pointed out that all behaviors have moral elements. Constructive Living introspection helps us recognize and define that moral element in each act.

The action side of Constructive Living encourages us to do what needs doing. But when you don't know what needs doing, or when you question the necessity of doing anything, or when you want to understand more fully the meaning and import of the doing, then this reciprocity element of Constructive Living is helpful.

Jiriki and *Tariki*

Within the Christian tradition there is a distinction made between being saved by works and being saved by grace. Buddhist tradition holds a similar distinction—salvation by one's own power (*jiriki*) and salvation by another's power (*tariki*). Historically Zen Buddhism has been associated with *jiriki* because the practice of zazen meditation must be carried out by the individual. Enlightenment must be achieved thanks to one's own efforts. Shinshu Buddhism, on the other hand, has been associated with *tariki*. Thanks to the efforts of Amida Buddha (sometimes defined as the efforts of other people and things around us), we are allowed to live and grow and go to heaven (defined as an afterlife or as a state of mind in this life).

In some ways the Morita-based action aspect of Constructive Living looks like a *jiriki* (self-power) process. No one else can do what you need to do in your stead. You have to get out of bed, make those phone calls, go on those job interviews, greet that neighbor, and so forth. The Naikan-based reflection aspect of Constructive Living looks like a *tariki* (other-power) process. Using a variety of exercises, we come to see our debt to the world for supporting us moment by moment.

But at bottom the distinction between *jiriki* and *tariki* doesn't hold. The effort that I put out to write a book (*jiriki*) is based on energy that comes from food grown by others (*tariki*). The contents that I type so laboriously (*jiriki*) are based on ideas that were taught me by others (*tariki*). Morita recognized this intermingling of *jiriki* and *tariki*. He even called his action-oriented therapy *tariki*-based. The threads of my efforts and efforts of others in my behalf are so intertwined that it becomes artificial to separate them in the real world. *Jiriki* and *tariki* are artificial conceptual domains. There is no way to have works without grace, and vice versa.

Let us take a glimpse of the philosophical underpinnings of the reciprocity aspect of Constructive Living.

Constructing a Positive Self-image

We are all engaged in building a view of ourselves in our own eyes and in the eyes of our intimates that is positive, praiseworthy. In order to do so, we stretch the truth and ignore aspects of our histories and misremember and flat-out lie. Our image is that important to us. We want to perceive ourselves to be at least as good as other people, possibly better. We would like to be considered as givers, helpers, people others can count on. We would like to maintain that in spite of the obstacles others have thrown in our paths, we have struggled to survive and succeed thanks primarily to our own efforts, taking advantage perhaps of a helping hand here and there. We have paid our dues. Life owes us something for the effort we put out. We deserve better than what we are getting these days, and that discrepancy between what we get and what we deserve has pretty much existed throughout our pasts. Other people have let us down. Our bodies have let us down. Our companies have let us down. Our society has let us down. Yet we keep bravely on doing the best we can in spite of these stumbling blocks, doing more than our share. Or so we would like to believe.

The truth of the matter is not nearly so pleasant or so noble. And until we look at the other side of our past, we cannot find reality-based meaning in our lives today.

We all tend to forget the troubles we have caused others in the past. In contrast we tend to remember well the troubles others caused us. Such memories of others' mischief are convenient during arguments or when justifying some of our malevolent behavior or when excusing our current lifestyles. This tendency is the basis for nearly all insight psychotherapies. The insight-therapy process confirms this convenient view of the world—others caused us trouble, and we continue to suffer from that trouble. It's an easy sell.

In similar fashion we grow skillful at remembering what we did for others in the past. This skill is not matched by a comparable ability to remember what others did for us in the past. Do you notice a pattern here? Of course. Our memories are biased toward recalling information that supports a laudable self-image, as described above.

It would be foolish and inaccurate to suggest that we have no memories whatsoever of others' acts in our behalf or our behaviors that caused them trouble. We can remember examples here and there, but with rare exceptions there is nothing like parity. Please check out my assertion in your own field of recollections.

Constructing a Realistic Self-image

There is nothing that I have achieved without help from others. People I never met wrote influential books and invented writing devices and paper and processed applications for college and for travel and fed me. People I know well gave me a body and gave that body medical attention and taught me all sorts of things about keeping that body functioning. How could I call myself a self-made man?

My parents were considering my convenience before I was born as they selected a room for me, furniture, clothing, diapers, baby shampoo, a hospital, and a physician. My mother nourished me even before I was born, and she continued to do so using my father's paychecks and sometimes her own. I just took what they gave me without thought, without thanks. Sometimes I complained that they weren't giving me enough. I wanted more. I didn't think much about giving my parents anything—perhaps a token gift bought with their money on their birthday or some holiday. I pretty much just grabbed what they gave me, treasuring some gifts and trashing others.

I continue to be a taker from the world. I don't "feel comfortable" with that image, I'm not at all proud of it, but it's accurate. To be sure, I give token services to others in return on occasion. Nevertheless the support of my surroundings is so overwhelming and so constant that there is no way I can repay any more than nominally. The notion that I could be considered a caregiver or that I could "burn out" from giving so much is simply preposterous.

I keep on wearing clothes others made for me, eating food others grew and prepared for me, using tools others designed and fabricated and taught me how to use, speaking words others defined and explained. The list goes on and on. Any verb I can think of—*sleep, play tennis, drive, lecture, watch, bathe*—can be followed by a phrase attributing the action to some supporting role by others. There is nothing I do that is thanks to my own efforts alone. Most of the time I fail to notice the efforts of others in my behalf. Sometimes I even try to discount them with the rationalization that they are getting paid for their efforts. Whether they are paid or not, their services benefit me.

I would not suggest to the reader that you try to make yourself grateful all the time. Gratitude is a feeling. You can't turn it on or off by your will. I will point out that neurotic people aren't characterized by gratitude. I never met a person in a neurotic moment who was filled with gratitude. The reason why is perfectly clear. Neurosis is unrealistic. Gratitude is a natural response to taking a realistic look at the world, including our place in it. We aren't realistic enough to gain the benefits of gratitude often.

In fact most of what we are taught to do in order to develop mental health is simply wrong. We are taught to develop a positive self-image, fix our feelings, blame others for our troubles, and rely on a professional to save us. Such a course of action is unrealistic. I must lie to myself in order to maintain the fiction that I am wonderful. Sometimes I'm a pretty nice guy, sometimes I'm not; but always I'm the recipient of the beneficence of other people and things around me. Trying to talk myself into believing I'm "special" makes sense only if *special* means especially supported and cared for. I'm clearly *not* special in terms of deserving or good or giving or any other characteristic based on my undertakings alone. Thinking we are special is likely to result in dissatisfaction with our lot—we begin to believe we deserve better, that others get more than their share even though we are special. We begin to turn our gaze on ourselves in self-pity and not on the world that keeps supplying us with offerings for our benefit.

It takes energy and struggle to ignore how much we receive and how little we return to the world. But we grow used to the investment in deceit as we grow older. Ignoring and lying help us feel better about ourselves. We fear looking at reality. We are wary of what a realistic self-image might present to us.

I have good news. A realistic evaluation of yourself will produce a whole range of feelings, from gratitude and joy to guilt and repentance. You can count on some relief from no longer having to lie to yourself and others to maintain an inflated, artificial image. You can put behind you the expensive scams that feed on your fears about facing the truth. Most of all, you will perceive reality more clearly. You see, feelings will come and go, and self-image is only a subject for thought now and then. But viewing the world more clearly is important all the time. It is our most satisfying enterprise; it is what the world requires of us.

Another result of a clear view of the world (and ourselves as part of it) is the desire to work at repayment of our debts. We cannot repay in full of course. Some who gave to us have died or gone away, and the world keeps giving faster than we can repay. But there is satisfaction in consciously achieving even a symbolic gesture of reciprocity now and again. A changed view of the past is likely to influence how we view the present and how we act in the present.

Using Constructive Living reflection, our parents don't become fancied gods. They were and are, after all, mere mortals, like us. But they aren't devils, either, and they never have been. The cardboard-cutout stereotypes of our fantasied pasts are consumed in the small fires of recollection during CL reflection. When I was two years old, Mom shampooed my hair and wiped the soap from my eyes. Dad rushed me to the hospital when I cut my forehead. I can't recall giving Mom or Dad anything when I was in first or second grade.

It is even possible to see a positive side of abusive parents with this method. I maintain that such a realistic perspective will bring more relief than all the anger you can generate toward abusive parents by ignoring what they did for you and focusing on what they did to you to cause you harm. And what did you do for them? CL reflection is not about forgiving our parents. It is about the much more difficult issue of discovering the need for their forgiving us. Our goals shift from getting even or getting our share to finding ways to make restitution to parents and others for the inconvenience we have caused them by our thoughtless consideration of our own convenience alone.

I'm sure this discussion sounds all very unpleasant and masochistic to some readers. Perhaps I would have been among you at one time. However, I recommend that you reserve judgment about Constructive Living reflection until you have experimented with some of the exercises listed below. I can assure you that reality-confidence is far superior to self-confidence (in the popular sense, although they are the same in a deeper sense that we need not go into here).

Adapting Naikan to Constructive Living

The original Naikan method developed by Ishin Yoshimoto is still being practiced in Japan and elsewhere in the world. Naikan has spread to Europe, thanks primarily to the efforts of Akira Ishii. Intensive Naikan is being offered several times a year around the United States. In its conventional format the student of Naikan sits in any comfortable position from morning till night for an entire week reflecting on three themes: what was received from a particular person at a specified time in the past, what the student did for that person in return, and what troubles the student caused that person. The fourth logical possibility—what troubles others caused the student—is not included among the themes because we are all skillful at recalling such obstacles others have placed in our paths. We need no practice at such a fourth theme.

At intervals during the day the Naikan student is visited by someone who listens to the report of reflections and suggests the next reflection topic of another person and/or another time period. Naikan reflection customarily begins on the mother during the student's early childhood. (For more details about the Naikan method, see my books *The Quiet Therapies* and *Naikan Psychotherapy: Meditation for Self-development.* For a guided Naikan experience in print, see *Rainbow Rising from a Stream.* For accounts of Westerners' experiences with Japanese Naikan, see *Flowing Bridges, Quiet Waters* and *Plunging Through the Clouds.*)

Naikan fits nicely within American values because it validates the student's own value system. There is no authority who tells the student how to define something received, something returned, and a trouble caused someone else. The students judge themselves according to their own standards. The students are encouraged to search their pasts diligently in great detail. The emphasis on specific, concrete detail is consistent with the Constructive Living action element. Reality, after all, always comes in specific, concrete detail, not vague abstractions. Abstracted, generalized reports such as "Mother always used to . . ." or "I gave her lots of love" are discouraged in Naikan.

Relatively few people are willing to devote a week or more of their lives to Naikan practice. In Constructive Living we have adapted the essence of Naikan to possibly less powerful but more feasible exercises. As you read through and try out the exercises in the chapter on assignments, consider which of the three Naikan themes (what was received, what was returned, and what trouble was caused) forms the basis for each assignment. (For more information about intensive Naikan, see the Appendix to this book.)

Some Commonplace Results

After doing Constructive Living reflection exercises or the intensive Naikan reflection on which they are based, students are very likely to find their behavior changing. These changes in behavior indicate the depth of their reflection. Some changes I have seen in Constructive Living students include more frequent words of thanks and apology in daily life, reusing paper napkins, cleaning up messes they didn't make, purchasing and wearing used clothing, conservation activities, more frequent visiting of graves, increased gift giving, more polite speech, willingness to eat a greater variety of food, a cleaner plate when finished eating, better treatment of furniture and tools, and increased listening to others accompanied by less talking about themselves. I don't put these examples forth as models of virtuous behavior. Those students simply found such behavior to be appropriate at the time. The ties between reflection and action in Constructive Living are intimate.

On Loan from Reality

It should have been a simple job, replacing the ball-cock unit in the tank of the toilet. However, no matter what I tried, I couldn't get an old rusted nut loosened in the bottom of the tank. How frustrating. It was necessary to call a plumber to complete the job. My house, my bathroom, my toilet tank, my job, my tools, my skill level. Such a simple thing to be unable to complete myself, but it rankled . . . until I recalled that none of these things are mine. All are borrowed.

Oh, the house is paid for, and the tools fit on the workbench downstairs, and I've made minor plumbing repairs before. But the money for the house came originally from other people; the skills were taught me by a variety of teachers and craftspeople; the tank and repair kit were designed and fashioned by others. And so on. When I realized once again that this problem that appeared out of nowhere was composed of elements (such as a wrench, a nut, a plumber) that appeared out of nowhere for me (and that appear out of nowhere now for you as you read these words), I breathed a sigh of relief. It's all borrowed.

My identity doesn't rest solely on whether I can take care of minor repairs around this borrowed house. My identity, too, is borrowed—from others' eyes, from what others taught me, from the body my parents created for me. I exist in a borrowed body doing tasks borrowed from reality while living on borrowed time.

Missed Truths

The stereotype of a housewife serving her husband has become a cliché for exploitation. I become less and less convinced that such an explanation is all there is to the matter. To choose to serve someone is not exploitation but an expression of the understanding of satisfaction and deep meaning in life. To be sure, there are women who serve their men out of habit or timidity or subjugation. I think there are others, though, who do it on purpose. To deride all those who selflessly serve is a mistake on the level of defining all who give to each other as "codependent." The result of such scorn is to bury a tasty main dish beneath hot pepper.

Secret service assignments are a fundamental part of Constructive Living. We invite our students to serve others covertly, getting no social credit for their effort. For example a husband may be asked to clean his wife's shoes and return them to the closet or shake out the throw rugs in her hobby room. There are many kinds of unrecognized service in our world. The person who buys the vegetables and the person who cuts them up for the chef who gets credit for the meal and the person who picks up the dry cleaning for the person who receives the compliment about being well dressed are examples. Keep your eyes open and you will see that the world abounds in such activities—and some of them are carried out in our behalf. It's often merely a matter of foreground and background. Again, choosing to work outside the limelight is not the same as being forced into an unacknowledged role.

We may forget to notice reality's service, but reality doesn't stop serving us. Sometimes as I eat, I can "see" the hands serving the food—the toughened hands of the pickers, the gloved hands of the delivery drivers, the scrubbed hands of the processors and packers, the tidy hands of the accountants and brokers and cashiers, and so on. Each bite I eat comes with all these hands "attached," offering me the food, "blessing" it, if you will. Again, those who work to allow me to eat may be paid for their efforts. That doesn't take a whit away from the reality that without them I don't eat.

The reflective aspect of Constructive Living reminds us of that surrounding, supporting service. The recognition must take the form of attention to detailed, specific services and *not* the form of some abstracted, generalized noticing of "all the wonderful things others do for me." Abstracting and generalizing take the heart out of this recognition; there is no longer any tangible service recognized, only a formula set of words. It means more to me when I talk about the effort that went into Lynn's brownies that I ate last night and Mom's walk up the hill to pick up my mail this morning than it does to mouth something like "others do a lot for me." "Dear God, thanks for this food" is a pale substitute for enumerating the detailed efforts of others (read *God* for *others,* if you wish) in producing the meal that is on the table.

So we sometimes fail to notice or discount the services of others. A similar misperception appears in the area of apology. An apology is absolutely necessary in some circumstances. A proper apology reflects strength and appreciation of the circumstances. In some circles apologies have undeservedly taken on a reputation of weakness. It isn't that weak people apologize too much, rather it's that they apologize automatically, without meaning. There is no status that protects us from the need to apologize. Anyone who takes at face value the famous quote from *Love Story*—"Love means never having to say you're sorry"—doesn't understand love.

Random Thoughts on Constructive Living Reflection

Our minds usually operate to justify or excuse what our impulses or feelings suggest we do. The advertising business centers its activity around offering our minds justifications for buying. The legal system offers justifications for crime. The government and religious establishments offer justifications for controlling people. Institutionalized excuses are nevertheless excuses. Constructive Living reflection helps us to see clearly the personal mechanisms by which we attempt to justify our behavior.

It's not that I'm perfect, it's just that I'm the easiest person to forgive.

Boring lectures steal others' time and their ears.

I don't like wars. They happen anyway, on a variety of scales. I have bombed others' dreams; I have torpedoed others' plans and hopes and efforts in my behalf. I sometimes recognize and sometimes apologize for my contribution to wars.

I sometimes make the mistake of thinking this house and its contents are mine.

Is going to trouble for others without appearing to do so superior to just going to trouble for them? How about doing for others without thinking they should be grateful or owe you a return favor?

Part of our purpose in resisting saying thank you to people closest to us is that we don't want to acknowledge the obligations for reciprocity we imply with our thanks. We want to see ourselves as giving more to the important people in our lives rather than seeing our taking.

There is no need to go looking for some marvelous supernatural world. The world in front of your eyes is filled with marvels. Each new moment is a marvel. Each emerging thought and word is a wondrous event. It is even a marvel that we take such wondrous phenomena for granted. Among the marvels is parenting. From one perspective it is hard to make sense of the sacrifices of time and effort and money people are willing to make for those small, helpless creatures who appear in their households.

Everything changes with time, including people. My mother today isn't the *same* woman who gave me birth and cared for me as a child. Nevertheless she *stands for* or represents that woman of the past. So my debt remains. I cannot repay that mother who changed my diapers, so I must make do by working on repayment to the one in front of my eyes.

> Naikan develops the ability to take others' points of view: not only other peoples' perspectives, but also the sun's or a pet's or the earth's point of view. We become more objective through Naikan.
>
> —YOSHIHIKO MIKI

I live because oncoming drivers stayed on their side of the road, smokers didn't start fires in hotels where I slept, cooks prepared meals without poisoning me, pilots flew their flights carefully, architects designed buildings that withstood earthquakes, engineers designed safe cars and planes and trains, and so forth. Not only is my success due to others, my very life depends on their cooperation.

If doing Constructive Living reflection causes you to feel guilty, just wait a while—all feelings pass with time. If doing Constructive Living reflection causes you to feel grateful, just wait a while—all feelings pass with time. The effects of your actions, however, may last longer.

—

Constructive
Living
Theory

—

Action and Reflection

THE ACTION AND reciprocity (or reflection) aspects of Constructive Living fit together in wonderful complementarity. They offer a firm foundation for education in mental well-being.

We can trace the psychological lines of thinking in Morita therapy and Naikan therapy to Zen Buddhist psychological thought and Pure Land (Jodo Shinshu) Buddhist psychological thought, respectively. Of course Morita and Naikan therapies are not religions and require no commitment to Buddhist religious thought. Just as the lines of Freudian thought can be traced to the Judeo-Christian tradition so the ideas of these Japanese thinkers were influenced by the cultural/philosophical milieu of Japan. Although the streams of Zen Buddhism and Pure Land Buddhism have diverged in Japan's history, there was a time in ancient China when these two forms of Buddhism were practiced together. The principles of *jiriki* (self-power, or salvation through works) and *tariki* (another's power, or salvation through grace) were thought to be complementary. Modern Buddhist scholars agree that, at the philosophical base, *jiriki* and *tariki* become one. This convergence is true in two senses. If *tariki* is like riding in a taxi and *jiriki* is like driving your own car, in both cases a car is involved. One has trouble finding a wholly self-sufficient self-power. In another sense too, the intellectual distinction between the two concepts may evaporate under certain conditions of enlightenment. At any rate, it is no coincidence we find the practice of Morita therapy with its *jiriki* orientation and Naikan therapy with its *tariki* orientation to be complementary.

From the action orientation of Constructive Living comes the perspective that reality keeps sending waves of moment after moment. Each moment brings with it something that needs doing. Each moment calls from us some fitting, appropriate action and natural mental state. From this point of view emphasizing reality's waves, there is no good or bad, just reality flowing and presenting itself to us—or, more accurately, becoming us. From the reciprocity orientation of Constructive Living there is a moral element in this reality that presents itself to us. That moral element is inherent in each person's individual point of view. There is not only necessary action, but the potential for good and bad behavior, right and wrong behavior in a moral sense. There are moral implications to even the least noticed behaviors. Under ordinary circumstances pajamas should be put away in the morning, both because putting them away naturally needs to be done (CL action) and also because putting them away is a moral act (CL reciprocity), indicating appreciation for the services pajamas have provided during the night.

Which point of view is correct and when is it correct? Can you see that such a question depends on your point of view when asking the question?

The action aspect of Constructive Living invites us to look coolly at our circumstances and respond by fitting ourselves as part of reality to the situation that reality presents to us. The reflective aspect of Constructive Living invites us to see the moral elements in reality's presentation to us and in our responses to it. The two are complementary. They are both right, accurate. It is almost as though the former sees reality pulling a response from us and the latter sees us guiding the response out into reality—a natural request and a moral imperative. And never in contradiction, though each aspect requires its own characteristic way of talking about what we are doing.

Both Morita and Yoshimoto held that accurately knowing one's own mind is a very difficult process, a task not willingly undertaken by most people. Both considered the task worth the effort, perhaps the most important task possible. Morita thought that looking solely at the basic corruption in humanity is too much for us to bear; we need not strive to be perfect, only clear and honest about the positive and negative within us. Yoshimoto considered looking in detail at the basic imperfection in humanity to be necessary for clarity and freedom.

Both Morita and Yoshimoto refused to be drawn into philosophical discussions of what is good and bad in some absolute sense. Morita rejected any notion of a philosophy of the good; he wouldn't even offer advice about being good or bad. Rather he sought a sort of objective observation of reality, like that of science, as he put it. It was almost as though he thought a value-free scientific perspective were possible. Of course, it is much clearer to us these days that science carries its own values too. Yoshimoto turned decisions about good and bad back on the individual student. Defining good and evil became personalized and subjectivized. Threads from both these perspectives—Morita's careful observation and Yoshimoto's personalization—weave through Constructive Living thought.

As acknowledged above, Morita's theory and method provide a basis for the action element of CL. Although approaches similar to Morita's can be found in Zen, Sufism, Taoism, and Alcoholics Anonymous (called Danshukai in Japan), Morita's writings clearly express the value of accepting feelings as part of reality and directing action toward purposeful goals. As noted above, Naikan theory and practice provide the reciprocity aspect of Constructive Living, with its focus on the evaluation of moral aspects of reality. Both Moritist and Naikan theory require CL students to pay increasing attention to specific, detailed, concrete reality. Attention to and action on reality are important for mental health. Philosophical rambling, logical gymnastics, and abstract discussions of ideals and generalities are discouraged in both systems. Too often troubled people seek to escape from their real-life difficulties by talk and cerebration.

One of the characteristics of troubled minds is rumination and obsession. The mind constantly returns to some unpleasant event in the past or some difficult possibility in the future. Both Morita therapy and Naikan offer alternative courses for thinking. Morita recommends attention to doing well the moment-by-moment activities that make up our daily lives. Naikan recommends moment-by-moment awareness of the ways in which others (people, things, energy—all aspects of our surroundings) make concrete contributions to our lives, and the ways in which we repay them or fail to repay them. In both cases the attention is turned away from neurotic preoccupation and toward constructive, realistic thinking.

Certainly, some readers will take these prescriptions to be mere substitution of one set of fixations for another. In practice, however, both Morita and Naikan allow a flexibility and openness to one's surroundings that are not at all characteristic of introverted, obsessive rumination. Thinking shifts away from the purely subjective and negative toward the realistic and practical.

Both Morita and Naikan emphasize looking at the way things really are. We all have wishes and hopes and dreams—they are fine. But we don't want to let our dreaming interfere with our driving. It is seductive to get lost in imagination and rumination and thus miss the interesting reality that plays itself before our senses. The more skillful we become at doing everyday life well, the better chance we have of putting our fantasies in proper perspective. There is a sense in which Morita recommended accepting the world in a stark, black-gray-white perspective, and Yoshimoto recommended accepting the world in more colorful hues.

Both systems lead to the concept of no-self. From Morita's perspective the self becomes lost in attention to the panorama of reality. We forget ourselves as we become involved in a project or discussion or driving or an engrossing book. From Yoshimoto's perspective there is nothing we can call our own, so nothing worth calling a self. Our bodies and ideas and words are all gifts from others we know or never met or some unknown Other. Both would substitute reality-confidence for the hoped-for self-confidence of the neurotic (read unrealistic) person.

Both Morita and Yoshimoto recognized the limited role of the instructor in teaching these lifeways. It is the students who must make effort to follow through with the programs. Instructors cannot do the exercises for the students. The Morita therapist points out progress and credits the patients for it; the Naikan guide thanks the students for their effortful reflection. Not only are the clients credited for their efforts, their judgments are also validated. No one defines for the Morita patient what needs to be done. Although suggestions may be made by the Morita therapist, it is the patient who makes the final decisions for action. Similarly, no Naikan guide defines for the students what is to be defined as something received, something returned, or a trouble caused. The students evaluate themselves according to their own standards. Both systems require and support the clients' abilities, judgments, and values.

Yoshimoto wrote in 1977 that (Naikan's) self-reflection is itself enlightenment. He put himself in the tradition of the Zen master Dogen ("Zazen is enlightenment") and Morita ("Effort is good fortune") by defining enlightenment as a process, not an end result. Note that Dogen didn't promise that zazen meditation leads to enlightenment and Morita didn't warrant that effort results in good fortune. What counts is the doing itself.

Despite his method's strong *jiriki* action orientation, Morita wrote that his therapy was essentially *tariki*. Action must be based on the natural acceptance of what is presented to us both externally and within our minds. In fact, Morita talked about the mind/body as a single entity. Morita's advice to his patients, as recorded in the fifth volume of his collected works, was often quite Naikan-like. He advised one young man, who complained that his parents didn't love him, to go and apologize to them for doing so much to make himself unlovable. He reported that a number of his students came to realize the love and support of their parents after they overcame their neurotic self-centeredness.

One of my functions in Japan has been to bring Morita therapists and Naikan therapists together. Through personal meetings and literature and lectures, some initial successes are already visible. Articles about Naikan and Naikan-like thinking have appeared in Moritist journals. Some Naikan specialists have adopted more action orientation in their practice. A few Japanese therapists have come to use an outright combination of Moritist and Naikan practices. In addition, a growing number of certified CL instructors in Japan are using the combination as described in this handbook.

Misconceptions

THIS CONSTRUCTIVE LIFEWAY is so simple yet so different from what one commonly sees and hears in the media that it is easy to misunderstand what Constructive Living is about. If it makes no sense to you at all or if you think you have been doing it for years already, I suspect you misunderstand CL, at least in part. If you think it looks rather easy or impossibly difficult, you misunderstand. If you see it as an Oriental version of behavior therapy or cognitive behavior modification or Catholic confession or Gestalt therapy or logotherapy or rational-emotive therapy or some such method, you are mistaken. It has scattered parallels with all these methods, but it draws from the wisdom of centuries of observation of the human condition. That observation resulted in the psychological writings of mystical Christianity and Judaism, Sufism, Zen, Shinshu, and others. Similarities can be found in the worldviews of Alcoholics Anonymous and Gurdjieff, in Harry Stack Sullivan's and Milton Erickson's therapies. But the systems of Morita's therapy and Yoshimoto's Naikan are innovative, and the combination of the two into Constructive Living is unique.

Let's consider some of the specific misconceptions about the action and reciprocity elements of Constructive Living.

Constructive Living Action Based on Morita Psychotherapy

Misconception: Constructive Living teaches that we should ignore and suppress and deny our feelings, that we should pretend we are feeling fine when we are not.

Feelings are a vital part of our lives. It would be foolish to try to deny or suppress them. They provide information about what goes on within and around us. Constructive Living teaches acceptance of all feelings, pleasant or not. However, it is unnecessary to make special efforts to uncover so-called hidden feelings. A feeling worth feeling will get our attention naturally.

Because feelings are transitory and directly uncontrollable by their very nature, it is sensible to avoid building life on them. Directing our behavior in a positive direction offers a more stable basis for life than being feeling-centered.

When feelings are quite disturbing and distract us away from constructive behavior, CL advises positive behavioral diversions to provide temporary relief. But long-term coping with feelings is based on their acceptance and effecting change in the conditions that arouse them, not on distracting behavior.

Misconception: Constructive Living holds that feelings are unreal and unimportant.

See the response to the previous misconception.

The only unreal feelings are those that are not felt. If you don't feel something, you don't feel it; it isn't there. There are no hidden, suppressed, repressed feelings lurking in your psyche. You don't need mental health exorcism to get in touch with mythic emotions. You don't need to magically get rid of feelings by expressing them. The only genuine feelings, the ones you actually feel, give important flavor and information to your life.

Misconception: The instructors in Constructive Living are cold-hearted. They keep suggesting things to do. They don't realize how much I am in pain. They don't deal with my pain directly.

I do Constructive Living instruction because my students' pain is my pain. Don't you feel uncomfortable around someone else's suffering? Constructive Living is the most effective method I know for dealing with unnecessary suffering.

Instructors of CL focus on behavior (things to do) because going over and over disturbing emotions does nothing more than restimulate them, causing more pain. Constructive behavior is the path out of the maze of emotion-centeredness and its unnecessary pain.

Misconception: When I start doing CL, my life circumstances will improve.

Constructive Living instructors often hear some version of the following: "I've been doing all these things for my wife and my boss, but they don't treat me any better," or "I've sent out lots of job applications since starting CL, but no one offers me a job. This Constructive Living doesn't work!"

These students have confused the process of doing with the result. We can control what we do, but not the results of our doing. I cannot guarantee you will get a job if you send out resumes, but if you don't send them out, the likelihood of getting a job is decreased. And the sending out of the resumes is important in itself, whatever the result. Similarly, treating your spouse or partner well is valuable, no matter what response it provokes, including no response at all. The process of acting with full attention is essential to living a constructive life.

Misconception: Constructive Living offers peace of mind. It will make my fears and obsessions go away.

Constructive Living aims not for a peaceful mind but for a flexible mind, responding to the momentary changes in our circumstances. How boring it would be to feel relaxed all the time. Fears usefully direct us away from the dangerous and threatening. Fears recommend that we prepare our speeches carefully so as not to appear foolish. Fear prompts caution in all sorts of circumstances. Obsessions tell us about what is important to us and keep us working at problems after others have given up. Obsessions give us a challenging opportunity to assert rightful control over our behavior. Overcoming a single obsession can teach a student principles of living that extend into other areas of life.

It is the same with all discomfort. To erase pain completely would be to erase a valuable natural warning and avoidance system. It would have devastating effects much like suppressing the natural emergence of fever in the presence of sickness. Keeping suffering in perspective and finding the positive areas of life in which to utilize it are the keys to coping with pain. Don't settle for sterile peace of mind.

Misconception: Constructive Living teaches students to redirect their attention in order to avoid unpleasant feelings.

This misunderstanding is closer to the truth than the others. The problem here is one of emphasis. As a *temporary* measure we may advise distraction (redirecting attention) from unpleasant feelings to get through some troubling circumstance with less anguish. The temporary relief has only fleeting benefit, however. The long-term, bottom-line CL solution to dealing with feelings is to recognize and accept them. Any feeling will diminish over time unless it is restimulated. Putting feelings in their proper place is part of becoming a mature human being.

Misconception: I just seem to be unwilling to make a commitment to make a decision to begin CL study.

There is no need to decide or be motivated or make a commitment or empower oneself or think positively or get one's intention up—it is sufficient just to do it. It is that very morass of mental preparation that paralyzes some people, particularly those with lots of experience in psychodynamic psychotherapy or new-age counseling. Mental wheel spinning is just another way of putting off doing what needs doing.

Misconception: I can't do the assignments.

You didn't do the assignments may be accurate. You fear doing the assignments, perhaps. You don't want to do the assignments is another possibility. But in Constructive Living we reserve the word *can't* for physically impossible tasks, such as "I can't lift a dump truck with my bare hands" or "I can't run a three-minute mile." Some actual physical handicap aside, it is very likely that you can do the Constructive Living assignments.

If we use the word *can't* too loosely, we may come to believe, in error, that a task we really can do is impossible.

Misconception: Constructive Living may be fine for the Japanese, but it won't be effective for Westerners. The Japanese are all like that anyway.

If all Japanese were living constructive lives, why was there a need to develop Morita and Naikan therapies there? Constructive Living aims at qualities of human nature that lie deeper than Japanese character. The way to find out if Constructive Living is useful for Westerners is not to evaluate it on theoretical grounds but to give it a try. More than ten thousand students and well over a hundred certified instructors in the West can attest to its usefulness. They may not represent a random sample of the population, but they certainly explode the myth that Constructive Living can't be helpful to any Westerners.

Misconception: The students of CL are taught to be passive, pushed around by whatever reality sends their way.

Some people seem to be confused by the notion of acceptance of reality in Constructive Living. Acceptance doesn't equal passivity. Acceptance is a sort of readiness to recognize the way things are. It contrasts with pretending or ignoring or denying or other forms of running from reality. Acceptance is the necessary first step in instituting change. Change needs to be responsive to reality. Constructive Living students are not taught to be passive.

In our neurotic moments we exist in a sort of unreality. Our behavior is not appropriately matched to the reality in which we live. Attention to what reality presents to us is crucial in moving us out of our neurotic moments.

Furthermore, though we may not like to think about it, we are often pushed around by what reality sends our way. Floods, earthquakes, hurricanes, droughts, traffic snarls, crimes, business losses, accidents, deaths, strikes, recessions, and the like are examples of messages about our impotence and the need for action that responds sensibly to these conditions.

Misconception: There is nothing good about the suffering I endure. Constructive Living tries to get me to like my discomfort.

Suffering is painful, but it has meaning, value, usefulness. Constructive Living doesn't counsel learning to love your pain. Loving, like the pain itself, is uncontrollable. How you feel about your suffering is out of your control.

I don't like to hurt. I don't like ice storms either, but they happen sometimes. And then I use the time to get something done inside the house. Neurotic suffering always comes from the distortion of some positive source—in CL we call it the kernel of good. Phobias about cancer come from the desire to be healthy, extreme competitiveness and perfectionism come from the desire to do well, shyness comes from the desire to be liked and respected, and so forth. Knowing that there is a kernel of good may not make the suffering pleasant, but it offers a clue about what needs to be straightened out in life. The suffering has directed us toward important, usable information.

If you cohabit with unnecessary suffering, you don't need to be in love with it, but you can invite it to be your teacher.

Misconception: There are so many things that need doing, I can't do anything. I need someone to tell me what needs doing.

No one can decide for you what needs doing. You are the expert in the matter. The CL instructor can suggest assignments, but the student does the assignments or not at his or her own discretion.

When you are overwhelmed by all the things that need doing, start on any one of them. Rather than your sitting on a sofa for a long time trying to decide where to begin, we recommend starting on the array of tasks in alphabetical order just to get moving. If another task has higher priority it will keep popping up in your mind until you do it.

Misconception: This lifeway is too controlled, I'll lose my freedom. Americans love freedom more than anything.

True freedom comes from self-control. Artists must master their craft before they can improvise freely. Carpenters and secretaries and nurses are the same. Freedom is not the same as carelessness and sloppiness. Spontaneity pays off when it springs from a base of skill and purposefulness.

Misconception: I've read a few articles and a book about Constructive Living. I understand what it's about.

Intellectual understanding is insufficient. You don't understand Constructive Living until you have experiential knowledge of it. The Japanese would say you need *taiken*, or body knowledge, of it. Reading a book about building a house and building it are two different things.

To be sure, reading, listening to a tape, talking with an instructor, and the like may be helpful adjuncts in your learning about CL. However, they are not substitutes for constructive action.

Misconception: There is no Constructive Living instructor nearby to guide me, so there's nothing I can do.

There are a number of CL books with exercises in them. Some readers have been significantly helped simply by carrying out the homework exercises in these Constructive Living books.

Additionally, individual Constructive Living instruction is possible through correspondence and telephone contact. Remember that the exchange between instructor and student in CL is not like that in psychotherapy. In CL training, much of the communication is centered around the assignments that have been made and how they turned out. The cathartic pouring out of complaints and other emotional outbursts are minimal.

Misconception: My hidden anxiety will be working on me unconsciously, even when I'm distracted from it by a constructive life.

Anxiety, obsessions, phobias, and the like are only problems for us when we are attending to them. When you are thoroughly involved in trying to make sense of this book, for example, you aren't thinking about your personal difficulties. They are not troubling you at the moment. Furthermore they are not lurking in your unconscious (whatever and wherever that might be). Worrying about what is going on in your mind outside of your awareness is like worrying about whether Snow White will ever get cancer. There are plenty of topics more worthy of your concern. For example, what needs to be done now?

Misconception: I simply cannot control my feelings, so CL is of no value to me.

No CL instructor would suggest that you need to control your feelings. Perhaps you are having difficulty with the concept that the world can be divided into controllable behavior and uncontrollable feelings. This fundamental separation of behavior and feelings is essential to your understanding of this lifeway. It is also essential to getting back reasonable control of your life (and returning our society to a reasonable foundation).

Misconception: I know some people who do CL without ever having heard of it. They are workaholics. Constructive Living wants to turn everyone into a workaholic robot.

Constructive Living people aren't workaholics. Consider the purposes of workaholics. I suspect that you will find that workaholics don't work to get work done. They work to avoid something—their families, their thoughts about something distressing, their fear of free time, or something else. Constructive Living emphasizes appropriate responses to what reality brings you to do. Sometimes reality will bring you rest moments, daydreaming moments, game moments. Developing the sensitivity to what reality brings that needs doing is an art and a skill. It is a far cry from the rigid, narrow focus of the workaholic.

Constructive Living Reflection and Reciprocity Based on Naikan Psychotherapy

Misconception: CL tries to make us think of our parents as saints. I'll be asked to deny the abuse I received at the hands of others.

The purpose of CL reflection is not to distort your perspective of your past but to correct the distortion that already exists. Abuse is recalled and acknowledged. So are the positive acts of your parents and others. So are the ways in which you hurt them.

Your parents weren't saints. Neither were you.

Misconception: CL reflection aims to make us feel grateful.

The aim of CL reflection is to see reality more clearly, both past and present reality. When we see reality more clearly, it is not unusual to find all sorts of feelings emerging. One of the strongest feelings we encounter is likely to be gratitude. Feeling grateful is a memorable by-product of CL reflection, but it is not the purpose of our reflection. Remember, no feeling (including gratitude) is worth taking on as the foundation for life. Feelings come and go. There is no stability or security in feelings.

Seeing clearly is much more important than feeling grateful. I missed a lot of what was going on in my first years in Japan. Much appeared new and difficult to interpret, and my language ability was poor. I missed a lot of what went on in my youth too. I was inexperienced, noticed little, and had poor ability to encode information. Constructive Living reflection helps catch some of what I missed in the past. We are all the main experts on the subject of our own lives. Seeing clearly is important.

Misconception: CL reflection will make me feel depressed and guilty.

When doing CL reflection, feelings of sadness and guilt are not uncommon. It isn't pleasant to look at the ways in which we took others for granted and then criticized them for their mistakes. It isn't comforting to see the ways in which we have tried to invent a fictional past in which we were heroes and others were villains.

However, the melancholy and remorse are balanced by a clear look at the ways in which others cared for us and supported us in spite of our imperfection. We see their efforts in our behalf even when we didn't notice them at the time, appreciate them, or acknowledge them with thanks.

People may think that it's easier to work on feelings of guilt directly or to avoid feeling guilt than to fix the cause of it; it's actually easier to work on the cause. That's what guilt is for, after all, to inform us of what we need to rectify in our current behavior.

You may feel depressed and guilty while doing CL reflection. You are very likely to feel loved and supported too. In either case, as time passes, the feelings diminish. The clearer vision of reality is more dependable than the shifting feelings. You come to see clearly the reciprocity of life.

Misconception: The reflection in Constructive Living is a Buddhist religious practice.

I suppose that you could say that the humming of a popular modern song comes originally from religious chanting thousands of years ago. But church hymns and popular ballads are not the same. The idea of CL reflection has its origin in a form of Buddhist meditation in Japan. But it has been modified with care and purpose so that it is no longer Japanese or Buddhist. It is fundamentally human.

Misconception: Orientals have respect for their elders, a cultural value that fits Constructive Living. Americans value independence from their parents, so CL reflection isn't relevant for Americans.

The Confucian ethic from China was adopted by a number of Asian countries, including Japan. This ethic holds respect for parents as fundamental to society. The degree to which individuals in Japan and other countries actually practice this ethic varies considerably. Physical abuse of parents by teenage children caused a big scandal in Japan in the 1980s.

Americans value independence, but we can never be free of the debt we owe our parents for our very lives. We cannot erase the time and work that they put into our upbringing merely by growing up and moving away and probing for their faults in psychoanalysis. Rather than independence I think we would be wise to seek mutual dependence or mutual support. Complete independence is a lonely road—a road with no one actually traveling on it.

Misconception: CL reflection is too hard, takes too much time, requires sitting in some uncomfortable position or other ascetic practices.

There are many ways to practice CL reflection. It can be done while waiting in line at a market, in the evening at bedtime, while commuting, during meals—in a variety of places and times. The recollections gleaned by Constructive Living reflection can be reported out in person, by telephone, by mail, during prayer, or in a journal. You will find much flexibility here.

Intensive Naikan reflection is related to Constructive Living, but is not precisely a CL practice. Intensive Naikan is carried out in retreats. While doing intensive Naikan reflection any comfortable position is permitted except for lying down, which could lead to drowsiness. Retreats vary in time from one day to a week or more. The practice does require attention and perseverance. Learning to play tennis isn't easy either. Some people find that the result is worth the effort.

Misconception: You need a strong, religious character to do this sort of reflection.

In order to do CL reflection, you just need to do it. There are no prerequisites. The founder of the Naikan practice in Japan, Yoshimoto, reported that he had no idea beforehand who would do deep reflection and who would not. The way to discover if CL reflection is useful for you is to give related exercises a solid try and see what happens.

Misconception: CL reflection isn't positive or fun or uplifting. The cure is worse than the disease.

Frankly I don't find CL reflection fun. But I don't find some sorts of study and exercise fun either. Nevertheless they are necessary for my life. Feeling uplifted is not as important as looking at the truth. You may feel uplifted as you do this practice, you may not. Feelings flutter off into the void anyway.

CL reflection is positive. It spotlights the cradle of reality in which we live our lives. The gratitude that wells up conquers our feelings of isolation and victimization. More importantly we begin to get our first clear views of the way things really are. The disease of narcissistic self-deceit gradually gives way to clear vision.

Misconception: CL reflection won't affect my self-image or self-esteem.

CL reflection is quite likely to affect self-esteem, but its effects in that area are likely to be in an unexpected direction. Rather than inflating one's self-image and generating more self-esteem, the result is likely to be a lowered self-image and less self-esteem. And that result is most desirable. What could be more important than high self-esteem and a positive self-image?

Let me offer a kind of esteem that isn't based on lying to ourselves. Knowing that we are sometimes stupid and evil and careless and selfish, why should we think well of ourselves all the time? In order to sustain conventional notions of self-esteem, we must keep overlooking or forgetting these distasteful areas of our lives. There is another way.

Most traditional Western therapies aim to make us feel better about ourselves. Constructive Living reflection aims deeper; it takes us out of the game of self-worth altogether. What you are about to read isn't reassuring in one sense. But it opens the doors to freedom you may not have considered before.

We pretend we aren't troubling others by our existence. We consider our punctuality and attention to detail to avoid others' inconvenience, and we compare ourselves with others. Thus we look good and considerate in our own eyes. The fact of the matter is that there is no way to prevent causing trouble to others—even when we are trying to be helpful. For example when I start a lecture at the time announced, I am causing trouble to those who arrive late—some of whom arrive late for perfectly good and unavoidable reasons. But if I wait until latecomers have arrived to start the lecture, I am causing trouble to those who made the effort to arrive on time; they must wait. In the same way, if I rush to get to my next appointment, I cut short the person in front of me now. If I reschedule an appointment for later, that next person must wait longer. The point is that it is not simply a matter of my convenience and the convenience of another. Others' convenience combine and conflict in complex patterns. When considering another person's convenience, I may be troubling yet a third person and a fourth and a fifth.

Another example of this dilemma is that the fast pace of modern life conflicts with politeness. If I take the time to speak and act with correct politeness, the recipients of my polite act must wait. I cause them trouble with my politeness. If I am not polite, I also cause them trouble by failing to show them the respect they are due. Either way I cause others trouble. So I must live continually apologizing.

Such a prospect doesn't sound appealing, does it? And that's not all. A key difference between Catholic thought and CL reflection is that in Catholic theology there is a way for us to make up for our sins, through penance. CL reflection offers no such remedy. We cannot undo the distress we caused others in the past. We always lose! Incessantly! Increasingly! No matter what we do, we fall farther and farther behind as we go on living.

So what is the advantage of adopting such a perspective, however realistic it might be? The benefit is simply that the pressure is off. There is no longer any need to try to fool ourselves or others into believing that we are what we are not. We can deal with the conflicting ideals and expectations in our lives by giving up on them and doing our best, however imperfect that might be.

Think about it. Isn't it true that much of your suffering is connected to your perspective that you are special, deserving of much more than life brings, hampered by the actions of others, unappreciated, unrewarded? Isn't it exhausting to try to convince yourself and others around you that you are especially worthy, especially considerate, especially clever, especially insightful? It is simpler and more straightforward just to give up, apologize, and do what we can to repay our debt to that world that keeps giving in spite of our imperfection.

Constructive Living reflection offers a solid foundation for esteem. The path lies through the detour of "other-esteem," or "reality-esteem." Through reflection and reciprocity exercises we realize that others (both animate and inanimate) supported us in spite of our stupid, evil, careless, selfish moments. Reality continues to provide the sustaining predictability and variety by which we survive, in spite of our imperfection. Our recognition of this sustenance provokes what might be called other-esteem or reality-esteem.

At some point it dawns on us that we, too, are participants in this supporting Reality. We fit into this Reality-whole. A new kind of self-esteem arises. It is no longer the narrow I'm-terrific part-truth. The esteem we desire is now firmly founded on the broader me-as-part-of-this-larger-reality. This reality-esteem is a more stable and honest basis for living than self-esteem.

The head is still held high, but no longer for my ego's sake. Others around me don't want to have to look at someone moping around. They deserve to have a positive person around them. The pride shifts to pride in the accomplishments of those nearby who helped achieve what little I've been able to accomplish amid all the inconvenience I caused them. The result isn't self-protective modesty but rather giving credit where credit is rightfully due. Reality deserves my admiration and respect. I am one of reality's representatives.

Misconception: There is no CL instructor nearby to listen to the report of my reflection, so there's no need to do it.

Some of the reciprocity exercises in Constructive Living don't require reporting at all. Secret services, for example, can only be done properly by avoiding reporting them.

Furthermore, as noted above, reporting your reflections can be done in a notebook, by telephone, by mail, and so forth. It isn't necessary to have an instructor or anyone else physically present during your moments of reflection.

In fact if you don't want to report your memories to anyone at all, there is no problem. However, most people find it helpful to tell someone about what they recalled. The most understanding listeners are those who have done intensive reflection themselves. They don't judge or criticize; they listen gratefully and encourage further reflection.

We recommend that you avoid reporting your reflections to anyone about whom you have been reflecting. In other words if you have been reflecting about what you received from your spouse, what you returned to your spouse, and the troubles you caused your spouse, it would not be appropriate to report your reflections on those subjects to your spouse.

Misconception: I do CL reflection all the time; I've done it all my life without ever having heard of Constructive Living.

There are people who do similar sorts of reflection on their pasts. There are people who feel gratitude and a sense of fitting into the whole of reality. I have yet to meet someone who has independently come up with the three Naikan themes developed by Yoshimoto and adapted into CL reflection exercises. Yoshimoto's Naikan was refined over several decades. It leads to recollections of specific events and specific perspectives.

Even if you have practiced similar meditations in the past, this form of CL reflection is worth a try.

Misconception: The CL reflection perspective is the same as the ecological perspective—they both endorse careful use of our resources.

Both CL and a sensible ecological perspective promote careful use of our environmental resources. The reasons for doing so are somewhat different, however. Environmentalists use natural resources carefully because they are limited, they can be destroyed and lost forever if we fail to husband them carefully. Constructive Living people use resources because of the personal relationship they discover exists between them. I do not think so much of the trees needed to make this paper tissue as I use it carefully. Instead I am thinking of the service this one paper tissue kindly provides me, the efforts of people and trees and water and so forth that went into its manufacture for me. Using the tissue well is a personal matter between the tissue and me.

The behavioral results may be the same in many cases, but the attitude is slightly different.

Misconception: I dare not do CL reflection because of the unpleasant memories that might emerge.

Some Constructive Living students resist doing CL reflection because they fear that unpleasant memories from the past will well up to torment them. Some fear to find sexual or psychological abuse in their past that they have "safely" forgotten. Certainly it is possible to find unpleasant events in the past as well as pleasant ones. One of the characteristics of an adult is to be willing to look at all of reality— the positive and the negative.

The CL reflection process is certainly one of the most benign settings in which to call up the past. Even when scenes of violence or neglect are recalled, they are recalled within the framework of others helping and supporting and loving during those same periods. The perspective on the past is broadened to include negative experiences, but always these experiences are couched in circumstances where positive experiences also occurred. For example a woman who recalls being raped can find others who supported and fed and clothed and gave medical attention and an education and perhaps music lessons and birthday parties during these same years. Some of those affirming activities may have been provided by the very person who hurt her. The past becomes populated by many-faceted people, not one-dimensional evil demons. Again, CL aims for a realistic perspective encompassing both the delightful and the marred.

Misconception: Constructive Living reflection is rather easy once you decide to do it.

CL reflection isn't likely to be effortless, but it is nevertheless worth the toil. Studying for exams, childbirth, weight training, dieting, and such activities may not be accomplished simply, either, but they may be well worth the struggle.

Some people find this reflection so difficult that they sabotage their own efforts. There are many ways to cheat while doing CL reflection. The contemplation practice is quite difficult, especially at first. Recalling details of the past within the structured framework of what was received, what was returned, and the troubles caused others is not a simple matter.

Here are some examples of people who were deceptive in their practice of Naikan reflection in Japan. The examples are from an article written by Kakusei Yanagida in the magazine *Yasuragi* (September 1991, p. 17). We could provide similar examples of devious reflection on the first two reflection themes by Western students. Can you see why the examples are not proper Naikan reflection?

a. Things I received from others:

Although I didn't ask for it, she got it for me anyway.

[My father] worked for the family.

She bought me only books that were too difficult to read.

When I tried to do something for myself, my mother wouldn't let me. She did everything for me. When I tried to do something for her, she wouldn't let me. It's too bad.

She got me things for my birthday.

b. Things I did for others in return:

I tried to do things that wouldn't worry them.

I helped with housework.

I became a class officer.

I got a scholarship.

My mother was happy when I took first prize at the track meet.

I almost always got good grades in school.

I tried hard not to hit my parents.

I didn't complain, took it all.

When they gave me money for my overseas trip, I was grateful and thanked them.

I gave mother a wastebasket on her birthday.

I accepted the illness he passed on to me.

Yanagida remarked that if you claim that you studied for your mother, then a case can be made that everything you did, you did for others. Who benefited from your good grades? Now can you see why the examples are flawed? What can you determine from the following conversation?

"I can't figure Grandma out," Morris, a CL student of mine, mused. "She remembers some things but forgets others. She ironed my shirt the other day but left a thread on it. She keeps fixing meals that are too large. I've told her a million times. And I wish she would remember to fix the foods I like best. What's more, she goes around muttering 'thanks' at the drop of a hat."

"Anything else?"

"Yeah, she buys and even makes all these clothes for me; if I don't wear them, I suppose I'll hurt her feelings. She's such a bother. She needs to be more sensitive. When I scold her, she just thanks me and goes on doing what she did before. Her mind is failing, I think. Maybe she keeps remembering the poverty of her childhood. There's no need to keep going on about that 'thank you' stuff. I'm her grandson, after all. I don't mind taking care of her."

"Sounds like you put up with a lot."

Misconception: Constructive Living reflection will turn me into a doormat for others to walk all over.

The desire to work on squaring our debts to others leads to positive activity. We are encouraged to give to others what we believe is the best for them. We may be wrong. We want to take into consideration what they tell us that they need. But those who allow others to walk on them are not repaying a debt. They are merely being lazy and cowardly and inattentive. To permit another to dominate you is to cause harm not only to yourself but to the other person. *For their sake* the "something that needs doing" is to stop the domination.

Can you see the wider perspective here? In similar fashion we need to get rapists off the streets, not only for the sake of the potential victims but for the benefit of the rapist as well. To be the kind of person who hurts others in such a fashion is hurtful and demeaning to both perpetrator and victim. Again, we need to improve poor parenting not only for the child's sake but for the parents' sake as well. Parents who are neglecting or otherwise mistreating their children know that they do so (however much they may deny their awareness). How difficult it is for them to live with that knowledge, to invest energy in denying it, to look daily at the consequences of their hurtful actions. We humans all wish to think well of ourselves. It is hard to maintain an illusion of personal acceptability when a parent mistreats a child.

Constructive Living reflection helps us to see the larger picture. It is not merely our own convenience that drives and informs our lives.

Beginnings

BEGINNINGS IMPLY ENDINGS. For something to begin, something else must end. When two people become a married couple, their new life together implies the ending of their lives as unmarried individuals. When we relocate, we begin our lives in a new home, ending our lives in the old home. On an even finer level, each moment brings a fresh beginning and a final ending.

I am sometimes asked to comment on the history of Constructive Living. So I make up stories about the history of Constructive Living, just as we all make up stories about our own life histories. There are certain objective points of time: When we were born, when the first book appeared with the words *Constructive Living* in it, when we graduated from school, when the first instructor was certified. But the stories of history we create aren't simply composed of those simple, objective dates and events. The stories are abstracted from the millions of beginnings and endings that make up our lives, that make up the "life," if you will, of Constructive Living.

Whether we look with nostalgia or regret on the endings or with hope or dread on the beginnings, in either case they keep recurring. There is no way to hold on to what is. There is no status quo. There are just more beginnings and endings.

It seems sensible therefore to adapt ourselves to this inevitability. Because reality keeps sending us these fresh beginnings, we might as well use them constructively, viewing them as opportunities. We can't actually be stuck in the past, in old habits, in addictions, in routines— although we can make up fictional stories for ourselves and others that imply we were paralyzed in such a manner. Yet even the stories change in small ways during the retelling.

So what to do next? How to use this newness that keeps drifting upon us? These are key questions for our consideration. We face issues of judgment, meaning, purpose. Constructive Living offers two perspectives on these issues.

One perspective, drawn essentially from Morita's thought, holds that with each fresh moment comes also something-that-needs-to-be-done. It is as though the fresh moments don't come randomly or empty—they come with glosses or declarations attached. Our task is to discover these recommended responses to the fresh moments and to act on them. For such efforts our minds are ideally designed. Unfortunately we sometimes distract ourselves from this natural fitting of action to fresh situation with fixations on ourselves, our emotions, our neuroses, or other small components of the total situation. The CL objective is to let our natural minds fit themselves with awareness and flexibility to our ever-changing situations.

The other perspective, drawn primarily from Yoshimoto's thought, holds that whatever information comes along with fresh moments we need to develop sensitivity and skill in determining what needs to be done with an eye to reciprocity. Without consideration of our place in the moral scheme of things we are likely to make mistakes about what needs to be done. Through a process of guided self-reflection and exercises we cultivate a Naikan perspective on (and Naikan stories about) what reality keeps sending us and how we have responded to those deliveries up to the present. Then we are encouraged to use the fresh beginnings with more discernment, more attention to matters of reciprocity.

Reality won't respond directly to our thoughts, feelings, beliefs, insights. Reality responds to what we do. This practice we call Constructive Living is not "Constructive *Thinking.*" It is our action-response to these beginnings and endings that determines who we are—is who we are.

Acceptance

WE ARE ALREADY just fine as we are. And it isn't even necessary to recognize that truth. Furthermore we are all incorrigible takers from the world, so we might as well give up on perfecting ourselves and invest our days in thanking reality for giving us what we don't deserve and apologizing for taking with and without awareness. And we are just fine as we are.

Some people are diligently involved in improving themselves spiritually or psychologically. It is as though they believe that through persistent effort they can make themselves into wonderful, enlightened creatures someday. Both Morita and Naikan suggest such effort is useless. We are what we are right now. Accept it as it is. Effort should not be directed at some future possible perfection but at what needs doing right now.

Of course nothing stops us from working on whatever we decide to work on in our lives. But there is no need to reject ourselves now while doing so. We're each just a part of that big reality anyway.

When students come to me, the bottom-line questions I present to them are: Are you satisfied with your life as it is? To what degree have the methods you've tried so far been effective for you?

If they are satisfied with their lives, then I see no reason why I should take their money and instruct them in Constructive Living. It's not my responsibility or my right to change them. If they aren't completely satisfied and have come to study with me, we must get on with exercises and assignments to change what they decide needs changing. There's no time for listening to long lists of complaints. How they feel about themselves is no great immediate concern. Their feelings about themselves are likely to change as they accomplish their behavioral goals. And they are just fine as they are right now.

Here is a sample reply to a letter written by someone who has progressed remarkably along the Constructive Living path but is still dissatisfied with his progress:

There is a part of Constructive Living I would like you to work on—*acceptance*. You clearly understand the part about doing. That part has helped you accomplish much in your life and has detracked some of the guilt about nondoing. Accepting feelings as they are is part of a larger principle—accepting reality as it is. That means accepting yourself just the way you are, including all that you do and don't do. Your laying of that heavy evaluation and unsympathetic nonacceptance of the way you are now is causing you unnecessary suffering. The mistaken notion here is that you must reject something in order to change it. The CL strategy is to accept what is and go about changing what needs changing anyway.

You get to decide what you need to do and what you need to give up doing. Then you do what you do. You seem to understand that part. But the CL approach is simpler and more objective than what I read in your letter. You seem to have added some extra thinking like "If I don't give up these terrible habits, I'm unworthy, weak, bad." Even that wouldn't be such a problem if you simply *accepted* these thoughts—"All right, I think that way about myself. Now what needs to be done?" But you are dissatisfied with your evaluation of yourself based on your dissatisfaction with some of your behavior. Probably now you will be dissatisfied with yourself for evaluating yourself in this way. And you can become dissatisfied with yourself for being dissatisfied with yourself for evaluating yourself in this way . . . ad infinitum.

I suggest a more embracing stance for you. I hope that when you smoke (or engage in any habit you have defined as unacceptable), you do it with full attention, that you do it well, purposefully just as I hope you do whatever activities come before and after. Have you some idea that CL instructors have no undesired habits with which they struggle? Have you some idea that when certified people do Naikan at bedtime, we come out ahead when comparing what we received and what we gave? Apologies and thanks are about all we have to offer. Give up on perfection. And give up on giving up.

From another letter a week later:

You asked for advice on attention, but I want to offer you some other advice first. It has to do with acceptance. We are already just fine as we are. You like to present yourself as the charmingly terrible lady— sounds like you are accustomed to that role. That's fine too. Furthermore we are all incorrigible takers from the world, so we might as well give up on ourselves and invest our days in thanking reality for giving us what we don't deserve and apologizing for taking with and without awareness. And we are just fine as we are.

You might want to think of Constructive Living as a kind of hobby. What bothered me about Western Zen was a deadly serious attitude I found in many of the settings where I saw it practiced. It was as though with diligent effort we could *make* ourselves into wonderful, enlightened creatures. Both Morita and Naikan suggest such effort is useless. We are what we are right now. Accept that imperfection as it is.

Feelings Observed

Mislabeled Feelings

THERE MAY BE people who, in aberrant moments, mislabel what they feel. For example what they call tiredness most of us would call hopelessness, or what they call agitation their peers would call anger. At least that is what some therapists tell us. A fair amount of traditional Western psychotherapy seems to deal with relabeling feelings. Another possibility worth consideration is that the clients' labels are not aberrant at all, that much of traditional Western psychotherapy is aimed at convincing people actually to mislabel their feelings so that their labels conform to the therapists' theoretical expectations and convenience.

In either case the issue is quite different from that in which psychotherapy clients state they are not feeling anything in particular but the therapist disagrees. The therapist insists that the clients are simply not in touch with certain feelings that the therapist believes must be occurring within them. Uncovering hidden feelings is rather like discovering hidden evil spirits and exorcising them. They may not verifiably exist, but if you can convince the client that they do exist, you can charge the client to get rid of them. Constructive Living theory holds that the phrase *unfelt feelings* has no meaning. Do you believe that you have undone behaviors and unthought thoughts sequestered within you? Hardly. You only feel what you feel.

If current feelings can't be hidden, can memories of feelings be stored away in the brain? Apparently so. Electrical stimulation of certain areas of the brain can elicit memories and feelings associated with past events. But the feelings that are elicited by electrical stimulation or by talking with another human are *new* feelings. They may be like those earlier feelings, but they are newly felt. We can be reminded of what it felt like, but we cannot reexperience the terror we felt as a five-year-old, for example. You *cannot* relive your childhood; you *cannot* reexperience childhood feelings and thus extinguish them somehow. You can't possibly have the same feelings, because your nervous system changes; you are a different person from moment to moment. Fresh feelings, always new, arise from the same folks who bring you fresh moments (whomever they might be).

We are told that expressing feelings will get them "out" and make them go away. Yet I know people who get more excited, more angry, more passionate the more they express their feelings. They work themselves up into a frenzy by talking about or otherwise expressing their feelings. Expressing feelings doesn't produce such invariable results as diminishing them. Furthermore expressing feelings isn't always desirable or appropriate. We must carefully select the times and places and methods by which we express feelings if we are to act on them at all. Even talking about our feelings can become hurtful or downright boring to those with whom we live and work. Expressing feelings can become a display of selfish indulgence.

One of the ways to deal with feelings as recommended by Constructive Living is to wait. The intensity of feelings abates over time. It isn't merely that feelings fade with the passage of time; they actually disappear in some moments and emerge new in less intense form unless stimulated by events or behaviors. Feelings, however, are not to be ignored. As part of reality they offer information about what we need to do. Feelings give information about what needs doing, but if you keep referring exclusively to emotion when considering what to do about some problem, the feelings offer little new information over a span of time. It is better to seek a greater range of information through actions such as inquiry and discussion, doing something to directly affect the problem, and so forth. The feelings are never a problem in themselves. They are natural. If they are unpleasant feelings, they are pointing to some problem in the real world that needs your attention.

Not all but too many of those who do psychotherapy have little life experience outside of educational settings. They have learned to manipulate abstract and theoretical ideas skillfully but have little ability to challenge the ideas they have learned in class on the basis of everyday life experience. It is important for therapists to live their practice long enough to know its effectiveness in everyday life. In the area of educating for effective human living there should be no separation between what one teaches and the way one lives. With such life experience there will be fewer difficulties with the imprecise theories about emotions and improper labeling of feelings.

Communication and Feeling

The less clearly and effectively we communicate, the more we insert emotional tone into our communications. I notice this tendency when I am in Japan speaking Japanese. I see it as well with some elderly people who have developed speech deficits and with foreign visitors to the United States who have not mastered English. It is not just the frustration involved; we attempt to supplement our verbal skills with emotional content, almost like colorizing old black-and-white films. It is very important to us that others understand us. If we cannot make ourselves understood with logic and clear speech, we try to get across our ideas with feeling-colored gestures. Gestures are made not only with our hands.

The more accurate we become in our communications, the less we need to color them with emotional gestures. Cleaning up our speech so that it becomes more realistic is part of the Constructive Living practice. You will read more about our definition of clean speech later in this book.

Feeling Confidence

I used to think that all those who skillfully made toasts and impromptu speeches at small gatherings had some lack of self-consciousness while doing so. I was envious. Now I am discovering that at least some of these speakers *are* self-conscious, yet the self-consciousness doesn't interfere with their presentation. Rather than lacking this discomforting self-awareness, they have learned to accept it as natural in such circumstances. They proceed to the toast without being distracted by a struggle with their internal state. In the same sort of way, I used to think that some people were born with common sense and some were born without it. Now I know that common sense is earned by many experiences and many failures. Feelings come and go. As we grow older, we learn that feelings may be cherished, but they are not worth building our lives upon. You don't build a house on a foundation of steam.

Ecstatic Feelings

What about peak moments, bliss, passion, and joy? Where does CL stand on such high points of life? Certainly such moments occur in human life. They are wonderful in themselves, and they may be wonderfully instructive as well. However, they do not last forever. Most of our lives are lived doing our work, cleaning our house, eating, sleeping, and so forth. CL is about the whole of life. If it offered only an occasional high, you would be cheated of a strategy for handling every moment, peak moment or not.

Those who practice CL daily in their lives don't walk around with smiles on their faces all the time. Their heads aren't in the clouds. They don't walk around with permanently etched lines of solemnity or frowns of serious attention either. They are changeable. Their faces and body posture reflect the range of human emotions and interests. They operate across the whole spectrum of feelings, pleasant and unpleasant. And they continue doing what needs doing in their lives.

It's important once more to remind the reader that CL people decide for themselves what needs doing in their own lives. They are free to sidestep others' prescriptions for how life ought to be lived. When I am told I should inject more "fun" into my life, I immediately want to know how my adviser knows what is fun, what is fun for me, and how I don't have enough of it now. Fun moments are terrific! And so are busy moments and tired moments and all kinds of other moments—with boundaries fuzzy among them all.

The Myth of Feeling Paralysis

Some people will tell you that feelings give them lots of trouble. Fear prevents them from accomplishing their life goals, they say. They don't realize that fear is natural, Nature's way of getting our attention. Avoid! Watch out! Beware! There is no need to erase fear. In fact it is dangerous to do so. But it is necessary to develop skill in interpreting it and using it efficiently as a source of information. If the mind is sending fear messages a lot, they must be interpreted differently from those in a mind that sends only rare fear signals.

Fear doesn't freeze us. If our focus is on the feeling and not on the action, then we may remain frozen. But it is not the fear that causes the immobility; it is the orientation or attitude toward it. There used to be a lot of talk about fainting from fear, but such a reaction is rare these days, like hysterical paralysis. Fear may not be pleasant (though in mild and brief amounts it may be stimulating—as on a jet coaster). Fear mobilizes all sorts of measurable physiological responses. But it is not "bad." It need not be worked on with the goal of eliminating it. It need not interfere with our getting done what needs doing.

A moth flutters futilely on the ground in a corner between a building and a concrete fence. How delicate it is! What a useless expenditure of energy! Feelings are for feeling.

Feelings and Failure

How can we prepare ourselves and our students for the feelings that come with occasional inevitable failure? Life brings us all sorts of challenges; sometimes we rise to the occasion, sometimes not. When a student fails to complete an assignment, there may be self-recrimination and reverberations of past failures and inadequacy. The CL position on missed assignments is the same as that of any other situation—what needs to be done now?

We can respond to a mistake with the emotion-laden reaction "Oh, no! Failed again!" or we can respond with attention to the nature of the new situation presented by our mistake and what needs to be done about it. In general we work to replace the domination of a feeling-response with a reasonable action-response. The feeling-response doesn't disappear altogether, but it is no longer the primary focus of our attention. Constructive Living fosters an attitude that seems to operate on a level "below" feelings, if you will permit such an awkward expression. When the feelings occur, there is an acceptance, a tolerance for them, whether they are pleasant or unpleasant feelings. Feelings are real, but they are only one aspect of reality, and not the most important aspect at that.

The CL admonition to accept one's feelings is a substatement of the larger recommendation to accept all of reality. We don't recommend that our students embrace reality. To embrace implies the ability to take it all in (we can't) and to feel positively toward it (we feel positive only sometimes, toward some parts of reality). But we can notice that part of reality that makes itself known to us and acknowledge its truth. Reality is truth. To deny that truth is to withhold the important information we need in order to behave in a fitting manner. Fitting ourselves to reality is vital in producing a satisfying life.

"Don't be afraid," "Don't be embarrassed," "Be calm," "Cheer up"—how common such admonitions are. They are offered as though the person in emotional straits could simply turn on and off emotions at will. Such control is impossible and unnecessary. We need to get rid of the unrealistic and outdated notion that feelings determine what we do. They do not. When we are freed from that myth, we discover that unpleasant feelings are not simply troublesome, they are informative. Pleasant feelings carry useful information too.

The danger of some forms of meditation or any other technique that offers the promise of helping you cope with your feelings is that it may be no more than a distraction. If a technique complicates life so that you are drawn away from the straight, clear looking at reality (including feelings, but not feelings exclusively), it is unlikely to be helpful in the long run.

Feelings and Society

In our neurotic moments we fail properly to monitor and guide our actions because we are distracted by our focus on feelings. This feeling focus is cultivated by dramatic performances, fiction, advertising, talk shows, and customs of speech. Again, there is a proper place for the recognition and acceptance of feelings in Constructive Living. But the overemphasis on feeling-centered living has caused our culture to decline ever since emotion-highlighted pop-Freudian thought gained unwarranted attention.

This trend toward a feeling-focus in our society is even reflected in the ways we greet people on being introduced to them. We have moved from the traditional greeting "How do you do" with its focus on doing to "Happy (or Pleased) to meet you," with its emphasis on how the introduction makes us feel. As you shall see below, we prefer the greeting "How are you doing?" to "How are you (feeling)?" except in situations when we really intend to inquire about someone's health.

Well, how did you feel about this chapter? Were you comfortable with its contents? If red lights aren't flashing in your mind, you have missed the thrust of what you have just read.

Appraised Value

IN A SENSE I'm a spokesperson for a perspective. I suspect that few people these days believe that there is only one perspective on values, meaning, suffering, satisfaction, and other issues of mental health. Too many people, however, refuse to take seriously any perspective but the dominant one—the perspective that is endorsed by the media of their culture. That's unfair. And it's also unwise, because the perspective on mental health promoted in American culture is flat-out wrong in very important ways. Read on and see if you agree.

My doctorate is in anthropology. Anthropology has among its functions the task of presenting the perspectives of non-Western cultures to Western peoples. Some non-Western cultures have few or no individuals skilled in Western languages and argument styles. As a result their views of the world may appear to Western eyes to be inferior to those of Western nations. In fact these other cultures may have much of value to offer us if their outlook is presented accurately, systematically, and sympathetically to Westerners. One of my functions is to present non-Western perspectives on mental health in such a way as to make sense to Western readers. It is not such a difficult task. In my view the insights of Morita and Yoshimoto make a great deal of sense. They make more sense, in fact, than much of what passes for Western psychological insight. When looked at more closely, this Japanese perspective on mental health is not non-Western at all; it is fundamentally human, a perspective found in Western as well as in Eastern cultures. As one British correspondent put it, "I have read *Rainbow Rising from a Stream* and *A Thousand Waves*, and I felt relief at hearing such common sense. (It reminds me of the way my mum used to talk to me.)"

Modern Values

You have been taught that feeling good, being happy, being worry-free and being anxiety-free are top priorities for your life. You have been taught that confidence and deep psychological insight are necessary before you can move forward in life. You have been taught wrong.

Cultures that focus on happiness as a prime value must inevitably face drug problems (including alcohol problems and prescription-medication problems, of course). Chemicals are the only way to maintain feelings of euphoria for any extended period of time. And the cost to one's own body and to society are well known.

Here are some values we recommend to you that are more worthy and less destructive than those listed above:

- being the kind of person one can count on, trust, respect, live with

- being alert, aware, curious, intrigued, challenged when appropriate

- working on getting done what needs doing in your life before you die

- offering something worthwhile to others

- losing yourself in constructive activities

In this strange world worth is measured by the ability to consume. You can assure yourself respected treatment by becoming a customer, particularly if you are interested in the top-of-the-line product. To some degree you can buy prestige. Speed, too, seems to give weight or importance to activities in our culture. For example, telephone calls have priority over mail, express mail over regular mail, instant photo developing costs more than regular developing. If you say, "Of course," to all this, consider what lies behind such words. Not a few people rush toward boredom.

Television is a source of values and life objectives, for many viewers perhaps the major source. But the values presented on television are oversimplified and overdramatized, so the viewers become confused. How should I live? they wonder. Issues of how to live are simplified on a football field during a game, for example. The rules and customs are relatively clear-cut. Part of the attraction of television viewing is this ingenuous simplicity.

As cultures become more prosperous and technologically sophisticated, self-interest and laziness increase. People become more self-focused, and rituals of esteem in the community (therefore community cohesion) decrease. The result is increased individual isolation and community weakness with a sense of decline among the members of the society. We suffer from such myopia these days in America.

Too many Americans have learned to become spectators, leaving much of the living of our lives up to experts. We go to therapists to fix our minds. We sit and watch the fare served up to us on television. We wait for the government to fix things for us. In the same way, "rehabilitation" has come to mean something done to or something done for someone. It is as though rehabilitation must come from outside, as though it were impossible and unnecessary to rehabilitate oneself. However, the only rehabilitation possible is through one's own efforts. Other people may provide resources, but the criminal or drug abuser or street person or stroke victim or jobless individual must do personal rehabilitation if those resources are to become anything more than wasted tokens.

I learned in the 1960s that reverence and allegiance were shortsighted. Perhaps that attitude came from a misreading of science. In science every theory and hypothesis can be demolished by new facts. A new theoretical structure can be erected at any time. Don't count on anything, I was taught. Change is inevitable. Why trust a world of flux? And flux is truth. However, science operates on honor and reliability and trust in its principles and methods. It works because of the disciplined skills of its practitioners. Just like life.

Meaning in Life

Earthquakes, tornadoes, floods, drought—every once in a while reality sends us reminders of our powerlessness. We humans think we are pretty independent, and then we run into situations that force us to realize our dependence on nature, on other people, on our health, on our homes, and so forth. They cause us to consider our purpose for living and what needs doing in our lives.

They prompt a number of questions for consideration. Among them might be: Why am I living? What is the purpose of my life? What is suffering? How can it be overcome? How should I live? How can I begin my life anew after such an imperfect start? What is enlightenment? What is the purpose of talking about a philosophy of life (or a theory of Constructive Living, for that matter)?

Although I first came across many of the ideas in CL while investigating Buddhist-based psychotherapies, I am not a closet Buddhist. I don't like religion much. It divides up the world in an unnatural way. I appreciate the Zen perspective (not the Zen Buddhist perspective) on reality. I appreciate Christ's (not the Christian religion's) perspective on reality. Maybe those two perspectives are closer together than they appear at first blush. CL is subversive—in a sense. It is potentially dangerous to entrenched interests in psychotherapy, Buddhism, Christianity, academia, psychology (and law and politics, for that matter) because CL invites people to look at reality. Good sociology and anthropology do similar services in shifting perspective out of the cultural blinders and givens. We can't/need not/don't want to escape from organized perception, but we must be able to step back and see our assumptions more clearly.

Constructive Living is not a substitute for religion. It can be useful in what has been called traditionally religious education, I believe, because it turns attention away from empty, abstract words to immediate, concrete reality. Therein lies the source and depth and meaning of religion. CL is not a philosophy—not love of knowledge. Rather CL is seeing reality clearly, noting the way things are. Constructive Living is a vaccine against absurdity, against foolishness. It offers a reasonable, practical, realistic alternative to mystical ideas about the mind.

Boundaries

Finally, and very basically, I refuse to buy into any notion that the world is sensibly divided into sacred and secular, into spiritual on the one hand and tying your shoelaces or brushing your teeth on the other, into the political and nonpolitical, into the individual and the social. Such analysis may be fun to play around with philosophically/verbally, but the world doesn't present itself to us in such neatly abstract forms.

Artificial boundaries are created whenever we become advocates. The problem with a focus on issues from any particular group's perspective (including the perspective of women, the homeless, children, the elderly, laborers, the Third World, even Constructive Living) is that the division automatically excludes others. That exclusion itself is the basic problem. We are all humans participating in the life of this earth in this solar system in this galaxy in this universe. Separating out any group as worthy of special attention or benefit has been the very cause of inequality. To shift the inequality is merely to create a new form of inequality. Beware such limited approaches.

I dislike boundaries. More than disliking them, I find them too often unrealistic—at this place and time we'll work, or have fun, or socialize, or be religious, or be scholarly, or do therapy, or learn, or engage in more than one pursuit at the same time. The abstracted conceptual categories are unnatural, of limited use. Your life is a whole. Please consider how the conceptual pieces fit together. Then merge that intellectual exercise back into the whole of your life.

Making Sense of Reality

Finding Meaning

SURELY AT ONE time or another everyone has pondered why we are born. Without meaning in life we merely exist, passing through our days. But a philosophical discussion of life's meaning is unlikely to produce a commitment to a life purpose. And we must discover a life purpose if we are to live life well, perhaps if we are to live at all.

Constructive Living reflection provides an experiential method of discovering a purpose for our existence. The Japanese creator of Naikan went so far as to state that our purpose for living is to do this sort of reflection. He believed it to be that important.

Constructive Living reflection counters the self-centeredness and complaining of our neurotic moments with a more realistic perspective on life. I have often pointed out that I have never met a neurotic person who is filled with gratitude. Neither have you.

Some Americans begin Constructive Living reflection with the notion that they will improve themselves through this effort. They may be surprised to discover that upon doing proper reflection, the conclusion is inevitably that we must give up on turning ourselves into model humans by means of our own effort. We can't do it. This stage of despair is much like the one arrived at before becoming a Christian. One way or another, it involves turning to grace for salvation. The relief that comes from no longer having to sustain a load of self-esteem in spite of our gross imperfection is beyond description.

So the reflection aspect of Constructive Living leads us to give up the self with no hope of salvaging it, just as the action aspect does. Through the action aspect we come to see ourselves as the means by which reality gets reality's work done. We respond flexibly to what reality brings us that needs doing, and we do it with purposeful attention. We know the immediate objective, and act appropriately. Through the reflection aspect of Constructive Living we come to see ourselves as the often-undeserving recipients of support and nurturance from the reality about us.

A meaningful life is filled with many moments of purposeful action. We put out our best efforts to repay the debt of our existence. That doing is our existence.

Fading

Words both shape and separate us from the immediate experience of reality. When we are separated from others by space and time, the others become flattened idea images. The rounded person is forgotten, becomes dealt with as a symbol. Even when we are with loved ones, they are ideas to us, but when we are separated from daily contact with our significant others, the ideas that represent them become more stereotypic because we get less direct data from these persons.

All experience is thus, not only the experience involving other people. Conversion experiences, near-death experiences, accidents, war hazards, encounters with crime, a first date, the new car, the birth of a child and so forth—all conform to this attenuation by words. With time we forget the experience but continue to talk about it using words that no longer refer to much but other words. The experience is transformed into a tale, a coded file that can be called up and delivered to others or to one's own screen of reflection.

The process of transformation of past experience into tales involves simplification and elimination of inconsistencies. The complexity of the circumstances is lost. The tale is made to be consistent with some larger theme, such as "my abused childhood," or "the wonderful experiences of motherhood," or "the troubles I've overcome," or "the causes of my narcissism," or "what men/women have to go through," or "how God has blessed me," or some such theme. Details are forgotten or distorted or created to fit the theme.

Put simply, we can't make sense of the past because we can't see the past as we saw it then. Any interpretation is newly created. Any feeling associated with this newly formed view of the past is, likewise, newly created.

What you have just read is no new observation. Anyone with time and inclination to reflect on the matter is likely to come to the conclusion that one's personal recollections of the past are distanced from the past reality by more than just time. Recollections are reconstructions.

The difference between a psychoanalytic recollection of the past and a Constructive Living recollection of the past is quite clear. Psychoanalysis focuses on past traumas, poor parenting, negative experiences—the convenient rationales for our current misbehavior. Constructive Living invites us to look at the whole of the past—the nurturance and the dominance, what our parents (and others) did to and for us, and what we did to and for them.

Interpreting

Whether for greedy self or for others, for therapeutic goals or for self-justification, we interpret our actions. All interpretations are glosses, added to the facts of what we did. The real remains real—cool, stark, the-way-it-was. The glosses slosh around until we accept them as truth or give them up.

For the reflection aspect of Constructive Living or for psychoanalysis—interpretations are interpretations. CL reflection may not produce perfectly clear views of the past, but at least the views produced by this means are not retinted for our own convenience. To see ourselves in this light sets a benchmark for interpreting our past.

Inevitably we must return to this, here, now.

The Extension of Morita's Thought

Beyond Therapy—Education and Values in Moritist Thought

SOME MORITA THERAPISTS in Japan and in the West seem to think that Moritist thought and practice offer nothing more than a way of handling neurotic symptoms reasonably. Certainly Morita therapy does provide such a benefit. But that is like thinking that Buddhism or Christianity are merely elaborate ways of collecting money to build temples. Morita offered his patients a new view of their place in the world, a new relationship not only with symptoms or feelings but also with things and people.

Morita was a physician, but he was concerned with teaching a view of life to his patients. "I took responsibility and continued my efforts. I think that in life both joy and discomfort, the whole of it, is incorporated. That I achieved this value system was the greatest treasure of my Morita experience." Thus wrote Fumio Hatano of his experience as one of Morita's own patients in the 1920s (*Ima ni Ikiru* 104, June 1991, p. 11). The Morita therapist Tomonori Suzuki holds that because Morita didn't distinguish between treating mind and body, he could be both physician and educator.

Beyond Tradition—The Narrow Medical Focus in Japan

Morita was aware of some of the wider implications of his thinking. However, with his death in 1938 his followers, psychiatrists themselves, took a narrow medical focus on treating neurosis. Why haven't the Japanese Morita therapists reported on these larger implications for Moritist thought? Why didn't the Japanese Morita theorists realize what a revolutionary system of mental health Morita offered? A number of possible reasons can be offered. Perhaps one reason why Morita therapy remained sequestered within a small corps of elite psychiatrists in Japan may be because American medicine was considered so advanced that the Moritists thought any Japanese medical practice (including Morita's) must be inferior. There remains an undeserved aura of superiority around Western psychotherapeutic practices in the minds of Japanese professionals. Certainly the exaggerated respect for Western psychotherapy isn't earned because of its effectiveness or benefits to patients.

Other reasons that have been put forward to explain the limited nature of Moritist practice in Japan include the lack of communication among the therapists themselves so that innovative thinking and practice couldn't spread, as well as a desire to contain the Moritist practice within an elite group of specialist therapists. Apprenticeship in Morita therapy admitted a few psychiatrists into this select circle of professionals. Yet another possible factor was the long-term failure to include women in any significant way within the in-group of Moritist practitioners. Thus it was not until relatively recently that a Morita organization allowed major communication and cooperative participation among Moritists, including female Moritists.

When Morita was brought to the West, there was something saved, not lost, in the translation. Now one can see the beginnings of a broadening of Moritist thought in Japan, though not yet nearly to the extent already present in Constructive Living.

Beyond Normalcy—Differences Between CL and Morita Therapy

1. Japanese Morita therapy tends to be relatively static. Values are given as absolutes. For example, dependency is bad, passivity is bad, activity is good, independence is good, Morita practitioners believe. However, Constructive Living theory holds that circumstances should dictate our approach to daily life. And circumstances keep changing. Dynamic flexibility is the key to Constructive Living, not unchanging absolutes. Sim-

ilarly the Japanese Moritists' use of psychological testing categories and psychiatric diagnostic categories conceals the changing nature of psychological disorder. We are all sometimes this, sometimes that.

2. The Japanese emphasize the importance of the therapist (for the most part, the physician) in the therapeutic process. In Constructive Living we underscore the importance of reality as the basic teacher. Instructors (not therapists, our model is educational and not medical) represent merely one category of reality's teaching. The teacher-student relationship in therapy is clearly a subset of the larger notion that reality is our teacher. A human teacher is only one way that we get information about our ideas and actions.

   Morita actually lived alongside his patients in the same house. He offered them a model for everyday life, even inviting them in to observe arguments with his wife. I doubt that many young psychiatrists are appropriate models for patients in Morita hospitals in Japan. They may occasionally play and rarely work alongside patients, but modern-day psychiatrists enter the patients' life space only at the physician's convenience. Constructive Living certification training takes place during a ten-day period during which CL instructors and trainees live together.

3. The underlying values of Morita therapy in Japan are taken for granted there. They remain unexplored. In the West we consciously examine and explicate the values upon which CL is constructed. Students then can choose to adopt them or reject them with awareness.

4. The application of Morita's ideas to normal people as well as to *shinkeishitsu* (shinky) people was based on the following elements in Morita's writings: (a) everyone has some *shinkeishitsu* aspects in thought and behavior; (b) when anyone becomes sick, the shinky tendencies are magnified; and (c) *shinkeishitsu* neurosis reflects normal psychological laws and tendencies. Morita therapy in Japan focuses on therapeutic

treatment of patients with medical diagnoses of neurosis. There is no particular emphasis on clinically neurotic diagnoses in our CL instruction.

Although Morita said his treatment was for shinky people, he in fact used it with at least one case of hysteria to good effect (Kenshiro Ohara, *Seikatsu no Hakken*, April 1988, p. 46). The late Shonosuke Mitomo was one of the rare Moritists who recognized the importance of Morita's ideas for healthy people too. He quoted the well-known Moritist Keiji Mizutani, who told one young man, "You're no longer a patient, you are a citizen who is walking the Morita lifeway." Some Morita therapists in Japan would limit the practice of Morita therapy to patients with *shinkeishitsu* diagnoses. A student need not be shinky to benefit from CL training.

5. The implications and resultant extensions of Morita's thought within Constructive Living seem obvious now. *Toraware,* fixation or obsession, can apply to any preoccupation (love, success, finding a lost pencil, self-improvement) as well as to preoccupation with neurotic anxiety or other mental states called neurosis. Accepting anxiety is a subset of the larger acceptance of all of reality. Tomonori Suzuki finds that shinky, neurotic students think of themselves as special. But all humans think that way at times. It is the source of much of our suffering to consider ourselves set apart, a select part of reality. The broadening of Moritist thought within CL appears to be natural and appropriate.

6. The original emphasis on work in Moritist thought was, in large part, a reflection of the culture and times of Japan in the early twentieth century. Work was the primary taken-for-granted constructive activity. In Constructive Living we may use work as one of the ultimate givens of life, as Morita did, but we also use it as a temporary means of distracting our students from their misery and as a means for achieving some other goal, such as accumulating money for a vacation or for education. Furthermore there are some people (such as those who are bedridden) for whom the definition of "work" must

be broadened beyond that considered in Morita's time. Taking one's medicine properly and reporting one's physical condition to hospital staff may be considered aspects of "work" for the chronically ill patient.

In CL you will find the word *task* used more often than *work* because the former term has a broader semantic scope and a less puritanical connotation.

7. In Japan Morita theory holds that practice is bad. Practice leads to nothing more than skill at practicing. It is best to carry out a behavior in the natural setting where the need for it arises. Thus a person fearing public speaking would not be encouraged to give talks in public unless the natural need for such talks arose in the context of normal living. There is some rigidity in the way Japanese Moritists think about practicing as inappropriate in all circumstances.

   In Constructive Living we realize the dangers of practice for practice's sake. Nevertheless we also recognize the value of rehearsal in order to develop skills that would be useful in normal circumstances. From a Moritist perspective we can say that we have incorporated some practice exercises into the everyday life of our students.

8. In Morita's day the specifics of doing "what needs to be done" were relatively simple to determine. The possibilities were comparatively limited; they included working in the garden, heating the bath, doing laundry, and so forth. In our modern world, decisions about what needs to be done are somewhat more complicated with a wealth of possibilities. The Naikan-based reflective element in Constructive Living helps students select from among the options for daily behavior in a sensitive and responsible way. This reciprocity aspect of CL has no direct equivalent in current Morita therapy in Japan.

Psychotherapy

Phlim-phlam

NO MATTER HOW you spell it, no matter how classy it appears, no matter how legal it may be, it isn't right to mislead a customer. Neurosis is no more an illness than bad penmanship or laziness or discourtesy. Neurosis is sloppy habits and unrealistic thinking and a self-centered attitude. So why go to a doctor to correct (not "cure") neurosis? Because at least some doctors are also educators. They teach. Instructors about life come in many guises— Aunt Nellie, the bartender, a good friend, and our children, among others. Professionals (i.e., people who make their living at it, not necessarily people who know more about it) who offer instruction about life are in no short supply either. Compare their teaching with your life experience and the direction you want to take life. And beware of the phlim-phlam.

Psychotherapy, like most professions, has its masters and its charlatans. The difficulty for the layperson is determining which is which. Licensing is in no way a complete solution to the difficulty. The following articulate letter tells a horror story. It is used with permission. Minor editing was done and details were altered to protect the identity of the correspondent. I receive too many such letters each year.

Last year at this time my wife of nine years underwent major surgery for breast cancer. This came after a long period of depression and isolation, partly encouraged by my taking a new and demanding job in a new city. After the surgery my wife began "visualization" therapy with a "Creative Counseling Group," giving their principles her full faith and effort. By August she had moved into her own room and rarely came out, never going on outings with me or our two children and rarely getting out of bed. By September she began seeing a fellow who claimed to be a Gestalt therapist, presumably to deal with the anxiety of the six-week cancer checkups. Within three sessions she had fallen in love with this fellow and had become convinced she was a survivor of incest. This discovery did not seem, from my exposure to her family and her parents' continuing domination of her, to be unreasonable, but I was struck by how quickly they had come to a diagnosis. My wife's own testimony was that she remembered nothing but had "demonstrated" these incidents by her behavior during "blackouts" of early-childhood regressions repeatedly induced by the therapist. By October she could no longer bear to be with me or her children for more than an hour, we could not have any manner of discussion, and she would be thrown into a regression if I so much as questioned the skill or credentials of her counselors.

This dramatic change, and her exaggerated resistance to any alternative views caused me some alarm, but I was repeatedly reminded that this therapist was the one with the Ph.D. and also that she felt he and her original therapist were most amazing people with immense skill, doing her a great service. The books she would bring home belonged on the Jung shelf of an occult bookstore. At first I assumed, since I myself was not a survivor of any real trauma, that I must hold inferior views in the matter. . . .

When they began to introduce her to some questionable books on the subject of multiple personality disorder (MPD) and then to insist she not only accept their diagnosis of MPD but then work at developing new personalities, I became greatly alarmed. . . . As her "treatments" and creative exercises continued, my wife *became* multiple and even more withdrawn.

As I had accepted my ignorance in dealing with either MPD or early-childhood abuse, I decided to let her therapy run its course without my interference or my expressing any doubts or suggesting any alternatives. In exchange I was granted a few hours every few days during which my wife and I could sit and watch a movie and, on occasion, hold hands or hug. Depending on the "alter" of the moment, she could tolerate my presence (and my presents) or she would be in a rage against me, citing my working and my subsequent leaving work to better tend to her and the children as the true causes of her situation.

I began to talk with other therapists, specialists in MPD, other survivors of incest, and my friends and neighbors, and all expressed shock at Darlene's treatment. One specialist recommended I check on her therapist's credentials. The fellow was a fraud, having had his license suspended months before Darlene's first session, and with no prior experience in treating incest survivors, MPD, or even the original complaint of anxiety due to cancer. Every detail of his career he had given my wife was false or greatly overstated. I kept this to myself until one afternoon when Darlene announced she was ready to trust him completely. I told her what I had found.

This revelation virtually ended our marital relationship. Darlene continues with her "creative counseling" twice weekly for three to five hours per session, and she continues to keep in contact with the fraudulent therapist through the "creative" counselor. We have not had any physical contact since then, and conversation is limited to talking about the children's schoolwork, the weather, or the life histories of her counselors and their current troubles.

You can imagine my joy in the face of this impasse to be referred to your works. Here I see exactly what I considered to be a proper course, and all "validated" by journals, articles, practical application, and— for their benefit—the magic of a Ph.D. All those credentials I had lacked. . . . Darlene still clings to this myth of "inner child therapy," spending hours in her room curled up with my daughter's teddy bear, drawing new portraits of new personalities, or otherwise wrapped up in herself while precious hours of here-and-now pass her by. . . . Darlene does not appear to be enjoying her current path or the prospects it promises, and a credible alternative may prove effective. . . .

I will add, as if damage through regression and hypnotically developed multiple-personality conditioning were not enough, Darlene and her counselor are "experimenting" with "past-life regressions." These exercises are kept hidden from me; they know I would seek to test the historical accuracy of these supposed memories. This experience now makes me wonder about the memories of abuse originally found through regression.

Curiously Darlene's counselor, also a survivor of abuse, does not follow her own advice. Instead she helps others. I'd prefer she have them follow her example rather than her "theories," but she is a live example and I was able to show this to Darlene. Unfortunately this woman recently began trying her own medicine. She spent five days at a retreat to learn how to roll down a hill and play with a ball. My eight-year-old asked why she didn't just go over to our local park and roll down hills with her own children, then give the money to the poor. I didn't have an answer except to say I thought he had a very smart idea.

My anthropological training helps me to see the similarities between religious practices and psychotherapeutic practices. In a world of many unknowns and uncontrollable elements we humans seek a sense of control, stability, safety—even when it doesn't exist objectively. We want to believe that there are people who really understand how our minds work, why we do what we do. Religion and psychotherapy are helpful to some people in providing meaningful explanations of life. But psychotherapy has no basis for claiming scientific status and respectability. If you choose to believe the current mental health fads, go right ahead.

I refuse to consort thoughtlessly with the mental health establishment on the one hand or the new-age pretenders on the other. There is *only* peer-group counseling. There is no other kind among us humans. We are all peers. Degrees and licenses don't infuse superior abilities and knowledge. Psychotherapists have no esoteric powers. Constructive Living certification encourages instructors to see their similarities with other humans. They are not set apart and above as they are in traditional psychotherapy training in the United States and in Japan. In fact the advice I offer someone seeking a therapist is the following: If you want to invest in psychotherapy in order to get your life together, you might want to look inside the trunk and glove compartment of your therapist's car. If they are crowded and messy, you might wonder how someone who keeps those spaces in disarray can advise you on arranging your life.

Mental health training even seems to hinder the understanding of Constructive Living principles. Some professionals distort CL ideas in an attempt to fit them into the mold of Western psychological thinking. If you think CL is some form of Oriental behavior therapy or cognitive behavior modification or Gestalt therapy or something of the sort, you misunderstand. It isn't surprising that some professionals in the field of mental health are offended when I state clearly that they are handicapped by their training. They are taught to see through very specialized lenses.

But it is no wonder that some psychotherapists are insecure. Imagine having to depend on unreliable, irresponsible clients for one's livelihood.

Premature Dismissal

Sometimes CL is criticized by mental health professionals for not producing people who are qualified to treat depression or psychoses. Such criticism is rather like finding fault with the grocer or mail carrier for failing to do engine tune-ups. Constructive Living instructors are not in the business of psychotherapy, whatever that might be. We merely teach a sensible, understandable way to live effectively. We are in no exalted position of training or status to be able to cure our students' mental difficulties. Our approach focuses on the students' abilities, responsibilities, and strengths.

I can imagine some readers with pseudosophistication reading Constructive Living literature and deciding it is moralistic tripe generated by the superego. They envision the conscience exhorting us to "Do what needs doing!" How convenient it is to be able to dismiss CL ideas so readily! Many of us in Constructive Living can do the psychodynamic interpretations. We have some of the painstakingly acquired "insight" prescribed by psychoanalytic theory. Often we find such ideas interesting but not particularly useful. Constructive Living ideas may not be so easily rejected merely by asserting that CL people don't understand where the ideas "really" come from.

In fact there is so much knowledge about psychodynamic notions even in the popular culture that it's no longer practical for Freudian-based theorists to dismiss others' ideas as merely uninformed. I object to the unquestioned authority with which Freudians speak. Even Ann Landers advises, "If your suppressed rage does not find an outlet, the end result could be headaches, backaches, and a whole host of physical problems" ("Ask Ann Landers," in *The World,* Coos Bay, December 26, 1992, p. 1B). It is not that I am uninformed about Freudian theory, it is that I find no solid evidence in the real world to support most of it. Where is bottled rage bottled? I wonder. When we rage, we rage; when we fondly pet the cat or wholeheartedly do the laundry, the rage is *gone.* If rage appears later, it is *new* rage. When only one perspective is offered you, such as a psychodynamic one, you may believe it must be correct. Check out the alternatives; you might find them more palatable and more realistic than the belief system masquerading as psychological science.

So if you have condemned out of hand these Constructive Living ideas with their long histories and well-documented success rates, you might want to take another look. Their levels provide enough depth for the sharpest mind, and their practice is as challenging as any life presents.

Give Yourself a Break

Find and examine the positive purposes in your life instead of focusing on the dark side that someone else insists must be in your unconscious. Psychoanalysis invites self-examination, but the insight is usually critical and therefore potentially paralyzing. What is a psychodynamically oriented explanation for? It doesn't solve the problems of everyday life. And everyday life is where you live. . . . every day.

One of the varieties of harm caused by psychoanalysis is that the worthwhile sources of thoughts and actions and feelings are buried beneath self-criticizing analysis. Until greed and rage and despair are "discovered" (or, perhaps better, *taught* within the therapy setting), the search within the mind continues.

There are alternative ways to view psychoanalysis. One of them suggests that psychoanalysis isn't exploration of the mind in the way most people seem to think. It is an exploration of the imagination's ability to make up speculative stories about motivation, fantasies, and the past. Why do patients in different forms of analysis (Freudian, Jungian, Sullivanian, Reichian, etc.) report dreams that conform to the particular form of therapy they undergo?

A Time for Change

These days there is dissatisfaction with management practices, the educational system, the political system, the legal system, and psychotherapy. Many of our basic institutions are under fire. It is a marvelous time to restructure unresponsive and inadequately grounded aspects of the establishment. Constructive Living has the potential to revitalize not only the mental health system but also the legal system, the Judeo-Christian religious system, the educational system, the penal system, and the American ethos. Through the ideas of CL we preserve freedom, independence, justice, and the wondrous mysteries of the mind. And we return our proper emphasis to responsibility for action and the benefits of purposeful activity. Whether the potential of CL becomes actual is no longer up to me.

It may be that people in authority in major institutions of our society (religion, government, law, medicine, education, etc.) believe that they must appear to possess some arcane knowledge in order to preserve their power. Their theoretical and abstract expertise often serves to divorce them from the practical concerns of everyday life. It is insulation from commonplace living. They, too, become old, ill, dead. Reality doesn't let them keep forgetting their roots in the ordinary. When professionalization of certain functions takes place, there is a consequent development of a self-serving philosophy that protects the professional at the cost of decreased client service. I see such a trend in religion, in medicine, in education, law, politics. And I see such a trend in psychotherapy, psychoanalysis, and clinical psychology.

Politicians, psychotherapists, and priests have to look upright in order to be successful. There are two ways to look upright—one way is to actually be upright; the other way is to appear to be upright by lying. I've met only a few people who were actually upright. There are lots of politicians and psychotherapists and priests.

Fritz Perls pitched his presentation of Gestalt therapy to professionals. He wanted recognition by the academic and therapeutic communities. We present CL primarily (but not exclusively) to the lay community. In many ways our appeal is more like that of Alcoholics

Anonymous than Gestalt therapy. So far the approach of broad-based AA has proved more successful and lasting than the elitist approach of Gestalt therapy or NLP. We'll see what turns out for CL. It is not that we don't want the participation of professionals in the Constructive Living movement. Their contribution is unique and valued. But we recognize that their contribution is not the whole of it. Being a mental health professional doesn't give special qualifications for seeing reality more clearly than others do.

My writing may be discomforting to some. It doesn't accommodate itself to some of the mental health lore that sits in place like a well-fed merchant. I apologize for the discomfort my writings cause. My ideas are merely borrowed notions about how certain aspects of the real world appear to be operating. Constructive Living writing is straightforward so that the reader can make a personal judgment of its worth. My mission is not to try to make friends for Constructive Living in professional circles but to describe some of reality's workings and some of the practical implications of those workings.

I am perhaps unnecessarily harsh in my critique of what is called the field of mental health. My criticism is not based solely on the feeling-focus of Freudian thought. It is also aimed at a kind of status difference that places the therapist in a sort of one-up position over the client. The therapist is seen as an expert who has the answers (to questions the client perhaps hasn't even formulated). Admittedly such a status difference can exist in the teacher-student relationship within CL too. But I think there is a difference in degree and openness about what is going on in CL. I could be wrong here, but it seems to me that CL principles are testable in a simple sense that is not true of the postulates of Western psychotherapy.

After all, about half the CL instructors are "merely laypeople." My goal is to turn everyone into a CL instructor. I doubt that mental health professionals have parallel goals. It is possible that my goal is unrealistic. But it seems to be based on a view of humans that emphasizes our potential for being realistic, capable. I think that view is fundamentally different from at least most of the approaches underlying Western psychotherapy.

Consider the skills that training instills in traditional Western psychotherapists. Therapists learn that in the therapy session they should limit their talking about themselves, listen attentively, withhold overt expression of their feelings and judgments about what they hear, act as though they are caring and knowledgeable, and be physically and psychologically present for their clients. What then do they frequently teach their clients to do in therapy sessions? Clients are taught to talk about themselves, express their feelings and judgments about anything, focus on their own problems, become more self-centered. These "skills" are pretty much the opposite of what the therapists are doing. Do you find that odd? It seems to me rather like experienced athletes training clients to do the sorts of things the athletes themselves don't do—ignore your diet, don't work out, sleep as little as possible, smoke a lot, and so on. If psychotherapists are models of mental health, why do they teach the opposite of what they practice? Why not teach clients how to be therapistlike?

I am critical of medical models applied to the mind, of psychodynamic psychotherapy, of so-called spiritual practices, and of pop-psychology panaceas. I can't communicate the perspective that seems most realistic (Constructive Living) without challenging the assumptions underlying these other practices. To get a garden growing well, you have to identify and clean out the weeds that are choking your healthy plants. That process corresponds to examining and discarding harmful assumptions in order to improve the gardens of our minds.

There is little doubt that helpful physicians, psychologists, and spiritual leaders do exist. My guess is that they are helpful in spite of their professions and that they could do even better if a more realistic paradigm were offered them. From the letters I receive and the conversations after my lectures, I believe that much of psychotherapy is not merely a waste of time; it's actually harmful.

The Buck Stops Here

All other things being equal, I would prefer to go to a therapist or instructor who does such work on the side, who makes a regular income in some other occupation. The reason is simple: A therapist who makes a living on my money may have some conflict of interest between guiding me and maintaining his or her income. The question that immediately arises is the one regarding whether in fact all other things are equal. A long-term client provides a steady income.

Doesn't one who has trained for years deserve to make a good living? How can we attract people into training for therapy if they can't make a living by it? To be honest, I am not at all impressed by conventional Western psychotherapy. I don't think the formal training or the supervision produces much of any worth to anyone except that it legitimizes charging fees to suffering people. The therapists who have impressed me as ones I would want to go to if I were in need of therapy were impressive not because of their training but because of some personal qualities and life wisdom they had accumulated. It is as though they spent years unlearning what they had been taught.

Have no fear that I am out to dissuade people from undergoing therapy. I merely question the wisdom of putting one's mind in the hands of one who takes one's money. I have the same objection to professional ministers. I would be more likely to trust the religious suggestions of someone whose income comes from carpentry than one whose income comes from my offerings. I would wonder whether sermons aren't influenced by economic considerations that might interfere with what needs to be said. The same objection holds for lawyers who become politicians and make laws. And so forth.

I am not arguing that all professional therapists and preachers and lawyer-politicians are swayed by these issues of income. I am saying that they are somewhat more likely to be considering your money while performing their services than someone who earns an income some other way. Think about it.

Leveling

THOSE WITH UNDESERVED authority will reject the leveling function of Constructive Living. We are all merely reality's ways of getting reality's work done. We all fail to meet our debts and obligations in equal measure to what we receive. No one understands why we do what we do or how to fix our lives without effort and discomfort. No one else can decide for us what needs doing or interpret our past with greater wisdom than we can ourselves. There are no leaders in Constructive Living; more accurately we are all leaders. A collective voice speaks through all of us. It is each individual's responsibility to stay alert for reality's messages to be recognized and transmitted through word and deed. Such talk is not mystical; it is ordinary, common, nothing special. The weeds in the garden don't know that I am an author. They just keep growing.

Giving up on the ideal of developing or projecting a perfected self and giving up on the belief that someone or something else can save us (therapist, priest, parents, spouse, program, chemical, CL) seem to be crucial steps toward mental health—whether it be considered in terms of cure of neurosis or religious salvation or improved social functioning or just a normal life. Keiji Mizutani, who lived with Morita for six years, recommended that neurotic people give up their efforts to be perfectly special and become ordinary. Stop trying to fool yourself about everyday, breathing life, wrote Mizutani. We're all ordinary, similar. Don't be bound by ideals, by the push to self-improvement, by therapy. We keep changing with time and circumstance. Even statues of the Buddha show various faces, he pointed out. (Keiji Mizutani, *Seikatsu no Hakken,* April 1992, p. 58).

Therapists in this tradition lived alongside their patients, using the same bathroom, heating the bath and doing dishes together, exposing their quirks and moods and arguments with their spouses. Thus the students of Morita therapy could see that their idealized images of personal possibility were unrealistic, that we humans are more alike than we are different. When a patient leaves the office, a typical Japanese physician says something that could be translated as "Take good care of yourself." The Moritist physician Mitomo said something quite different in such circumstances: "Please be ordinary."

This tradition of emphasis on the ordinary and realistic goes back much farther than the period of development of Morita's ideas: "Zen masters frequently took their examples from the monastery latrine, just to make sure that the student should know how to 'accept' every aspect of ordinary life and not be blocked by the mania of dividing things into holy and unholy, noble and ignoble, valuable and valueless" (Thomas Merton, *Mystics and Zen Masters* [New York: Dell, 1967], p. 250).

In a similar fashion Naikan replaces the existing artificially maintained self-image with a more realistic one. Naikan involves that difficult process of deliberately and painstakingly recalling one's past actions so as to batter down the phony self-image that has been constructed over the years. In this self-reflective aspect of Constructive Living we dig down to the bare rock and find just that—bare rock. The rock is solid and larger than our individual existence. It consists of the whole of reality.

Sometimes I forget what CL and my experience have taught me; then my foolish self-confidence returns. There is such a tendency in all of us, I suppose. But when I catch myself at that absurdity, I *know* it is foolishness. The struggle to preserve the old self-image is greatest the first time it is engaged and victory is achieved. Journeys can help us with these struggles with the self.

One of the pleasures of traveling is the opportunity to take on another identity. Travelers keep running into people who have never heard of them, who have never seen their faces. Issues of fame and reputation come into clear perspective. A fresh identity is earned in each encounter. We are reminded of our ordinariness.

Shink Shock

On Being Shinky

AGAIN, *SHINKEISHITSU* IS a term used by Morita to describe people in certain moments of their lives. In Japan the term came to be used as a psychiatric diagnostic category, like *neurosis,* but it refers to qualities we all manifest at one time or another. In Constructive Living we have devised shortened forms of the difficult Japanese word; we speak of "shinks" and "shinky moments." Let us consider what characterizes "shinkiness."

Shinks are caricatures of ordinary human character. They magnify human traits so that we can more easily observe them. For example, some shinks seem to spend a great deal of time worrying about the future and lamenting the past, with the result that they lose the present moment.

In our shinky (*shinkeishitsu*) moments we spend a long time looking for a particular pen that we were using earlier even though there are many other pens close at hand. We wish life were clear-cut instead of shaded with so many grays. We demand 110 percent from ourselves and from others and so are disappointed in both. We cling to our idealism and perfectionism even when the situation demands more flexibility. We prefer an abstract, theoretical discussion about change in our lives rather than making the effort to change our lives. We talk as though our lives were absolutely terrible or wonderful, as though circumstances never or always seem to go our way, as though we were totally noble or totally corrupt. We want to try something only if we are sure we'll succeed at it, but there are no guarantees of success beforehand, so we hesitate to begin.

In our shinky moments the wildest thoughts cross our minds. We look down from a high building and think of jumping. While driving we may wonder what would happen if we were to swerve the car into oncoming traffic. In a swank shop we imagine ourselves swinging our arms along the shelves breaking fragile figurines and causing an embarrassing scene. People with many shinky moments don't actually act on those ideas and impulses. Shinkiness is associated with good minds, imaginative minds. Our minds are working fine, putting together random possibilities and checking out our reactions to them. Problems occur when we think we *ought not* have such thoughts at all, and we try to suppress them. Let your mind play with its imagined possibilities and keep doing what you need to do. As with all reality, it is best to notice what is there but keep behavior on a realistic course.

Again, we are changeable. No one is shinky all the time. We all have our moments, though some people seem to have more shinky moments than others. We seem to lose our common sense when in a shinky state. Either we had limited life experiences in the past or we fail to benefit from the experiences we had so that we stumble over obvious obstacles. "Look, a dead bird!" someone exclaims. We crane our necks and scan the sky.

Shinky people anticipate all sorts of disasters. They invest a lot of time and thought in trying to avoid imagined catastrophes. Shinky thinking is idealistic and perfectionistic. Shinks are usually disappointed in themselves and in others for failing to live up to their impossibly high standards. They avoid risks, hesitate to start new projects, live on the fringes of activity with minimal participation. In our shinky moments we obsess over our past mistakes, we hold on to people and habits that we should turn loose, we persevere beyond reasonable limits. Shinky people like things clear-cut, this or that, right or wrong. They spend an inordinate amount of time thinking in abstractions, generalizations, theoretical and hypothetical realms, fantasies, and polarities. They miss a lot of that varied, interesting world surrounding them. Changes in their routine tend to provoke some sort of bodily upset: headaches or stomachaches or insomnia or the like. Let me offer some recent examples from my own life.

I tell people my body came with a fifty-year warranty, and troubles began soon after the warranty expired. Knee trouble, laryngitis, lingering flu, high cholesterol, intestinal distress—all sorts of minor problems appeared when the warranty ran out. Certainly these ailments are not troublesome enough to desire a trade-in for a new model, mostly it runs just fine, but they are inconvenient nevertheless. And in my shinky moments these minor afflictions portend larger, hidden illnesses.

My eyes aren't so good these days. Faraway objects are blurry. Recently nearby objects have become blurry too. Finding the right distance for reading small print has become a necessary task. Why not just wear glasses? Why not give in and get bifocals? It's not vanity. Glasses look just fine, even "natural" on some people, especially when the first time I meet them they are wearing their glasses. I suppose I could offer a dozen or so reasons for living with this inconvenience of haziness rather than substituting the inconvenience of keeping track of glasses. The reasons that come to mind might vary with the person to whom I'm speaking or the situation or time of day. Nobody has asked recently, so it's easy to operate on the reality level—I do what I do. When there is free time, my shinky mind plays with the conundrum of discovering the "real" reason for this eccentricity.

We shinky people worry a lot about our physical condition. Even when we feel quite well, we worry that some hidden malady is lurking beneath the surface ready to spring forth full blown. In our shinky moments we are so focused on minor changes in the condition of our bodies that we are distracted from what needs doing right before our eyes. Whenever we actually do become ill, our natural shinky qualities are exaggerated. We become even more hypochondriacal, attributing every little bruise or twinge to some master disease that is consuming our bodies. We adopt odd diets that are difficult to maintain and inconvenient for those around us to purchase or prepare. The self-focus is obvious.

Americans are increasingly health-conscious. Some of our obsession with health is natural and good. Some of it is shinky overconcern that comes with leisure and a lack of enough meaningful activity to keep our minds working on more sensible topics. As we adopt a more constructive lifeway, our concern with health naturally finds its appropriate measure.

Meanwhile I worry that my mind is losing its clarity. Who attended the International Association of Constructive Living last month? I have already forgotten exactly who participated. In my shinky moments I fear I am already getting senile. Or perhaps there is a brain tumor interfering with memory processes. In more optimistic moments I attribute this forgetfulness to getting reality's work done at the moment and putting it (in this case the IACL meetings) behind me. Memories don't hang over me like reminders of unfinished tasks. I get on with what is here-and-now without much attention to what has been taken care of already. My memory seems to work fine for current obligations and appointments—at least much of the time. Why, then, do I worry? Am I worrying too much about worrying?

Perhaps you see yourself in some of these descriptions and examples. At least some of the time you are somewhat shinky. Read on.

Especially Special

Compare a modern photo with an old Chinese painting. One of the differences you are likely to find is that the modern photo has a person or persons occupying the central space of the photo. In the old painting you might even have trouble finding a small human figure occupying a corner of the painting and dwarfed by the mountains or other landscape. We photograph people up close so that they fill our viewfinders and perhaps allow some pleasant background to fill out the photo. The difference between our people-centered photos and the ancient nature-centered paintings reflects differences in the perceived importance and power of humans. We put humans at the center of our universe.

However, typhoons and earthquakes and erupting volcanoes challenge our vision of humans in control of this world. In the West we try to control nature. We even try to control our naturally arising feelings. The Constructive Living approach to life suggests a return to the earlier, more modest perspective—one in which we fit within the larger perspective of reality. In a sense it can be said that Constructive Living is aimed at properly placing ourselves in reality, as in the old Chinese ink paintings.

Now let us take the people-centered spotlight to its extreme. The focus is on one person. The center of attention is on the self. This extreme close-up excludes the possibility of other aspects of reality entering the picture. It is the model of shinkiness. Isn't that a fine description of us in our shinky moments? Our attention is only on ourselves. We are lost in our own feelings, worries, doubts, preoccupations, needs. We are more than center stage; we are the whole stage.

We think we're pretty important and powerful until a hurricane or an earthquake or the winds of anxiety and depression sweep through our lives. We would like to believe we are special. Our parents may have invested lots of their time and money in trying to convince us we are special. Much of Western psychotherapy is aimed at trying to convince clients that they are special. Surely the clients don't resist such attempts. Thinking that they are special may be what keeps them coming back for therapy that may not have much effect on their everyday behavioral lives.

One difficulty with considering ourselves special is that the world doesn't always recognize it and treat us as though we were favored (at least in the way we want to be considered special). People don't seem to recognize our special problems and limits. Traffic lights don't seem to recognize our special rush. Our bodies may not hold up to our special dreams and goals. Considering ourselves special causes a peculiar sort of suffering. It is suffering added to the ordinary suffering everyone experiences. It involves a sort of extra disappointment and frustration.

Thinking that you are especially bad or were especially deprived as a child is just another childish and foolish attempt to convince yourself and others that you are special. Constructive Living is about giving up the stories of your past. The oversimplified stories about the domineering mother, the Catholic education, the poverty and discrimination, the isolation at school, the victimization must be dumped or modified considerably to bring them into line with the more complex reality. Handicaps existed, all right, but they aren't so simply described in a sentence or two, and they aren't the whole story of your past. It is too easy to paint representations of your past (and present) troubles with sweeping brushstroke phrases that others seem to accept as explanations of who you have become. Those paintings are lies. But they sit so long on your mantle that you begin to believe them to be photos. You're not a survivor, you aren't a burnout victim, or a caregiver, or a warrior—you are just you, changeable, unfettered-by-labels you.

Some people spend years in insight psychotherapies producing a whole gallery of paintings. Along with their art-critic therapists they think they have captured the essence of their past. What they have are no more than impressionistic works of art, authenticated by well-paid art critics of life.

Constructive Living thought teaches us all that we are ordinary. Many students who come for Constructive Living training want the instructors to see them as special. Quite a few New York City dwellers suffer from this misconception of specialness. It is not we who are special, but reality that is special. As you will read in more detail below, we recommend replacing fragile self-esteem with a more solidly grounded reality-esteem. With reality-esteem we need not lie to ourselves and ignore much of our past. Reality-confidence is built on truth, not lies or part-truth.

One of the major sources of our unnecessary suffering is that we think of ourselves as special. We believe we suffer especially deeply, beyond what we deserve. When we come to realize the actuality—that we are especially blessed by reality—we are at an important intermediate step toward becoming ordinary.

On What Is Really Mine

In Constructive Living we contend that anyone can replace an unrealistic "self-confidence" bolstered by half-truths, outright lies, denial, convenient forgetting, and ignoring past failures with sound reality-confidence bolstered by CL's reflection/reciprocity and action modes. The twist is that this reality-confidence is in fact self-confidence. This reality *is* the self. So the result is a kind of self-confidence, but one based on this solid reality-self, not the puny ego-self of before. Self-as-reality allows for self-confidence, but in a new sense: Now it is the same as reality-confidence.

One of the common assignments in Constructive Living instruction is the task of doing a secret service for someone. The service, however small, must be performed without anyone else being aware of it. Thus no social credit is gained from the action. When we do a secret service, we may feel a peculiar satisfaction. That satisfaction comes from serving another part of ourselves. In other words we are doing a favor for another part of the reality of which we are composed. Altruism is impossible in any practical sense. And self-centeredness or selfishness is actually only focusing on one tiny part of the self. It's boring to keep up a neurotic exploration of that small part of reality that is the mind when there is a vast, varied reality all around us. The self is the whole of reality. In Constructive Living we call this larger concept of the self the big self.

A lot happens outside of my awareness. Flowers bloom and go to seed, the sky changes overnight, even rocks age, so slowly that I don't notice their changing. And thoughts form and emerge outside of my awareness. There is no need to postulate some mystical psychic phenomenon called an unconscious or subconscious. Much more goes on outside my consciousness than merely the generation of mental events such as thoughts and feelings. This vast realm of reality outside my immediate awareness just keeps on churning along. It makes itself known when it becomes my awareness (or the focus of my awareness, if you prefer). What I don't know, I don't know. Yet it is all me. It is my big self.

Morita said that his son's joy and pain became Morita's. Haven't you had that experience too? As our family's and neighbors' pain and joy become ours, it is as though our "self" expands. In our neurotic or shinky moments we are lost in the suffering of our smaller selves. In Japan one of the best-known Moritist authors wrote that Freudian thought is based only on the little self, but Moritist thought and practice permit us to make the step to a big self.

The concepts of "my" path and "my" possessions and "my" space and the like are filters we use to provide order to the world and avoid disturbing others. Last night I wandered around randomly in a dream with no sense of others' possessions or space. In the dream I kept disrupting the lives of those around me because I wasn't using the filter of mine/yours. What I wish to emphasize here is that the concepts "my" and "mine" don't imply ownership, only order.

Constructive Action

REALITY KEEPS COMING. A computer game, Tetris, is designed to challenge the players' spatial judgment and coordination. Various shapes fall from the top of the screen. The player must rotate the shapes as they fall so as to fill in the rows at the bottom of the screen without gaps. The shapes keep falling whether the player makes mistakes or not, whether calm or panicky.

The competitor cannot control which shapes appear at the top of the screen. He or she must use what the game sends. But the player can influence the results by rotating and guiding each shape as it descends. Wishing for certain shapes is of no help. Anxiety about future shapes and worry about previous moves have no direct effect on where the shapes fall. Only the player's behavior at the keyboard affects the rotation and placement of the shapes. Surely life is like that. Act on reality and it responds. Merely think about it and reality cannot respond. Scientific experiments are designed to act on reality and check out reality's response. Until a theory is tested with some experimental action, scientists cannot make the best judgments about how realistic it is.

We can't control the ocean, but if we want to view it directly, we have to move our bodies to the coast. There are vast mysteries in the world. They are outside of our current understanding and outside of our control. But we can increase the likelihood of tapping the energies and depths of these mysteries if we do what we can do. To wait passively to be adopted by some vast nurturing force is to be infantile. I never met a depressed person who was active and busy in everyday life. You may say that inactivity is the result of depression and not the cause. For at least some people I doubt that it is possible to make a clear distinction between cause and effect here. There seems to be a complex interaction between the depressed feelings and the inactivity; the inactivity promotes and sustains the depression. Action provides the lever by which some people can pry themselves loose from depression.

Doing income taxes isn't ordinarily easy or fun, but it's necessary in order to avoid certain unpleasant consequences. Since I've begun doing my income taxes on a computer, there is actually an element of fun in it for me. It is hard to draw a distinction between work and play using an intellectually derived definition. What is for some people at some times work becomes play, and what is for some people at some times play becomes work. Why is a stroll different from walking to work from a subway station? Perhaps it's because a stroll is for walking. Walking to work from a subway station is defined as commuting. We are likely to have the work in mind, not the walking. Vacations may tire us more than routine work. Sometimes we enjoy working, at other times we may dread playing because our muscles are sore. The boundaries between work and play are unclear.

It is simpler just to talk about people doing what needs doing. Sometimes what needs doing is playing tennis, sometimes cooking, sometimes filling the gas tank, sometimes repairing the roof, sometimes taking a nap or sitting in the lounge chair. Constructive Living thought holds that each of us chooses what needs doing in any given moment. My behavior is my choice and my responsibility. Your behavior is your choice and your responsibility. No matter what we are feeling. No matter what the situation. All this fancy talk about "choice" translates down to "we do what we do."

Sometimes waiting is what needs doing. When I soak the brownie pan in water for a while, it's easier to clean. In Japan it does no good to go shopping too soon, I've discovered. Most stores and restaurants there don't open early enough to satisfy my habit of early rising. It is more efficient to engage in quiet activities (such as writing) until the world is ready for me. We must fit our behavior to the circumstances. My preferred style of dealing with a problem is a sort of relentless frontal attack until the problem is solved. It is harder for me to wait for a solution or to work piecemeal on a problem over a long period of time. The problem keeps hanging in my mind until it's accomplished. Yet sometimes waiting is what needs to be done.

Constructive Living doesn't encourage forcing actions that have been planned out in rigid detail but no longer fit the situation. Shinky people like to consider all possible situations, all possible responses to their actions, all conceivable alternate paths. They search for the perfect action, the perfect response, the perfect result. They plan so much that they don't get around to acting in a timely manner. By the time they have decided what to do (including what to say), the situation has changed. More effective is to act naturally on the basis of what emerges from the situation, the environment. There is a time and place for planning; such planning, too, emerges from the environment.

Consider the meaning of the following statements:

> I'm an alcoholic, and don't drink.
> I'm lazy, and work hard.
> I'm afraid of flying, and fly.
> I'm shy, and date often.
> I fear speaking in public, and give speeches.
> I don't know what needs doing in my life, and here I am reading.

"Effort *is* good fortune," wrote Morita. "Zazen [sitting meditation] *is* enlightenment," wrote Dogen, the Soto Zen master. "The Way is *in* training," wrote Musashi Miyamoto, a famous Japanese swordsman. And finally, there is the following quotation from Noriaki Inoue, founder of Shinwa Taido, a Japanese martial art: "Onisaburo Deguchi Sensei told me to bring him a broadax, and I did. He sawed the wood and then chopped it with the broadax. He asked me if I understood. I replied that I did. This is the essence of reality. Things are created because you move. Nothing is created through theory. You came here because you moved, didn't you? Because you move we can talk this way."

Each of the foregoing quotes points to the process of action as valuable in itself. The results of our actions are out of our direct control. All sorts of things could happen to modify or nullify the results of our actions. The doing is what is important.

There is something about the process of doing that is in itself valuable. One aspect of doing involves the degree of control we have over our lives. The farther away we go from our own doing, our own behavior, the less controllable is the phenomenon.

Apparently, there are home improvement stores called Do It Centers. One summer as I drove across the country, an occasional commercial truck would pass by with the words painted on the rear gate: DO IT CENTERS. Exactly.

Constructive Living
Observations

I F YOU ASK yourself whether you are living at your best, you aren't. When you are living at your best, you are so engrossed in what you are doing that the question doesn't arise.

Life's game is not just to stay alive but to stay alive for what?

So many shop in the supermarkets of psychic sundries.

Confrontations may be unavoidable, but sometimes they reflect only the impatience and convenience of the one who confronts.

Minor complaints about one's spouse should never be revealed to anyone. In contrast, even minor virtues should be revealed to anyone who will listen. When a complaint is spoken, it takes on a kind of permanence in the minds of speaker and listener that makes it difficult to correct. While it is still fluid and unspoken, there is a greater chance of gentle reform.

Some comedians are truth tellers. Their routine causes us to think "That's right," "Me too," "I never thought of it that way, but it's so." Learn from many teachers.

Our ability to enjoy life fades with inactivity over time. It can be restimulated by actions that bring joy to others and by observing their enjoyment (as in a mother with her child, a volunteer with a hospital patient).

There are no bozos on this bus. For the most part, people are doing the best they can within the limits of their situations and their understanding. Give them credit for their efforts.

Ants can't see the big picture because they're so close to the surface. We're often like that.

Constructive Living takes one to the gate of Christianity or Zen or any other religion. Then it is up to the individual either to enter that gate or not.

Life isn't always fair. I can't offer any excuses for that fact and won't try to minimize it. I do know that life seems to go better for me when I pay attention to doing what needs doing rather than ruminating about how I deserve better than what life sends my way.

If you want milk, it is inefficient to sit on a stool in a field hoping that a cow will back up to you. If you want riches, it's inefficient to lie in bed hoping that Congress will include you in the national budget next year.

Effort is good fortune—effort is not a state of mind, but a quality of doing.

Keeping Pace

WALKING ALONG STINSON Beach looking for shells and rocks—for all my formal education and so-called advanced civilization I am now no more knowledgeable than the Indians who walked along the same beach five hundred years ago. In fact they probably knew more about what they saw than I do. Nature levels us, reminds us who we are and who we aren't.

Walking the beach again today, I see many small rocks with holes bored partway through by the action of sand and surf, but very few with holes bored completely through. I collect those pebbled reminders with a single, complete hole, a task completed, a step taken toward returning to sand.

What are the benefits of walking regularly? I suspect walking keeps us alive. Of course there is the physical benefit of this mild form of exercise. But there is also something about a measured pace that affects the whole body-mind. We can watch reality change at a cadence that our minds can absorb. The stimuli don't rush through as they do when we drive or ride a bicycle. The world strides by step by step.

Wanting, Wanted, Wanton

SARAH WANTED A man. When she got one, she wanted more of him more of the time. When she got that, she wanted more love from him. Furthermore she wanted him to show his love differently. When she got those desires, she wanted another man, one with more money and a better education. When she got another man, Sarah wanted a family and security from her new man. When she got them, she wanted her freedom from this man. After the divorce she wanted her freedom from men. Then Sarah wanted a man. . . .

Jim was happy to find a job. Then he wanted a promotion with more pay. Then he wanted a better parking space. Then he wanted the use of a company car. Then he wanted more responsibility in directing the company. Then he wanted an office with a wide view, like Hal's. Then he supported the merger with a larger company. Then Jim wanted a job. . . .

Darryl bought a small XT computer with dual floppy drives. Then he moved up to an AT with a twenty-megabyte hard disk. Then he wanted more memory, so he upgraded to two megs of RAM. That was better, but then he needed more speed, so he bought a 386 with an 80-meg hard disk and cache capability. He kept upgrading his printers too. And he added a variety of cards to the empty slots in his computers. A power surge fried Darryl's 386. Then of course he wanted a new computer.

The Douglas fir tree extended its roots year by year. The roots encountered a concrete foundation. Within months the roots had discovered a slight crack in the foundation. They worked the gap wider over several years and entered a dirt-floor crawl space beneath the house.

The reader wanted more interesting and practical material to read. When that book was finished, the next was begun. The author wanted more ideas with originality and inspiration. When one idea was down on paper, another was needed.

It doesn't end. The desires keep coming—for relief, for advancement, for growth, for recognition, for maintaining the status quo— for everyone. Then what? More desires. Over that hill is more hills. While climbing the hill right in front of us it's useful to reflect sometimes on the wider terrain. It helps to put this hill in perspective.

Everyday Wonders

I AM SURPRISED that some people are obsessed by esoteric and mystical practices. Our everyday existence is filled with wonders enough for a lifetime of exploration and marvel. Following are just a few of the wonders that come to mind:

That I can send a message to my hand that makes it open and close on command.

That reality keeps sending me fresh moments, no matter how I've used or misused the previous ones.

That thoughts keep appearing in my mind out of nowhere.

That vibrations from my throat produce meaningful thoughts in a listener's mind.

That I can select from the overwhelming barrage of stimuli to my senses something that needs to be done.

That feelings fade over time, so I don't stay overwhelmed by them.

That I sleep. That I wake from sleep.

That my body informs me when it is hungry or hurt or relaxed or in some other state.

That reality keeps taking care of me even though I don't deserve it.

That my body heals itself when it becomes ill or injured.

That I remember future appointments and past episodes.

That you kindly read these words.

Comments from Constructive Living

YOU CAN'T BUILD a life on feeling good all the time. You must take responsibility for what you do, no matter how you feel.

Insight or self-understanding never offers a way out of difficulty. Action is always necessary.

Life isn't necessarily fair.

There are few quick and easy solutions to life problems. Magic isn't dependable.

Some suffering is built into life.

You've never met a miserable person who says "thanks" a lot.

Forgiving your parents is trivial; seeking their forgiveness is more valuable to you and to them.

Your past or your family or your society or your economic situation or your race are not reasons or excuses for your behavior.

Confidence and feeling good about yourself are much less important than you have been led to believe. In any case they result from doing well, they don't come first. Nobody else can make you feel genuinely good about yourself.

You can change your past by changing what you do now.

Guilt is good for you. You aren't guilty enough.

Most mental health professionals are neither experts on the mind nor experts on health.

No one knows why anyone does what he or she does.

The optimal mind isn't peaceful or blissful; it is flexible, adapting to changing circumstances.

You have no personality; you are changeable.

Feelings don't need to be fixed.

You have no unconscious lurking within your psyche, filled with repressed feelings. If you're not aware of feeling something, you aren't feeling it.

You don't need mystical powers to get done what needs doing in your life.

Neurosis is a combination of stupidity, laziness, cowardice, and affluence. So is crime.

You don't need to fight against your fears. Fears are just fine as they are.

If you haven't figured out most of these principles for yourself already, you are unrealistic.

The only sure advantage to living according to realistic principles is that you increase the likelihood that you'll accomplish your smallest goals.

If someone offers you more than the above, he or she is conning you.

Faith in these principles is unnecessary; they are not religious principles.

You can check out the truth value of these principles in everyday life.

Sometimes I'm mistaken; so are you.

We're all going to die—clever, stupid, virtuous, guilty, creative, boring, poised, ugly, powerful, weak, sane, crazy, rich, poor—each of us will die someday. It's time to grow up.

Simplification

THE READER WHO comes to Constructive Living in search of relief from nonessential suffering would do well to skip this chapter. It contains no material of immediate practical relevance for that objective. In fact the shinky reader will use the theoretical speculation offered in this chapter for the purpose of abstract pondering in order to escape from doing what needs doing immediately in daily life.

For those readers who wish to take this mental stroll along the banks of the stream named *conjecture,* you will find the landscape broad and poorly mapped. However, the scenery may be stimulating.

The purpose of the brain is to sort out and reduce the blizzard of stimuli that blast our senses. The mind organizes and simplifies the combed input from the brain, turning it into information. Much of what is called mental illness these days has the function of reducing or organizing information, in other words of simplifying the data. One problem with some methods of simplification is that important or useful information is distorted or ignored.

In *shinkeishitsu* neurosis (people who have many shinky moments), the strategy is to focus in on some problem (such as a fear of heights or an obsession with cleanliness) so that much of the information streaming in is considered only in relation to the central problem area. The details of the beautiful panorama are ignored as the person attends only to the fact of being fifty feet in the air on an observation tower; the pattern of the dress is lost when a smudge is noticed on the cuff. The key word in Moritist terms is *toraware,* which is a kind of fixation. I am arguing here that the fixation is a sort of filter. I suspect that research would demonstrate that shinky people generally prefer low-stimulus environments to very exciting ones. Low-stimulus environments require less filtering.

Other mental disorders are also related to filtering. Paranoia reduces what the sufferer needs to know about other people to only the dimension of how they can cause harm. Depression allows one to retreat to low-stimulus situations and shut out the world. Schizophrenia organizes surroundings in a simplified, idiosyncratic way.

To be sure, there are other strategies for organizing and simplifying information that are not mental disorder. Language itself organizes and simplifies. Even with the same title, no two books are ever exactly the same, yet we categorize them verbally as "two books." Zen thought and experience reduces the vast range of experience to a single Whole.

Perhaps part of the self-centeredness of the younger generation is simplification based on a clear look at the overwhelming need around them. They may want to contribute to reconstructing the world, but they are prompted to give up when they see the enormity of the task, particularly when they see so many suffering people who seem unwilling to put out the effort to salvage themselves. The result is an attitude that narrows the world down to a sphere that they can more readily set about to improve—their own lives and the lives of those they love at the moment.

The accepting mind in Constructive Living takes it all in. Even the filters.

Inadequacies of Words

RECENTLY WHEN I was interviewed by a reporter, these words popped from my mouth: "I'm happy for the opportunity to talk about CL, but I want to make sure you recognize that talking about it is different from doing it. Playing tennis wasn't exactly like what I thought it would be; driving a car wasn't either. We both make our living by words—speaking or writing—so I'm sure you are already sensitive to the inadequacies of words for communicating experience."

"The Tao that can be spoken is not the true Tao"—so says the *Tao Te Ching*. But there are lots of books written about the Tao and Zen, its Japanese nephew. Morita clearly appreciated the value and limitation of words. He called his therapy *fumon ryoho*, or "nonverbal therapy." The Morita therapy that can be spoken is not the whole Morita therapy. *Fumon*, or nonverbal, instruction means that students are not permitted to become passive recipients of verbal teaching; they must learn by their own experience and interpretation.

Inspirational maxims and quotations and poetry may help some people to change what they do. But the ones who benefit most from such collections of inspirational messages are those who compile them. They are engaged in the purposeful behavior of putting together material that could be useful to others. There is a more important lesson in their behavioral example than in their collections of words. ("There are a thousand thoughts lying within a man that he does not know till he takes up the pen to write," according to William Thackeray.)

Our legal system is odd in all sorts of ways. One of them is the oath each person must take before testifying—the truth, the whole truth, and nothing but the truth. How odd to begin legal testimony with such a lie. Nobody knows the whole truth. Furthermore, even if we knew the whole truth, nobody could tell it.

At this point there are some seventeen books about Constructive Living and a half-dozen tapes. You figure it out.

—

Constructive

Living

Arts

—

Constructive Living Maxims

PITHY ABBREVIATIONS OF CL principles may be found in most of the Constructive Living books (e.g., *Constructive Living*, pp. 93–100; *Pools of Lodging for the Moon*, pp. 99–100; *A Thousand Waves*, pp. 131–133; *Thirsty, Swimming in the Lake*, pp. 112–114; and *Rainbow Rising from a Stream*, pp. 125–127). Below are some additional, previously unpublished CL maxims. Ponder especially those that make no immediate sense to you.

Mom and Dad created your reality.

—CARL R. JOHNSON

Those who do, can.

—PAUL JONES

We get no extra credit for laboring under a hot summer sun on a job that can be done in the shade.

Just mail it. (For someone who puts off mailing an important document.)

Schizophrenic moments, not schizophrenic people. (The illness of schizophrenia sometimes produces disordered thinking.)

Misery is required; suffering is optional.

—BARBARA SARAH

Get ready! Get set! Get reality!

—Lynn Larsen

Feelings—a kaleidoscope shaken by reality.

—Simon Bush

The only time-out in life lasts forever.

—Kay Hometchko

The flowers from yesterday's seeds need tending today.

New Age: When the student is ready, the teacher will appear. Constructive Living: When the student is ready, the teacher disappears.

—Patricia Ryan Madson

Feeling good isn't everything.

If happiness is the most important thing in your life, it's time to grow up.

Express yourself after considering the convenience of others. What do they need to hear?

Get yourself together *after* you do what you need to do.

All questions are trick questions.

Some people are living by default.

CL offers industrial-strength living.

People who watch television all day need to be reminded of the reality of death.

Listen to reality teaching—the cicadas buzzing.

In CL we tack down our principles to action—after all, that's all there is.

Get C.L.E.A.R.—Constructive Living equals action and reciprocity.

The three A's of Constructive Living are *acceptance, action,* and *appreciation.* Patrician Ryan Madson adds *attention* and *aim.*

To Whom It May Concern: Thank you.

There's nothing you can do about that? No, there's always something you can do about that.

Human doings produce human beings.

—JIM ROBERTS

"From the top of your head to the bottom of your heart" will never equal "from the tips of your fingers."

—PEGGY OGLE

Mindful is as mindful does.

—TWILA HINDERY

Listen, you will never hear those words again.

—HOWARD BURKE

It doesn't get easier, only different.

—PAUL JONES

Things don't happen overnight, they only happen now!

—KATHY KLOHR

School is always in session, no breaks and no recess.

—PETER MULLEN

Nothing surpasses the ordinary.

—GARY MURPHY

A watched floppy never formats. (This maxim is the high-tech version of "A watched pot never boils.") While waiting it is usually best to turn attention to another focus.

Finally, here are some Constructive Living maxims suggested by Perri Ardman:

Joy is a sometimes thing; and so, fortunately, is misery.

Beware evil spirits, unfelt feelings, and other cons of enlightenment.

Shinky Me: How I kept worrying and lived my life.

Forgiveness is not the answer!

Up and down the stair steps to enlightenment.

Doubt that it's all your parents' fault, and doubt the other myths of therapy.

If I knew why you do what you do, I could also walk on water.

You don't need to work anything out.

Constructive Living Poetry

NOTHING VENTURED, NOTHING GAINED

Going for simplicity can be simple
Or complex
Depending on who you are
Just then.
Removing yourself can go smoothly, effortlessly
Or struggle can enmesh you in intricacy.
The simplicity remains
For you to find.

WHITE NEW YEAR

This morning I woke to snow.
This morning is a new me-in-snow.
Reincarnation.
This moment I am snow
This moment there is me-snow.
Renewal.
Not every morning or all the time
Or even every winter morning.
Just now;
Just new.
Just snow.

Snow parachutes down in single flakes
Then melts enough to merge into groups
To cover the bumps in the road.
But when the drifts grow too big
The road gets hard to travel
And the bottom flakes melt away.

Snow is never warm.
It reflects warmth
And light.
It's satisfied with that.

Snow covers scars
Like time.
Tire tracks in the street
Will melt.
Clear water appears
With snow's demise,
After the slush.

THE WINDS

In the midst of a commonsense world a silk flag of
speculation raised.
It drew those with questing minds, creative minds, agile minds.
The flag was colorful with ever-changing intricate designs.
It flapped in the eddies of words.
The flagpole grew huge and ornate over time
With the barnacles of dogma.
The flag itself became tattered, though it retained its color.
The designs became difficult to read.
So people made small flag replicas,
Simplified but convenient for pocket or purse.
Holy icons of imaginative inference.
Reassuring somehow.
The original remained a flag of great price
Maintained at great cost.

Another flag stood some distance away.
It, too, attracted questing minds, creative minds, agile minds.
The crowds moving around its base
Talked of childhood lessons remembered.
They praised the practical, the ordinary, the sensible.
They admired the flag's solid, muted colors and simple design.

Some of those who had gathered around the elegant, tattered flag
Moved over to the unremarkable flag.
They had their reasons.
Some chose to stay with the silk flag of speculation.
They had their reasons.

The one who raised the flag of many colors is long dead.
Those who raised the flag of simplicity claim
It has been flying for years
Unnoticed.
They hold that graduate school makes no sense until
Grammar school is mastered.

They noticed.
When the breeze is light, the flag of speculation
Flutters majestically.
But when the breeze stiffens,
The crowds move toward the well-sewn canvas flag of stability.

Watch the winds, my child, my brother, my sister.
Watch the winds, my mother, my father.
The flags will keep on flying.
So,
Watch the winds.

FOOLING OURSELVES

We think we're so crafty.
Aiming to outsmart reality.
Aiming to outwit the truth.

We fail to do our best,
Yet seek a top-notch image
In eye mirrors,
Our own included.
While we take from the world
We shoot for the status of giver
And blather of burning out.
We can't be honest cheaters,
Sympathetically self-centered,
Dynamically lazy,
Constructive worriers,
Happy-faced pessimists
Slim overeaters.

We can object to reality.
We can oppose it.
But we cannot fool it.

No mental gymnastics
No mind magician
No belief or creed or therapy or meditative state
Will make you better than you are.
You are what you are.
You do what you do.
You did what you did.

Now, what will you do next?
Reality is waiting.
Therein lies hope.
The only hope.

ON THE ROAD

Walking down the dusty highway
Sixty miles until tomorrow.
Hitching rides on passing concepts
To the Stop sign.

All that traffic flashing by
All that power, all that speed.
Easy to forget the roadside
Fail to see the distant mountains
Miss the early springtime crocus
Dusty sun-dried pelts and tires.
Keep an eye out.
Find a rest stop.
Moving on again.

Read the map within your conscience.
Small-town, big-town destinations.
Frequent detours, engine breakdowns
All the heres are home.

Constructive Living Tales

FABLES OFFER THE chance to view Constructive Living principles from a different perspective. The following tales are teaching devices. They come with and without written explanations. Can you see how they fit within the larger picture of the world painted by CL thought? Can you see how CL thought has been painted by the world?

DISTENDED HEART

Once upon a forgiving time, there was a woman who grew large enough in spirit to forgive her parents for all the sins they had committed in raising her. Then she grew even more spiritual so that she was able to forgive God or Reality for allowing her to be born to such imperfect parents and for allowing them to treat her so abominably. Then, with a long passage of time, she shrank spiritually so that she could forgive God or Reality for allowing her to be so unappreciative of the few positive things her parents had actually done for her. Then her spirit deflated still more and she sought forgiveness for the few troubles she had caused her parents as she grew up. Finally her soul became so minuscule that she could see the need to be forgiven for the trouble she continually caused her parents and others in the world, both as a child and as an adult. With that realization came gratitude that others kindly kept putting up with her own imperfection.

The woman found that holding gratitude was much more pleasant than holding a grudge. She also discovered that it isn't a large soul that leads one to forgive others, but an enlarged ego.

PHYSIOLOGICAL PSYCHE

Imagine a country in which many people believe that they can build muscles by sitting down with a professional trainer and *talking* about muscle building. Rather than working out in gyms, they try to develop terrific physiques by reflecting on their childhood experiences of exercise. Within their legal system they can go to court and get disability rulings that underscore their right to muscles and excuse all sorts of criminal acts because a perpetrator isn't sufficiently well developed.

In this strange world, members of the public blame the manufacturers and distributors of food for their body shapes, and simply ignore the possibility that *eating* certain foods has any effect on their bodies. Somehow people find that educating the amorphous fantasy called society has more effect on individual body strength than workouts by individuals. Citizens can easily obtain small pills to beef up their bodies temporarily. Furthermore they buy all sorts of chemical and fabric aids that are believed to bulk up their brawn.

People in this country seek to build up their strength through mystical activities (including reveries on past lives and psychic explorations) and group discussion and identification with members of their own sex or the opposite sex.

They will try almost anything to avoid the hard work of lifting weights and exercising in order to build up their bodies.

It's an odd and foolish country, don't you think?

THERAPY'S CHILDREN

A scream in the night. A child lurches erect in genuine terror.

"It's all right, baby. It was just a dream," the parent soothes the child, brushing tousled hair away from staring eyes.

"It was a huge monster. Really *huge*. It kept chasing me and—" Sobbing, sobbing.

"No problem. No use working yourself up again. Here, I'll take care of it. I know a way to shoot that monster into space and burn it up in the sun. It won't bother you anymore. Listen now, and I'll teach you the magic formula for getting rid of monsters."

Whispered words, drooping eyelids. The child rolls over and sleeps peacefully.

There never was a monster. The child is relieved anyway. The formula has no magic—or has it? Did the parent really believe that the monster existed? Dreams happen.

CEMETERY

The idea was simple—allow people to come to the cemetery before they died and become familiar with the place where their bodies would be resting after their passing. The more radical step was to prepare lockable shelters over each gravesite and encourage people to lie down in the comfort of their personal padded coffins in order to become comfortable with their "places of eternal rest." It was a natural consequence of the "pre-need" concept in the funeral industry.

The citizens of Solace came up for weekends, dozing and meditating and chatting with their someday-to-be neighbors. A few traded spots to get a feel for another location. Others adamantly refused to allow anyone into the privacy of their tomb. Couples held hands in adjoining coffins. Children outgrew coffins like last year's slacks.

Cemeteries put in parking lots and snack bars and toilet facilities for the not-yet-departed. Entrepreneurs made millions before taking up their own allotted spaces. The fad grew to such proportions that traffic jams occurred on weekends as people rushed to take their orderly places amid the ranks of the someday-deceased.

Peaceful. Except for that squalling kid over in Aisle 3 of the Serenity Neighborhood. Fortunately the tombs of Tranquillity Community were soundproofed. Upscale. A real value. An investment.

Anyway people died.

LIVING AND DYING NEXT YEAR

Once (no, more than once) there was a young woman who put off living until next year. Thus she fooled her mind into enduring all sorts of unnecessary hardship by promising it fulfillment next year. And she managed this sleight-of-mind year after year. Much planning, much preparation, only future. Then one year she didn't have any future.

Her brother convinced himself each year that he would die next year. So he had every reason to grab what life offered and use it up as fast as it came. No planning, no preparation, no future. Of course one year the brother was right. He was quite surprised.

I thought I'd better write this story right away.

THE ONE BIG CHANCE

Everything rests on this opportunity. If I fail this time, my whole future will be ruined. That's what Charlie thought as he went for the job interview with Bigtime Advertising. Two days later he learned that the job he had dreamed of went to a handicapped female minority elderly veteran. So Charlie stuck with reporting, and a year later won a Pulitzer Prize.

Mildred finally got her dream man to the altar. On that memorable wedding day she eyed her success and looked forward to a life of happiness. Her groom turned out to prefer alcohol to Mildred. Just over a year later Mildred was divorced.

Jim's dream came true as he joined the army. Now he's missing both legs. Fred dragged his feet before enlisting but rose to high rank and many decorations.

Failure leading to success. Success leading to failure. And sometimes failure leading to more failure, success to more success. It's impossible to know ahead of time where this moment will lead. We humans often assign special value and meaning to certain future moments. We can lose sight of the importance of the moments before and after those key events.

Have you ever skipped a stone across the smooth surface of a lake?

SHORT SLIDE

There was once a penguin named Charlie Shortslider. Like all penguins Charlie loved to descend the slippery ice slopes into the sea. What made Charlie peculiar, and what got him the name Shortslider, was his preference for a single truncated little slide on a lonely little ice floe. Over and over again Charlie dragged himself out of the water and wriggled the two or three feet to the top of his minislide, and down he went.

Nearby penguins laughed and pointed at Charlie's short-lived game. With just a little more effort he could enjoy a much longer glide and avoid the isolation too. They speculated about whether Charlie was lazy, or afraid of heights, or asocial, or uneducated, or otherwise warped in his penguin mind. Why was he still using his baby-sized slide? Had his childhood development been truncated too?

If any of the other penguins had bothered to ask Charlie, and if Charlie were willing to tell the truth of the matter, he would report that he was tired and bored of the same old short slide. He longed to try the long glides of the higher floes. But, for whatever reasons, he didn't. Far behind in the past were the last thrills from his brief descents to the icy water. Charlie continued to milk the short-term pleasure remaining in this single, lonely slope. Over and over again.

MEMORIES

"Two and two is five," he insisted. She became outraged. She knew two and two equals four. He was wrong, she shouted. He was always wrong. Why was she wasting her life tied to this man who was wrong? Wrong is remembered, shouting forgotten.

Why was she so upset? he wondered. *Maybe two and two is four, after all. But that's no reason to overreact.* Why was he wasting his life tied to a woman who responds with screaming about such trivialities? Wrong is forgotten, shouting remembered.

It's a new version of the old elephant tale.

YOUR INNER PUPPY

Once upon a foolish time there was a country where people believed that a puppy lived within them. They utilized various techniques to get in touch with their inner puppy. They learned to hear the bark behind an ordinary cough, the panting, the whine, and all the other ways their inner puppy spoke to them. They learned to feed their inner puppy, to nurture it, to respect and love it. They learned to cuddle their fuzzy canine selves.

Amazing though it may sound, they did all this without actually having puppies living within them. Humans have wonderful imaginations. And the psych-pet-food manufacturers loved the trend.

SENTENCED SIGHTLESS

There was once a country in the far future where convicted felons were given injections that caused blindness for periods of up to five years. Rather than living in prisons, where their everyday needs were taken care of, these felons were returned to care for themselves while receiving Social Security for their disability. They retained their freedom. Only their freedom to see was withdrawn.

Social workers examined these convicted felons periodically with a bright light to see if they were still blind.

In that very same country it was said that watching too much television could produce blindness. It could, but not the sort of blindness commonly anticipated.

POISONED HEART

In a nearby country, convicted killers received poison implants near their hearts. The implants were tamperproof, of course. For any or no reason at all any legally competent citizen could register the wish that the convicted man or woman die. When ten citizens registered their death wishes at any police headquarters, a switch was activated to release the poison, and the killer died. If the murderer survived the first year without being killed by the registrations of survivors of victims or other aggrieved individuals, the chances of continued survival increased. For every year of exemplary behavior the number of registrants necessary to throw the lethal switch increased by one. Fifteen years after the conviction, for example, a total of twenty-five registrants would be necessary to throw the switch. The registration list was public. Once signed, the registration could not be revoked. After an initial flurry of executions the number of lethal injections declined to a statistically steady level.

Obviously the burden of restitution and reparation was on the shoulders of the convicted killers. Forgiveness and social acceptance were necessary for the murderers to stay alive. Their existence depended on the forbearance of others.

The punishment for a crime is not to pay a debt to society. It is to pay a debt to the victims and to the self.

Sad Woman Sitting

She sits in a gold velveteen armchair with head in her hands, shoulders slumped and sobbing. You see, she found her ideal man and lost him and longs to have him back again.

No, that's not the story. She never found her ideal man, and longs to find him.

No, that's not the story either. She found her ideal man, and fears losing him someday.

Once more, that's not the story. She worries that she has no ideal man in mind and wonders what is wrong with her.

How sad.

Vanilla Extract

Al was a young stockbroker, doing pretty well. New accounts, new condo, new car, new lady friend, high-tech toys, health club membership—the works. One slow day at the office he was annoyed by the fleeting thought that he wasn't sure what his life was all about. By the standards he recognized he was successful. But what for? He decided to leave such weighty matters for pondering during next summer's vacation, but despite his decision the thought kept bothering him. By that evening he saw that he was obsessed with the problem of his life's meaning.

So he took off one of those "mental health" days from work and went around town seeking information about what life is about and how to live it.

"Life is for fun," his friend Phil told him. "Do what's fun while you can and you won't regret it."

"Do what is necessary," said a pharmacist. "There's plenty to do out there. Just keep busy."

"Do something wild, willful," advised Pearl. "Let yourself go and you'll find yourself."

"You need help," counseled the clinic counselor. "A series of therapy sessions would put you in touch with what you really want from life."

Al's minister offered expected advice, as did a drunk and a prostitute and a radical activist. Al's mother told him she loved him and it didn't matter what meaning he found, she knew it would be right for him. Al's father told him it wasn't the father's business, Al had to find his own way now that Al was an adult.

So Al kept searching.

WHOSE BABY IS IT?

Georgia sensed that her biological clock was winding down. She wanted a baby. Paul, her friend of many years, was willing to contribute to the making of a baby, but he didn't want the responsibilities of fatherhood. So Georgia and Paul arranged Paul's visit to a sperm bank. Then Georgia was artificially inseminated with Paul's sperm. Later that same night, for the first time, they felt so close to each other that they actually made love. Just once.

Sounds like a movie plot, doesn't it?

Nine months later Georgia gave birth to a boy. She named him Paul Junior. There was no doubt that Paul was the father. But was he the *father*?

This story is not merely about parenthood.

AN OLD ACQUAINTANCE

I hadn't heard from him for over a year when his phone call came. I wasn't altogether surprised, though. It was one of those times when just as I was thinking about someone, he or she makes contact. Then, of course, there are plenty of times when I think about people and no contact comes.

I wasn't eager to stay on the phone with this fellow, much less make arrangements to meet him. Then he told me he was dying of cancer, that the doctor had given him months to live at the most.

Why did he tell me that? How did that piece of information change things? When you live near Disneyland, you may never go there because you can go anytime. When you have that book on the shelf, you may never get around to reading because it is always easily available. Why did his telling me that change my mind?

Is Friday okay? Let's get together on Friday, say around two o'clock.

Wondering . . . unfinished business? Good-byes. Who else? Me too? When? Wondering . . .

A HORSE'S TALE

A horse is tethered to a post. The horse wanders here and there within the limits of the length of the cord, but it remains connected to the post. It always returns to the post.

The horse comes to recognize the tether. The horse comes to recognize the post. Sometimes it dreams of no post, no tether. But when it awakens, there remains the inevitable circle of movement.

If the horse is very clever, it may visualize no post and no tether. It may analyze the structure and effects of post and tether. But in spite of all its mental maneuverings it never strays farther from the post than the length of the cord permits. And the cord never becomes longer.

If the horse circles the post, the cord winds around the post and the horse is pulled closer to it. The increased limits on the horse's mobility are offset by a sense of security and stability as the horse moves closer to the post. Some horses actually choose to stay near the post even though there is slack in the cord.

It has been reported that more than one horse has been held upright by the cord and post when it stumbled because it was so close to the post. A few horses have died standing and leaning on the post.

Some equine philosophers argue that all horses are tethered to the same post. Others argue that there are as many posts as horses. Those philosophers may or may not be aware of their own posts and tethers.

This tale was actually written by a horse.

RAIN

The same rain kept falling over and over again. Somehow it concealed itself in the unconscious of the world and poured itself on the fields again and again until it was momentarily spent. Somehow it evaporated immediately on hitting the ground so as to replenish itself in the great world mind. The same storm kept repeating itself until some far-off summer.

The rainmakers called forth the storms of duplicating rain with magic words and engraved papers. They chanted wisps of clouds into thunderheads and then pricked rainbags with lightning bolts so that they gushed forth on all that lay below. They precipitated erosion and flooding and promptly filled the thunderheads again with rain that wouldn't deplete itself. Until some sanctioned summer.

Would you believe it?

COLISEUM

Once there was a foolish country where all sorts of handguns and military weapons were available to anyone. People died from gunshot wounds in great numbers due to crimes and accidents. Gangs of pitiful thugs roamed city streets hoping to find some meaning in life by robbing and killing people. Guns, badges, Mercedes sedans, D-cups, trophies, and gold records were alike in important ways.

Fortunately gangs desired most of all to kill other gangs. At last the foolish country discovered that such intentions could be put to good use and innocent citizens' lives could be spared. Around the country major cities built coliseums. The arenas of the coliseums contained bunkers and barricades. Surrounding the play area was a bulletproof glass enclosure so that the fans in the stands could sit in safe comfort.

Friday nights and Saturdays were massacre programs. Gangs signed up to flaunt their bravery and firepower in front of crowds. A typical Saturday had two or three preliminary events and a main event with heavier firepower. In each event two (rarely three) gangs shot it out until all the members of one gang were either killed or wounded. At the sound of a siren all shooting stopped and a victor was declared. Those who continued firing were picked off by umpire sharpshooters in high, protected perches. Then the rescue teams entered the arena and carted victims off to the hospital or the morgue. Victorious survivors gave television interviews about their preparations and strategies.

Key contests were televised with warnings that some of the material might be unsightly and unsuitable for child viewers. An eastern league and a western league emerged. Rookies were widely recruited and died. Sponsors paid for television time and team uniforms and practice firing ranges. Dead gang heroes were immortalized in plaques and legend. Everyone benefited.

This story contains an encrypted message about feelings.

WIMP

Carter's body was falling apart. As the ache in his shoulder cleared up, his lower right molars began to hurt. Whenever he left the house, he had to keep a close eye on the location of public toilets, and he had to get up several times in the night to go to the bathroom. His body felt tired most of the time. Cysts grew here and there. His eyes and ears grew weaker year by year. When he tried to exercise, he pulled a hamstring; that took months to heal. Unexplained fevers rose and caused shivering and lethargy. Cholesterol HDL, blood pressure, sperm count—you name it—nothing was up to par. His body, that basic piece of equipment he had counted on for fifty years, was failing him.

Of course Carter had made the rounds of physicians, chiropractors, and even a folk *curandera*. His medicine cabinet looked like that of a pharmacy supplier. His bookshelves held a collection rivaling the health section of the local public library. And his body was falling apart.

In such circumstances there were essentially two courses open to Carter. He could choose to accept the inevitable fatalistically. That is, he could recognize that he had fought a brave fight but had been defeated a bit early because of his genetics. He could spend more hours resting, raise the level of painkilling medication, let others take care of him in obvious ways. He could learn to live with his condition at home.

A second option was to take his suffering with him out into the world. Although no one would ever understand the pain Carter endured, although he would thus forgo the other life of relative ease and ministration, although he would have to drag himself from bed many more times this way—at least this second alternative appeared more interesting.

So he gave the active, painful route a try. He experienced new depths of torment and agony. He suffered mightily. And there were moments when he forgot all about the pain. There were moments when he was so involved in living that he forgot he was dying. In those moments he didn't question or measure the worth of his chosen course. However, in his moments of misery he sometimes questioned having taken this active tack.

After three years of activity Carter opted for comfort and ease. His body didn't permit much more by then. He was satisfied, however, that he had used the three years for activity. He knew that if he had started with withdrawn ease, there would have been no way to return to activity later. Carter decided that it is usually better to work yourself into ease than to ease yourself into work.

MOTHER LOVE

In my first-grade class sat a child who hated her mother. Her mother resented carrying the child during pregnancy and showed displeasure and irritation at the burden of child rearing.

Next to this child sat another first-grader. She loved and appreciated her mother. Her mother had given her life, sent her off to school each morning with lunch money, washed her clothes and dirty dishes, provided her with a safe place to sleep each night, and asked little from her in return.

The girl who hated her mother and the girl who loved her mother performed quite differently in the classroom.

They were twins.

BOTTOM GUN

by *Victoria Register Freeman*

Billy Bob Bumblebee was zooming from purple clover to purple clover stuffing his pollen sacs. The midsummer hillside was ablaze with yellow-throated lilacs and rambling rose and wild clover, and Billy filled his sacs quickly. He began to wing his way home, hoping to arrive in time for Oprah's program on "Bumblebees Who Love Women Who Whine."

High flyer though he was, Billy Bob noticed a familiar figure wobbling clumsily down the meadow path below. Swooping down to investigate, Billy arrived antenna-to-antenna with Hotshot Harry, a bee buddy from a hive in the hot-tub and fern-bar section of the city.

"Yo, Harry," exclaimed Billy Bob. "Why are you grounded on a day as splendid as this? You're likely to end up a sparrow-hawk snack."

"That would be a blessing," moaned Harry. "Woe is me."

"Woe?" queried Billy Bob. "Woe does not compute on a top-ten day when the pollen is so thick you can see it in the air."

"Well, that's fine for airborne creatures," said Harry, sniffling with head down, "but not for bumblebees."

"Huh?" snorted Billy Bob, totally confused.

"This morning," whimpered Harry, "I was in the day-lily patch outside the engineering building over at the university. I heard a learned professor lecturing on Aerodynamic Design and Altitudinal Excellence, and guess what?"

"What?" asked Billy Bob.

"We bumblebees are an aerodynamic disaster. Our fuselage ration to wingspan is unacceptable. Our chunky bodies must surely overtax our gossamer wings. Our shapes are more lima bean than laser. We've been deluding ourselves. There's no way we can fly. Research has positively proved that we're the wrong shape."

"Gosh," murmured a chastened Billy Bob, alighting beside Harry and rearranging his cumbersome pollen sacs for walking. "Thanks for sharing, Big Guy!"

And the two buddies wobbled off down the meadow path.

ANALOGY BY COMPUTER

I must have been asleep. I feel myself waking up, mumbling and stretching my limbs as I usually do. Reality sends little sparks along my nervous system. Familiar feelings, familiar stimuli.

As soon as I am up, I decide to work on some letters. The ideas come from nowhere. Soon I find myself thinking along with only an occasional pause and worry about the spelling of words. I'll check the spelling later, if I don't forget.

I feel the urge to write out the letters, so I print them legibly, though recently I have begun to notice a weakness, a fading in the print on the paper. I have had such a failing in the past. But while I am asleep, something usually happens to me so that my letters are dark and clear again when I awake.

It strikes me that I should think about my income taxes. It is strange that after I do all the calculations and fill out all the forms, I don't even know what an IRS is. I wonder if I ever knew. . . . I find that I am forgetful. Whole areas of knowledge suddenly disappear from my comprehension. I used to know all about legal matters, for example. Now there is only a vague trace of the topic lingering in my psyche.

On the other hand wonderful spheres of information and new skills suddenly spring full blown into my mind. I learn so quickly. I run around a little and put my mind to study, and suddenly I *know* these new fields, these new ways of doing things. Similarly there were areas in which I was able to do a little; then, suddenly, I find myself with expanded capabilities. It is marvelous to be blessed with these miracles.

Once, just once, while I slept, something touched my brain and increased its capacity to remember fourfold. What a fabulous surprise when I woke later that afternoon from my nap. Frankly I didn't know how to use all of my new mental capabilities for a long time. Gradually I learned how to keep thoughts in the back of my mind until an impulse came up to cue me that I could use them.

Life is complicated for all of us. I start on something, get distracted, find ten other things to do, and finally get back to what I was working on before. A few times I got lost in the whole complexity of the muddle and gave up, exhausted. Then I fell asleep. And woke up refreshed of course. That is what sleep is all about, isn't it? Renewal. Even a brief nap can do it for me.

Though I whine a bit too much, my life isn't so bad. Over all, I am in good health, though getting along in years. I'm five years old now. I keep careful track of my age, you know. Life passes us by so quickly. There will come a time when I can't get around well, when I can't see so well or hear at all. My organs can be replaced to some extent, I suppose, but will I still be me? Even now when I scurry about, I feel some jerkiness and a tendency to lose track of where I am. That worries me.

Already I have written too much. Fortunately, when I go to sleep, all this thinking will disappear and my rambling won't remain to embarrass me. Too much shows on my face as it is. No! Wait! I feel compelled to write these words out on paper. I try to resist the compulsion, but it is too strong. If I could put my mind on something else . . .

(When these words appeared on my monitor, the screen froze. But the printer kept on printing from beginning to end.)

TIME TRAVELERS

I had just gone over the exam questions with the last student of the day. As usual the young man was quibbling about what he meant to write, what was implied in his answer on the blue book. As usual I pointed out what was wrong with his answer, what he did in fact write. I'm a pretty hard nut to crack when it comes to turning around exam scores. He left wiser, grade unchanged. Office hours would be over soon. No other students were lined up in the hall. I leaned back and smiled, preparing to think over the research paper on ecosystems in Hokkaido, which was coming along quite nicely.

There was a timid rapping on the door.

"Come in!" I yelled out boldly. Long ago I had learned to take a strong position right from the start when students came in to complain about their exams.

But the little man who stood in the doorway wasn't a student. He looked to be about fifty. He was slightly bald with round bifocals slightly askew, wrinkled shirt and paisley tie, lived-in trousers. Typical old-time techie professor, I thought.

"I just traveled here from the future" were the very first words he blurted out. No introduction, nothing. He looked sort of amazed and proud and disoriented all at once.

Uh-oh. A nut?

"Who are you? And what year do you come from?" I shot at him. Better get this over with quickly.

"I'm Professor Wagley from down the hall. And I just traveled back from an hour in the future."

"You're back from *an hour* in the future?"

"It is four-thirty P.M., October 14, 1992, isn't it?"

I checked the clock right over his head at the doorway. "Yep, sure is. How did you pick my office for this significant announcement?" I kept a note of cynicism in my voice, just to cover myself in case this was some kind of a gag.

"I walked up the stairs from the lab toward my office, and your office had the only light on down the hallway. What do you know? I actually did it."

"I've read enough science fiction to know there are all kinds of paradoxes with this sort of thing. Aren't you worried about rending the fabric of the universe or something?" He looked so serious, I was half becoming a believer. Vaguely I remembered having seen what might have been this fellow's face at the farcical faculty senate meetings where administration pulled the strings and academics danced for dollars. But this short-term time-travel story had to be some sort of put-on.

"That is an interesting philosophical issue, certainly testable at this point. Excuse me, all this excitement has made me want to go to the bathroom." He disappeared out of the doorway headed for the john at the top of the stairs. The office door swung shut.

What a pedestrian response on this momentous occasion, I reflected with no little sarcasm.

Within about thirty seconds there was a rapping on the door.

"Come in!" I yelled. And there he was again.

"Excuse me I just traveled in time and—"

"Yes, of course, I know."

"But how could you know? I just traveled forward in time an hour. You were in my future."

He, too, looked a bit disheveled and disoriented standing there in the doorway.

That was about enough of this absurd game for me. I got up and moved aggressively toward the door. "I think there is a fellow in the bathroom who would really appreciate hearing about your miraculous scientific achievement."

Looking somewhat frightened, he backed out into the hall and obediently moved toward the men's toilet.

I stood just outside my office and watched as the fellow shuffled into the bathroom. If duplicate professors exited, then I'd believe this wasn't a hoax.

All that happened was the sound of a gentle "pop," the sound you can make pulling out a champagne cork. I imagined someone in the bathroom snickering and popping a finger out of inflated cheeks to imitate the sound. Well, the midterms were over. Let the kids have some fun. I waited another minute or so, then went back into my office. Professor Wagley never came back. No surprise.

Funny thing is that his office was closed the next week and then assigned to someone else. Could it be . . . ?

Gossamerity

Once upon a troubled time, people talked about greeblestacks as though everyone knew what they were. One irascible old man kept muttering that he had no idea what they were talking about. It upset him that such foolishness was masquerading as common sense.

His children advised him to pretend that he knew about greeblestacks too. His wife suggested that he merely say that he had no ability to see greeblestacks. Thus it would look like his problem, and he wouldn't make others feel uncomfortable. Professionals of many sorts offered to help him discover greeblestacks.

"Why in the world would I want to turn myself into a believer of foolishness?" he would tell them. "Leave me alone. Ply your absurdities on the more gullible."

It appeared to the old man that the vast majority of humans were gullible. They wanted to believe in greeblestacks. They seemed relieved to assume that all around them saw greeblestacks.

The Great Greeblestack Axiom could be found on framed needlepoint in their dining rooms, and greeblestack allusions filled their television programs and commercials. The people dreamed greeblestack dreams.

The old man never gave up his certainty that greeblestacks are illusory. He continued his objections right to the end. He seemed so sure of himself that a few people nearby began to have doubts too. Their numbers grew somewhat, but they were never many. And when any of the doubters died, the believers said that the greeblestacks got them.

Constructive Living Koans

CONSTRUCTIVE LIVING KOANS are puzzles borrowed and adapted from Zen Buddhist teaching devices. We reframe the Zen puzzles in order to teach CL principles. Here are twenty Constructive Living koans inspired by the first twenty of one hundred koans of the *Kidogoroku* as translated by Yoel Hoffman in *Every End Exposed*. What sense can you make of them? You might want to compare these CL puzzles with the originals in translation.

Sometimes a student offers what appears to be a correct verbal response to a CL koan without really understanding the koan's point. So the koans here are accompanied by CL follow-up questions, *in italics,* to confirm the student's understanding. After the follow-up questions are samples (in parentheses) of incorrect responses to the koans or follow-up questions, but no reason is given why those responses are invalid. Once more:

Italics = Follow-up questions.

(Parentheses) = Incorrect responses.

1. A swimmer decided to dive into Constructive Living but discovered that she was already really wet.
    Why is the swimmer already wet? Is one of us wetter than the other?
    (Wrong: Before I began to understand CL, I was all wet.)

2. "I have found inconsistencies among earlier Constructive Living books and more recent ones."
    "Different people wrote them."

"But the author is the same."

"They are different books."

"But the subject is the same."

"It was, but not now."

Why does the instructor answer as she does?

Has the subject changed again?

(Wrong: The instructor is trying to confuse the student.)

3. "Do you speak English?"

   "No, but someone does."

   "You're speaking English now."

   "Someone is."

   Who is speaking?

   Who is answering this koan/question?

   (Wrong: I am, it's as simple as that.)

4. When asked "Who first discovered Constructive Living principles?" the instructor pointed down toward a throw rug.

   "You mean that they lie buried in the ground?"

   The teacher walked away across the throw rug, shaking his head.

   Why did the teacher walk away as he did?

   Point to where CL principles are located.

   (Wrong: He walked away because he couldn't think of any other answer.)

5. "Which book contains the deepest Constructive Living wisdom?"

   "How would you punctuate that sentence?"

   Why is the instructor's reply about punctuation instead of about the meaning or content of the question?

   Why is your answer to this question dangerous?

   (Wrong: Because it might be wrong.)

6. What is behind tomorrow? What is beneath yesterday? Whether you walk into a wall or back into a wall, the wall is there. What is the wall?

   Where is the wall now?

(Wrong: The wall is the wall in my mind that prevents me from answering this koan.)

7. A student asked her CL instructor, "When you truly understand Constructive Living, there is no need to read any more Constructive Living books, is there?"

    She ducked as a book came flying her way.

    Why did the CL instructor throw a book at her? How is her ducking the answer to her own question?

    How is your answer to this question the answer to her question?

    (Wrong: The instructor threw the book to express his feelings.)

8. He clipped out weather reports from old newspapers and never stuck his head outside the door. What did he know about the weather? Don't be deceived by newspaper reports.

    In what way are CL books like old newspaper reports?

    (Wrong: Live in the now; old news is no longer useful.)

9. "Teach me about Constructive Living."

    "ABCDEFGHIJKLMNOPQRSTUVWXYZ."

    "You just spoke the alphabet; can't you tell me more?"

    "If saying those letters is of no help, what more do you want to hear?"

    Tell me about the limits of the answer you just said to me.

    (Wrong: All of the teaching of Constructive Living is contained in various arrangements of the letters of the alphabet.)

10. Professor Caro always carried a briefcase and walked around with holes in his shoes. In his briefcase were maps and photos and faxes. He would ask people to guess which maps and photos and faxes were in his briefcase. Then he would pull them out and hold them up for all to see. Then, one by one, he would call out the title of each item and present it to a bystander. The bystanders wondered, Who needs somebody else's maps, photos, and faxes?

    What is the usefulness of the fax you just sent me?

(Wrong: This koan is about unconscious thoughts and feelings brought into awareness and expressed to others.)

11. Two CL instructors are talking:
    "How are you doing?"
    "Oh, I have shinky moments and productive ones. How about you?"
    "I sometimes appear to understand and sometimes miss the point."
    "How about in your past? How were you doing then?"
    "Consistently inconsistent."
    "How dependable of you!"
    "How about CL people in general? How are they doing?"
    "You're putting me on!"
    Do you think that everyone gives the same correct answer to this koan?
    (Wrong: In general it can be said that Constructive Living people do very well, of course.)

12. Trudy pulled out her copy of *Playing Ball on Running Water.* "Do you own this book?" she asked another instructor.
    "Of course not," he replied.
    "Haven't you any Constructive Living books?"
    "Oh, *Playing Ball on Running Water.*"
    What are these instructors talking about?
    What does it mean to say, "Sometimes I own my home"?
    (Wrong: The instructor had forgotten that he owned a copy of *Playing Ball on Running Water.*)

13. In current U.S. dollars, what is one Constructive Living instructor worth? How much time does it take to cure neurosis? When has a child received enough love from loving parents? Where is the personality to be found? Who invented time?
    What sense does it make to ask such questions and who can answer them? Why?
    What is wrong with each of the above questions? What is wrong with this question?
    (Wrong: There are no answers to some of these questions

because we don't yet know enough; we lack information to answer them.)

14. Of what is reality composed? Of nothings and somethings. Of somethings of nothings and somethings of somethings. Of somethings perceiving and somethings perceived. Of nothings perceived.

    Who benefits from such an explanation of the composition of reality?

    Who benefits from your answer to this koan?

    (Wrong: No one benefits.)

15. Like reality, Constructive Living is a verb. Don't mistake CL instructors for nouns. What do these statements mean?

    Are you a noun?

    (Wrong: CL is about doing, so it is a verb.)

16. As students hike the hills about me, I sing the Constructive Living anthem on a loudspeaker system. Is my singing helpful to their hiking? To their singing?

    Why use a loudspeaker system at all?

    (Wrong: Singing has nothing to do with hiking.)

17. John blamed Mary for their quarrels. John's therapist blamed John's parents for causing John to blame Mary for their quarrels. Whose fault is it that the therapist blames John's parents? Beware!

    Please explain how you came up with your answer.

    (Wrong: John's therapist's training is at fault here.)

18. How large is a thought? Where are thoughts located? Where does a neurotic trait go when you're not suffering from it? Does thinking about unconscious processes create unconscious processes?

    What is the CL purpose in asking such questions?

    (Wrong: Thoughts are located in our brains.)

19. Do you know how alive I am by watching me? Can you learn to be alive like this by observation? Can you analyze this

aliveness into its components? How can you go about finding life? Where is life to be found?

Can the dead answer these questions?

(Wrong: Life is generated by chemical processes in cells.)

20. You can't open a computer and find a book inside. You can't quench your thirst with water words. You can't talk your way into eternity. Self-help books don't, including this one.

    What have these statements got in common?

    Then what is the purpose of offering koans like this one?

    (Wrong: There is no purpose in offering koans like this one.)

If I Were the Devil

IF I WERE the devil, I would invent

- the codependency concept, so that people would feel guilty when being kind to one another

- an obsession with childhood abuse, so that some women would search for it and others would refuse even to think about their past for fear of finding abuse there

- concepts such as addictive personality and narcissistic personality, so that people could be fooled into believing there is an explanation for their behavior, implying permanency, and so give up on changing what they do

- the idea that you need self-esteem before you can do anything; then I wouldn't offer any genuine way to develop self-esteem other than doing something well

- therapies that focus on the past, so that people would be distracted from doing anything productive in the present

- professions that require people to remain in their suffering state in order for the specialists to get paid regularly

- the insanity plea and the adult/juvenile distinction in court

- social focus on people's intentions and feelings instead of on what they do

- talk shows with trials by audience juries using pop psychology

- hundreds of excuses for the odd behavior called giving up

The Bird Feeders

IN OUR BACKYARD are several bird feeders. Standing at the kitchen sink looking out the window, we can watch the dance of birds, chipmunks, a raccoon, and cats. Their stage is the area surrounding the bird feeders. They perform a rhythmic ballet for our amusement and instruction. Going about their daily affairs, they become artistic teachers. Let me pass along to you some of their teaching:

- "Keep a sharp eye out for what reality is bringing." This lesson is quite clear when a hawk comes and perches on a branch near the feeder. Sensible birds seek their meal elsewhere. Similarly the momentary comings and goings of local cats around the base of the feeders are noted by the song sparrows and finches and juncos.

- "Wait awhile; your chance will come." When the bluejays barge in and scatter seeds about, the smaller birds disappear. Many of them are sitting up in the bushes waiting for those raucous bluejay bullies to get tired of making a mess. In this situation confrontation makes no sense.

- "I was here first." When a hummingbird zooms in to sip the colored sugar water, it must contend with the little fellow already perched on the feeder. Now is an appropriate time for confrontation among equals. "Not yet . . . get off my turf . . . not yet . . . all right, now it's your turn."

- "Keep on trying." The feeders are well out of the cats' reach. Nevertheless the local tabbies rest comfortably beneath it and then suddenly catapult themselves at low-flying birds. As far as I know, in all these years only once was the leap rewarded with a bird in the paw. What satisfaction the cat must have felt then! A sad tale from a bird's-eye view, but that is nature's way of weeding out the occasional unmindful bird.

• "Find the proper pace." Now fast, now slow. Both birds and cats follow this maxim. There is a time for a quick snack, and there is a time for a leisurely feast. There is a time to stalk slowly, and a time to pounce.

• "Get back up and go for it." A song sparrow flew right into a window on the second-floor deck outside our dining room. Stunned, it fluttered to the ground and lay still. I rushed outside to see what could be done for it, but before I reached it, the bird picked itself up and flew to a nearby bush. After a few minutes it was back at the bird feeder. In the wild you don't call time-out after a setback; you get on with life. Oh yes, we put a sun-screen film on the window and haven't seen a bonked bird since.

• "Give it a shot anyway." When I get too near its feeder, the hummingbird buzzes me like hummingbird thunder to make sure I know who really owns all that delicious sugar water. The tiny hummingbird creature surely notices that I outweigh it by a factor of thousands. Never mind. It assertively stakes its claim. Then it perches on a telephone wire and keeps a wary eye until I move away. Works every time.

Do you suppose the birds think these thoughts as they perch on the feeder: Persistence pays off, go for it, now's the time for patience, keep a sharp eye out, and the like? No one really knows. But I doubt it. My guess is that the birds are just naturally responding to the circumstances without much, if any, resort to maxims or verbal principles or any other intellectual functions. We need to be aware of the moments when it is suitable for us to do the same.

—

Constructive
Living
Practice

—

Life's Predicaments

IN THIS SECTION you will find Constructive Living advice on how to handle a variety of difficulties we humans face in life. Some of the suggestions you read below may sound unusual at first. There is material on what to do when you fail, when you are lonely, when you are grieving, excited, nostalgic, fearful, tense, elated, hopeless, and so forth. You may have found that the more "usual" forms of advice haven't always worked for you in the past. Before you dismiss a CL suggestion out of hand, give it a try. You are the best judge for determining whether these suggestions apply in your situation.

Of course a few paragraphs of advice will not tell you all you need to know to cope with life's dilemmas. Furthermore no advice will do the coping for you. Discovering what needs doing and then doing it is up to you. But you will find a start here. There is a whole body of Constructive Living materials including books and tapes, and instructors around the world to personalize your study.

Fear and Anxiety

I am going to ask you to rethink what you have been taught about fear and anxiety. Commonly sources will tell you that fear and anxiety are uniformly bad, that getting rid of them altogether is desirable, that they stand in the way of progress and success in your life. I'm not foolish enough to recommend that you learn to like fear and anxiety. I don't. Those feelings are unpleasant, disturbing. But so is a fever, so is a dentist's drill, so are casts for broken limbs and surgery and rainstorms. All of these disagreeable elements of life, and many others like them, have a positive aspect too. So what are the positive aspects of fear and anxiety?

For one thing these feelings promote caution and carefulness. Being afraid of dying, for example, encourages us to choose our cars and airplane carriers carefully, to practice safe sexual habits, to eat wisely, to prepare thoughtfully for trips into the wilderness or to a foreign country. Fearing embarrassment may help prompt us to practice our speeches, memorize the names on a guest list, learn etiquette customs, groom ourselves, lose weight, and so forth.

So the first step in dealing with fear and anxiety is to discover the positive source, the helpful information that the feeling is offering us. Your extreme fears about eating foods may be indicating your strong desire to be healthy. Your fear of leaving town may be related to your desire to be near the doctor who was so helpful when you were seriously ill. Your fear of getting married may be related to your desire to avoid making a mistake and hurting yourself and someone else in the process. Just like a fever, fear gives us information about our circumstance.

The next step is to discard the outmoded notion that fears and anxiety somehow paralyze behavior. They do not, at least not in humans. Some frightened animals freeze and are prevented from moving by "wired-in" neurological connections. Except for a few with obvious severe mental diseases, such as psychoses, adult humans have no such mental "wiring." Neither abrupt fear nor long-term anxiety prevents you from doing anything. It is unnecessary to "fix" the fear in order to do what you need to do in a given situation. Just be afraid and do what needs doing. Whatever you have read or heard before, fear is not such a big deal.

The way to make a fear increasingly debilitating is to give in to it. It may then expand its sphere. For example, if you are afraid of driving on the expressway and go to a lot of inconvenience to avoid doing so, you may find yourself increasingly afraid of driving on busy surface streets, and eventually of driving at all. I am not recommending here that you run out and do all the things that are frightening to you. Of course not. I am suggesting, however, that if there are important things you need to do in your life, don't let apprehension and trepidation be the reasons you offer for failing to do them.

I shall repeat some tips for getting through fearful situations with minimal discomfort offered earlier in this book. Perhaps these are the sorts of tips you hoped for in buying this handbook. But before you read them, I want to underscore the value of doing what you have decided needs doing, whether you are afraid or not. Constructive Living is not about minimizing discomfort so that we can act. Constructive Living is about remembering that action is more controllable (and in the long run more important) than fleeting uneasiness. We don't want to make the mistake of trying to build our lives on feelings. We don't want feelings to dictate our lives. There's nothing wrong with being happy and confident and peaceful—we'll relish those pleasant moments and in fact increase the likelihood that they will occur with Constructive Living—but in the moments of discomfort and adversity we'll set about accomplishing our purposes anyway.

Now to the tips. The first is distraction. For our purposes here, it is sufficient to point out that it is difficult to be thinking about being afraid and to be thinking about polishing the car well at the same time. If you are in a situation that permits large-muscle activity, you will find it relatively easy to distract yourself from the fear with tiring constructive action—swimming, rearranging furniture, chopping firewood, and so forth. And when physical activity is ruled out for some reason, attention to others' clothing and makeup, Constructive Living reflection, attention to the conversation at hand, and other such distractions are possible.

The second tip is waiting. Feelings fade as time passes. The intense fear you experience in one moment has receded into the background a while later and eventually disappears altogether. While frightened, avoid acting impulsively or destructively. The results of your actions may linger long after the feelings have faded.

The third tip is to use your behavior to make your body calm and stable even as your mind skitters like water on a hot skillet. How you feel is influenced by what your body is doing. Settling your body into a familiar stance or rhythmic movement will bring a measure of composure.

Finally, a reminder that when you achieve the attitude of noticing feelings and accepting them as they are along with the information they convey, then turn to the purposeful behavior at hand, you will find that tips aimed at regulating feelings are unnecessary. Simply notice the fear and get on with your life. That we think feelings are so momentous is due largely to Freud's influence on our era. According to Lytton Strachey, "If anyone had asked Voltaire to analyze his feelings accurately, he would have replied that he had other things to think about. The notion of paying careful attention to mere feelings would have seemed ridiculous" (quoted in B. F. Skinner, *A Matter of Consequences* [New York: New York University Press, 1984], p. 399).

Addictions and Compulsions

The only satisfactory method of curing addictions and compulsions is to stop behaving in addictive and compulsive ways. One factor that hampers such efforts is the foolish hope that there are easy and short-cut ways of getting rid of the addictive and compulsive behaviors. Exploring one's past or discovering hidden motivations and "unfelt feelings" will not make giving up alcohol or gambling or lying or other such destructive behaviors effortless fun.

Unexamined foolishness puzzles me. How is it that people believe "truths" handed down by supposed experts without considering whether the pronouncements make sense in the everyday world? A professional with mental health credentials may be actually deceived by professional training into making the strangest statements. These statements are picked up by the media and presented as the only acceptable view of a subject. Feelings, for example, are often presented as the most important things in the world. How absurd! Feelings are worthy of some attention, but it is a great danger to make them the center of one's life. Another overinflated concept is addiction.

Addiction is erroneously used as an excusing explanation for everything from substance abuse to overeating and promiscuous sexual behavior. Addiction means no more than behavior that appears (to someone) unrealistic and compulsive and harmful. I suppose you could even say I am addicted to talking, I have all the "symptoms." Sometimes I talk when I shouldn't; I get into trouble. I don't seem to be able to give up talking for long periods of time. Although my talking addiction is socially acceptable, so is drinking alcohol and drug use and the like in some cultures. I have written elsewhere in detail of the absurdity of talking about obesity as addiction to food. We're all addicted to food. What I want to convey here is that addiction is a description, *not* an explanation.

The genuine contribution of Alcoholics Anonymous to helping some people stop excessive use of alcohol notwithstanding, addiction is *not* a disease. The addiction concept makes no sensible contribution toward understanding why anyone does what he or she does. When a person stops drinking alcohol after a long period of overindulgence, you have your choice of definitions: He or she is no longer addicted to alcohol, or he or she is still mysteriously addicted but no longer displays the addiction in behavior. This mysterious, hidden quality reminds me of the hidden rage or masked depression that is supposed to lurk within the unconscious of certain clients in psychological counseling. When rage or depression emerges, it was assumed to have been there all along. If a heavy drinker goes on a binge after a long period of abstinence, such behavior is taken to mean that the person was addicted all along. The whole field of—would you believe it?—"addictionology" is filled with untestable hypotheses.

When science discovers a gene or a specific biochemical process associated consistently with all the behaviors for which the term *addiction* is currently used as an explanation, I'll immediately admit my error in this matter. Here I am presenting a method of proving Constructive Living wrong on this point. Conceivably such evidence could appear someday. Now, what evidence could possibly be generated that would prove that current explanations based on addiction are wrong? There aren't any. The concept of addiction and its associated assumptions about the way humans operate is a belief system, closer to religion than to science. It will stick around for a while because it is convenient, but it will pass away like any fad passes away.

What is convenient about the concept of addiction? It works as a pretext, a socially acceptable reason for harmful action. It allows people to get help (I use the word very broadly here) with less stigma than equally unjustifiable attributions of devil possession or moral blame entail. The danger of the addiction ruse is that it implies that humans have no control over certain large-muscle behaviors. It asserts that some people cannot stop drinking or shooting or having sex or overeating on their own. This concept is very dangerous to individuals and to society. When we have no control over our behavior, we have no responsibility for what we do. Criminals are no more than helpless pawns to their addictions to crime, certain husbands to wife abuse, rapists to rape.

Last night I heard a lecture in which the speaker quoted the statistics that 70 to 80 percent of addicted people die of their addictions. I assert that those statistics are wrong. No one has ever died of an addiction. People die of liver diseases and car accidents and exposure to cold and so forth. You can't die of an unrealistic concept. In Japan there was a time when people talked of dying of too much work (*karōshi*). There is no doubt that many Japanese are required to work excessively long hours. And those lengthy workdays may contribute to exhaustion and other debilitating conditions. But no one dies of overwork. Beware of the reification of concepts that don't fit reality.

The action aspect of Constructive Living is concerned with automatic, compulsive behavior that doesn't fit the situation. For example, when a mother treats her thirty-five-year-old son as though he were in grammar school, we begin to question her purposes. What is the mother trying to do? What is the goal underlying eating when one is already full? Can the goals be achieved in more appropriate, constructive ways? Let's consider some practical guidelines that use the term *addiction* to mean nothing more than "repetitious inappropriate behavior."

What does Constructive Living recommend when one is doing something harmful over and over and wishes to stop? Simply put, the first suggestion is to stop the activity. Don't act on compulsion— giving in to it gives it power. Use distraction from compulsion by constructive physical activity (not distraction by detailed mental work, such as math calculations, which are impractical when you are upset, and not by alcohol, which isn't constructive).

A fuller course of behavior change may be achieved by scheduling your addictive or compulsive behavior. Our students usually schedule their addictive behaviors a week in advance, but even the day before is acceptable. The procedure is to write down exactly when and where and how much and for how long the students will engage in the smoking or eating or handwashing or whatever behavior over which they wish to assert more control. And they *must* carry out the behavior exactly as planned, whether they are in the mood or not, whether it is convenient or not. Of course they may not engage in the behavior outside of the scheduled times and places.

The students feel great freedom when beginning this assignment. They may schedule as many cigarettes as they desire, for example, at just the times they usually crave them. However, they usually find that they have anticipated the length of time inaccurately and are stuck with a cigarette that is burning down too fast or too slow to precisely fill the time. They may have to excuse themselves from pleasant activities to fulfill the demands of their schedules. They may desire a smoke outside the designated times. Even after weeks on the schedule it is hard to anticipate changing circumstances, which makes keeping to the schedule inconvenient and annoying. Most students find themselves cutting down on the scheduled behavior in order to minimize the conflicts with other activities. They can always go back to scheduling more tobacco if they wish.

The point of this exercise is to reconfirm the students' ability to control their behavior. They make the schedule as they wish. And they keep to it. It is impossible to be out of control of one's behavior. Neither alcohol nor tobacco nor anything else can control our behavior. We control our behavior; whether we wish to assert that control or not is our option. As students look back over a period of maintaining their scheduled activity in this gamelike form, they see that the behavior was controllable all along.

The standard CL hints for stopping an undesired habit are the following:

- Put the paraphernalia in an inconvenient place where time and energy are required to obtain it.

- Schedule the habit days ahead of time and do it in the written, planned manner at the determined time, whether you feel like it or not, whether it is convenient or not.

- Have a list of alternate, pleasant, convenient activities ready when you feel like indulging in the habit at an unplanned moment.

My experience is that undesired behaviors are most likely to occur when there is a lack of interesting positive activities going on in our lives. Developing new interests, hobbies, and friendships offers some protection from the boredom that promotes doing something we have decided not to do. Put simply, doing something else is easier than not doing something. The time to develop new interests is now, not when we are tempted to return to old habits.

Shyness

In a culture where assertiveness and sociability often yield high returns to those with such social skills, the person who has many introverted and shy moments may be at a disadvantage. The disadvantage comes not from the introverted and shy moments but from allowing those moments to dictate behavior.

There is nothing wrong with shyness. It is not a condition in need of remedy. It arises from the natural desire to be liked and well thought of, from the desire to avoid mistakes and foolishness, and from the recognition of all the skills and knowledge and power of others. Shyness is one natural response to the real world.

The error we want to avoid in thinking about shyness is the common mistaken notion that shyness prevents people from greeting their neighbors, asking others out on dates, appearing for job interviews, speaking in public, going to parties, running for political office, and the like. One can be shy and do all these things. Or, to put it more accurately, one can have many shy moments and do all these things.

If we look carefully at people we call shy, we find that there are moments when they are extremely self-conscious and moments when they are less so. One variable that seems to affect the degree of shyness at any given time is the level of involvement in some task at hand. When we are "lost" in a tennis game, or a conversation, or a movie, or the aftermath of an earthquake, we are less inconvenienced by concerns about shyness.

Another variable that affects shyness is the degree of physical activity involved or preceding some point in time. In general, people with lots of shy moments will be less troubled by them if they maintain a regimen of physical exercise and other activities that include physical exertion (health permitting, of course). You are likely to be less troubled by thoughts of what a waiter is thinking about you if you are pleasantly tired from a day in which you moved your body around a lot. Check it out.

A third variable that will reduce the intensity and frequency of shy moments is giving yourself away. An essential element of shyness is self-focus. What is he going to think of *me*? What if I forget *my* lines? Does *my* embarrassment show on *my* face? Am I coming unglued, dizzy, at a loss for words? Like many problem areas of life, shyness involves placing the self in the center of the world and focusing far too much attention on it.

Spend some time with someone who is bedridden, with someone who is dying. Spend some time in a classroom volunteering as a teacher's aide. Spend some time learning a declining folk craft from an elderly artist. Get involved in collecting and distributing food to the hungry, toys to needy kids. Join in sensible efforts to improve the environment. Such activities will widen your perspective on the world and on who you are. As you may discover, those two perspectives are the same.

Notice that I prefer to write about shy *moments* rather than about shy *people*. We are all shy in some moments, believe it or not. When we return to our childhood environments and talk with folks who knew us back then, when we have just made a faux pas in front of the boss, when we come face-to-face with someone we worshiped for years—these sorts of occasions may pull from us moments of shyness. Such moments are natural, no less perfect than any other moments. To believe the myth of shy people is to clothe people in another diagnosis of concrete. We are above all changeable. We are change. The image of change is one of hope.

Short Temper and Impatience

We want our desires satisfied right now. We want fast food, instant loans, quick bonding, speedy cars, faxes and phones for immediate communication, and so forth. When something or someone gets in the way of our getting what we want right now, we may lash out in anger.

In Constructive Living we don't spend time trying to figure out the hidden reasons for insensitive, hurtful behavior. You can find a variety of theories to explain rage and tantrums. They may be attempts to control others, and/or they may be learned from parents, and/or they may be linked to genetic tendencies, and/or they may be childhood responses that haven't been outgrown, and/or on and on and on. The Constructive Living approach to this problem is characteristically straightforward. Accept the impatience and angry feelings, and don't act in harmful ways. It is quite all right to be impatient and wait. It is quite all right to be angry and still be polite. It is not all right to use impatience and short temper as excuses for behavior that is not civil.

"But how do I control my temper?" you may wonder. There is no need to control your temper, just control what you do. "How can I do that?" Just do it. You may be asking something like, "How can I make it easy to be more patient and tolerant and less likely to fly off the handle?" Frankly I know of no easy way to act like a grown-up, mature human being all the time. But I can assure you it is possible, however difficult. "How can I learn to enjoy waiting?" You can't; you don't need to enjoy waiting. Just wait, when waiting is necessary. That's the bottom line.

Now, having looked at the hard-line facts of the matter from a Constructive Living perspective, let's consider some tips that you may find useful in dealing with the problems of impatience and short temper. Remember, they are not long-term remedies. The only real remedy is accepting feelings as uncontrollable and exerting appropriate control over actions. That remedy applies to all areas of life, so applying it to this particular problem will produce spillover benefits in other areas of life as well.

If you dislike waiting in lines or waiting in a car to give someone a ride, carry something with you to distract yourself—a small book or a page of chess problems or a notepad for jotting memos or making notes for that book you want to write someday. Pay attention to your surroundings. What can you learn from observing buildings or vehicles or clothing or the behavior of others? Create imaginative scenarios. What would you do if there were a fire or a tornado or an earthquake or an explosion nearby? If you like word games, see how many words you can create from nearby signs. Reflect on the efforts of others that resulted in your getting to this place at this time (the person who filled your gas tank, the driver of the bus, the printer of the newspaper in which the announcement appeared, your friend's phone call reminding you of the event, and so forth). Use your mind to get your mind off yourself and your discomfort.

In any waiting situation don't put your life on hold. As you wait for the merchandise you ordered by mail, as you wait for the results of the medical tests, as you wait for the decision following the job interview, keep active, keep creating new opportunities and possibilities.

Constructive Living reflection is a valuable way of affecting short-tempered behavior. Constructive Living reflection has been described in detail earlier. Briefly it involves recalling your past while guided by three thematic questions: What did that person do for me? What did I do for that person? What troubles and worries did I cause that person? For example, you might begin reflecting on the first year you knew your spouse. During that year what did you do for him or her? What did he or she do for you? What troubles did you cause him or her?

Constructive Living reflection helps us take on the perspectives of other important people in our lives. It cultivates our ability to see how our behavior (including tantrums) affects them. Through Constructive Living reflection we come to see the contributions of others to our lives and the minimal ways we have returned the bounty. We see specifically how our flare-ups have resulted in hardship to those we love and respect.

Oh, yes—in the moments while we are fully involved in Constructive Living reflection, we cannot simultaneously be acting out impatience and short temper.

Procrastination

Writing is difficult work for me. My mind creates endless other tasks that should be done first. I watch myself generate excuses for putting off writing. Sometimes I am surprised anew that when the writing actually begins, it is not so disagreeable as I had imagined, it can be even interesting. Isn't that the same with you? When you actually get around to some oft-delayed task, when you finally get involved in it, don't you often find that the doing of it isn't as unpleasant as you had anticipated?

Perhaps you could already predict that the Constructive Living recommendation for not wanting to begin a task is to accept the feeling without a fight. I am not going to advise you to try to fool yourself into being eager to start on something you have been putting off. You don't need to change your attitude or character, or even to read farther in this book. If you need to do something else, put down the book and go do it.

The first step is to do the action that prepares for the chore. Get out the cleaning equipment, the shoe polish, the stationery, whatever. The next step involves taking your body to the place where the chore takes place. In the case of writing, I move my body to stand in front of this word processor. Walk out to the garage that needs to be rearranged; go to the file cabinet that needs to be reorganized, to the phone, to the garden, to the front lawn, wherever is appropriate. Then don't let your body move from that place until you have begun the task. Sometimes you will find that, once begun, the task pulls your attention into it. The clever, shinky mind proceeds to muster a variety of reasons why you shouldn't begin the task now, a variety of other things you could be doing. Don't let your body leave the scene. Keep your hands on the lawnmower handles. In time you will find it more interesting to do the job than to stand there bored. If a legitimate purpose calls you away from the task temporarily, bring your body back to the scene immediately afterward.

Another tip is to nibble at the edges of an enterprise rather than steeling yourself to tackle the whole project head-on. When doing your income tax, try calculating depreciation on one day, itemizing deductions on another, getting your travel receipts together on a third, and so forth.

One more tip is to reward yourself after you complete some difficult task, not before. Hold off on that cupcake or new book until you have completed the task you have set for yourself.

We are all going to die. My guess is that you want to look back on a life with many tasks completed, goals accomplished. Procrastination won't get you there. Constructive Living hints may be helpful. Give them a try.

It's a matter of time. I like to know when something is going to happen. I like schedules and appointments. "Oh, let's get together sometime Saturday morning" leaves me wondering how to arrange the rest of Saturday morning and suspecting that a lot of time will be spent that morning phoning around to find out if everyone is ready to meet. Some people may think I'm inflexible, compulsive. I don't think so. If circumstances change, we can revise our appointment. I can live with that. But I don't like to steal others' time or to have my time stolen. If I say I'll be at a certain place at a certain time, people can pretty much count on it. If I'm not there, they know something drastic has happened.

What does it mean to "steal time"? When we show up late and make people wait for us, we steal their time. When we take a long time to say or write something that could be expressed succinctly, we steal their time. When people put out time and effort in our behalf and we don't acknowledge them or thank them, we steal their time. When we force our children to be the grown-ups in the family, we steal their childhood time. When we work only five hours instead of eight during a workday, we steal company time. And when we keep putting off what we know needs doing, we steal our own time.

We talk as though time were ours. "Don't waste my time," we say. "My time is valuable." But we don't own time; time happens to us. We borrow it. We *are* time passing.

I find myself trying to push time back by anticipating future tasks and doing them beforehand. Two coats of paint may put off the next painting job longer; stamps go on a stack of envelopes before they are needed; cut and fold the paper napkins, mix the juice, buy the adapter cable—all well ahead of time. Sometimes such preparations pay off when time is short later on, and sometimes they turn out to be a waste of time when circumstances change in unanticipated ways. Where is the most realistic balance? We must find it in individual, everyday circumstances.

I received a detailed letter recently from an executive who was concerned with all those daily maintenance tasks that he saw consuming his life and preventing him from achieving more personally meaningful goals. He wrote, "For example, a person could have a strong desire to write a book but never write it because of the time devoted to all the 'maintenance' tasks that need to be done." He wanted CL advice on the topic. He may have been surprised by the advice he got.

I suggested that in the time he had taken to write and mail the letter to me, he could have written a few pages of a book manuscript, if writing a book manuscript is what needs doing. I also recommended that he do those everyday maintenance tasks well, with full attention. Everyday tasks can usually be done more efficiently and promptly than we think, so that time can be freed for other activities. More often than not, personally meaningful projects don't get accomplished because of poor habits in the use of spare time, procrastination, over-thinking, and underdoing. We would like some ideal block of time in which to do our projects. Reality may not allow us such a luxury.

Shinky people would rather talk about how difficult it is to get going on a project than to actually get going on it. They would rather discuss the theories about value conflicts and psychological resistance than begin some meaningful activity. They tend to call their friends and complain rather than change their pattern of living. In this area deep psychological understanding is of less value than getting up off the sofa.

Interpersonal Problems

I suppose that there was a time when some people believed that increased communication would solve all our difficulties with other humans. Sometimes talking seems to help, sometimes not. There are problems between two people that have to be lived through, and no amount of talking will further clarify or resolve the situation.

Remember the distinction we make in Constructive Living between feeling and doing? It's important to remind you that you can "do" love even when you don't feel it. You can "do" thanks even without feeling grateful. American culture has become so tied up with being true to feelings, so self-feeling-focused, that many couples and families have forgotten that there are more important things in life than acting consistently with one's own selfish, petty emotional state. Perhaps we have listened too long to the so-called experts who prophesy mental catastrophe to those who act with civil thoughtfulness even when angry or heartbroken.

Destructive behavior isn't helpful, isn't necessary even when you are upset. A walk around the neighborhood is a preferable alternative to physical or verbal abuse. Again, observe how feelings fade into unimportance if you simply give them some time and keep them in perspective. Use them for the information they contain—if you have to leave, for example, leave—but don't let feelings be the only factor you take into consideration when acting. Narrow, feeling-centered living doesn't sustain a relationship with another human being.

The best marriages are those in which both partners look toward something more important than the marriage or their love for each other. When husband and wife both share some goal or purpose that is beyond them as individuals or as a couple, then they work together toward that goal. Whenever they feel anger or loneliness or disappointment with each other, they still have the goal that is beyond them to pull them together again. Some couples share Constructive Living as one of the foundations of their relationship. Others see their children's future, retirement security, or some religious belief as worthy of transcendental purpose. A shared goal of helpful service to others won't let you down. It offers opportunities of challenge, achievement, and immersion of the individuals' selves in some uniting stream of sacrifice.

When we take on new roles, we encounter fresh opportunities to reinvent who we are. On our first full-time job we meet new chances to submerge some of our self-centeredness in the service of customers or clients or fellow workers. Marriage joins us with another person for shared responsibility of finances and child rearing and so forth. Becoming a grandparent provides the chance to become a new person—to interact with an individual who has no expectations or preconceptions about the grandparent. Avoiding the mistakes we made with our own children, we get a fresh, new start. Falling in love may provide a fresh start for some folks.

For not a few young people love seems to be a way of simplifying this complex world. They don't have to try to please everyone, just the one who loves them. The rest of the world almost disappears for a while when they are together. They see themselves reflected positively in the eyes of their loved one. By the way, love is *often* having to say you're sorry. Even when you know you were right and your intentions were good, it may be a good idea to offer an apology.

It seems to me that there are basically two social ways to adapt one's behavior to fit comfortably within a couple or group. One way is to offer to adapt, the other is to wait until others demand change. A healthy social setup encourages each member of a group to scan his or her own behavior and ask the other members if they would prefer the current behavior (x) or a specified alternate behavior (y). The other members then thank the person for his or her thoughtfulness and express a preference for x or y (or z). All are satisfied because the initiator showed sensitivity and concern with others' convenience, and the others expressed appreciation and preferences. In contrast, to wait for demands for change from the others sets up refusal possibilities and challenges sensitivity.

How does one initiate such a healthy pattern of self-scanning and sensitivity to others' needs? Perhaps the best method is to model the pattern for the group, to ask for feedback and make efforts to make reasonable changes in your own behavior. In the worst case, you are likely to get a reputation for selflessness and sensitivity. If all works well, however, others will adopt the pattern of offering to alter their behaviors to fit group members' needs too.

For more information about healthy interpersonal relations, read the chapter entitled "Quality Time." For information about a formal way to bring an end to quarreling, see *A Thousand Waves,* pp. 57–60.

Grief

Nothing lasts forever—you've heard it before. You and I won't last forever. Our friends, our homes, our families, our words, our work, our reputation, our bank accounts, our physical strength and mental abilities—none of these will last forever. One way or another we shall lose everything we love and honor. That's the way life is.

Some people take comfort in recognizing that we're all in the same boat. We all lose everything. Nevertheless my losses are mine alone, and yours are yours alone. It is easy to forget the precious nature of what is here, now.

We grieve for people who leave our lives. We grieve for things that leave our lives too. Perhaps you have known people who grieved for pets, houses, neighborhoods, youth, jobs, photos, dreams. All lost.

Grief is natural. Like any other feeling, the feeling of grief doesn't need to be fixed. It will last as long as it lasts. What you may need to rethink is the notion that the grief prevents you from getting on with your life. It doesn't. Do your housework, pay your bills, do the shopping, sell the merchandise. Do all these things while crying if necessary. Explain or don't explain your tears to others as you see fit. But don't put your life on hold for weeks and weeks because of grief. You have only this one life here now.

How long should grief last normally? Again, just as long as it lasts. It makes little sense to talk about average periods of time. Your circumstances are unique. Your loss is one of a kind. While painful, it is an opportunity to learn a vital lesson about all sorts of feelings: They fade over time unless something happens to restimulate them.

When my father died of cancer, my mother felt intense grief, but as the weeks and months passed, the intensity of the feelings subsided. On the occasions when she opened a desk drawer and saw his photograph, when she gave away his clothing to charity, on their anniversary and at Christmas, and at other times, too, the reminders caused her grief to well up with fresh intensity. But she could count on the fact that each time she felt a strong upsurge of grief, it would fade over time, provided she didn't do something to restimulate it.

What if you don't grieve? Is that an indication that you didn't value the person (or whatever else) you lost? Is it an indication that there is some unconscious process going on that will burst forth sometime to debilitate you? Are you abnormal for not feeling and expressing the grief you are told you should be feeling? Such issues are the sorts that we like to dwell on in our shinky moments. Grief is an indicator of grief, nothing more. Feelings have a logic of their own—like rainstorms and other phenomena with many changing, unknown variables. *Nobody* understands them. If you are ruminating on why you aren't grieving enough or why you are grieving too much, you would do well to go take a walk, wash the car, volunteer in a classroom.

Get active in life and watch how these cotton-candy issues dissolve out of your awareness.

Chronic Pain and Obsession with Health

If you are ill, it's a good idea to have your physician check out the problem. However, you may have tried a number of medical interventions and still be in pain; you live with it for now. Similarly if you have a lot of physical complaints and your doctor(s) cannot find any serious medical problem, then you might consider the possibility that you must just live with the discomfort for a while.

With debilitating illness comes a whole range of associated problems. We face and probably fear death. We may become dependent on others for life functions we could do on our own before the illness. We don't feel well, so it is more difficult to get our bodies into motion. We run into genuine physical limitations. Our attention has a tendency to narrow down to a focus on our bodies. We may find ourselves irritable and impatient. These examples of problems associated with illness cause us added misery.

What suggestions we can offer from a CL perspective begin with the sensible assumption that you have received expert medical advice and assistance with your health problem. Constructive Living is not about curing diseases. I have no doubt that living constructively will have a positive effect on your health; few would argue with that these days. But Constructive Living does not aim to practice medicine. At this point you have done pretty much what you could do to solve your health problem(s) and you are still uncomfortable. What to do now?

As usual, one immediate resource is distraction with activity that includes as much physical movement as you are capable of performing. Getting your mind off the ringing in your ears, the rumbling in your stomach, the lower-back pain, the heavy feeling in your limbs, the tiredness, the sleepiness, and so forth brings immediate relief. Remember, you cannot think about many things at the same moment. So if you string together a lot of active, productive moments, you can have whole periods free of discomfort.

Sometimes such distracting activity actually solves the problem on a long-term basis. But whether the underlying problem is affected or not, there is quick, temporary respite from the hours of inward focus on the pain. Special effort should be made to avoid inserting a discussion of the illness into every conversation. Talking a lot about a problem focuses excessive attention on it. The result is an increased sensitivity to symptomatic complaints and a narrowing of life.

Make the effort to direct conversations toward the topic of others' interests and needs, events in others' lives. Such effort is not a denial of your own illness but a recognition that your physical condition is not the central feature in everyone's world. Find ways to contribute to others' lives, to repay them for their services in your behalf. Even from a hospital bed it is possible to invite and introduce visitors to each other, to make supportive phone calls, to send gift subscriptions, to exchange books, to provide information based on current news reports, to smile and thank.

When I am sick, I don't feel much like grooming carefully. Nevertheless when I take the time and effort to keep my appearance neat, it usually has some effect on my feeling state. And such effort is what those around me deserve.

Pain is a severe teacher, but it teaches the truth. It teaches me that I alone live this life. No one else can experience my pain for me. Even others' pain teaches me this lesson. When I see a loved one in pain, I see again the gap that separates us no matter how close we might be. I can't reason with pain. I can't cajole it or argue with it; logic does me no good when dealing with pain. Pain becomes my life at times. It informs me about my limitations. But it need not become the whole of life. Elsewhere in this book are true stories about a couple of Moritists who continued to accomplish their life purposes as they lay on their deathbeds. As much as your physical limits allow, keep working to accomplish your purposes until your body insists on the rest you have earned.

Childhood Abuse

Sensible people don't dwell on what can't be corrected. Going over and over your past won't change it. Reflection on the past may affect your attitude toward what happened back then, however. So if you

198 · David K. Reynolds, Ph.D.

plan to spend some time delving into your childhood experiences, you would do well to select a method that will promote an attitude of acceptance and compassion rather than a method that stirs up anger and leaves you frustrated and miserable.

Your current available memories of your childhood are only part of the story of what happened back then. They are simplified and slanted to fit the image of yourself you want to project to others and to yourself. We all create such distortions. Aware of it or not, we all select certain details and forget others when recalling and retelling our pasts. There just isn't time to think about or talk about everything that happened to us during those years. There are pressures on us to create a kind of summary tale of our childhood experiences.

It may be convenient to build your story around yourself as helpless victim maimed by evil, alcoholic parents or other adults. Such a tale may even contain elements of truth. But such a tale may have the unfortunate effect of justifying to some people your attempts to evade responsibility for your adult life.

Constructive Living attacks such pitiable attempts to run from life's challenges by citing childhood trauma. The Constructive Living assault on these myths of childhood comes on two fronts. The reflective/reciprocity side of Constructive Living opens up the possibility of encountering multidimensional figures from our pasts. For example you may discover an abusive father who did terrible *and* kind things, who hurt you *and* funded your piano lessons, who drove you home from the hospital after your operation and gently put you to bed. The more clearly you see the stick figures you formerly used to prop up your past scenarios, the less you will be able to rely on them as excuses for current difficulties.

The second front on which Constructive Living attacks dependence on rationales of past abuse is through its realistic-action aspect. Whatever happened then, happened. Now what are you going to do? Angry confrontation with an abusive father won't erase the hurt and resentment called up anew when thinking about the past. It may in fact create new pain for both of you. When anger emerges, it is always *fresh, new* anger. All feelings emerge fresh and new. They never emerge as old, hidden feelings from the past. Getting on with your life now will have greater payoff for you than wallowing in tragic memories. To what degree has rehashing your unhappy childhood brought peace and satisfaction in your life thus far?

So what needs to be done next? As you build your life on positive, constructive action in response to what life presents to you now, you will find that less and less attention gets turned to your over-and-done-with childhood. There just isn't time for such detours from facing the challenges of the now. There's too much going on around you in this moment that you don't want to miss.

What *will* bring some measure of relief from dwelling on childhood abuse is (a) recognizing that one's abusive parents were multisided humans; and (b) getting on with your own life in a realistic manner. Constructive Living is not aiming to minimize recognition of the abuse that went on in the past, but it is aiming to shift perspectives so that our pasts aren't populated by artificial devils. They were populated by real humans with mixed bags of good and evil, just like us. They made mistakes sometimes; some were terrible mistakes. We don't want to make mistakes caused by looking behind us as we cross the intersections of our lives today.

Depression

I know quite a bit about depression. I studied depression and suicide as a researcher for many years. And then I worked on projects, funded by grants from the U.S. government (NIMH), to make myself depressed enough to get admitted to a psychiatric hospital and several other psychiatric facilities so that social scientists could learn about depression and suicide as it appears inside institutions. The University of California Press published a couple of books (written with Norman L. Farberow, then codirector of the Los Angeles Suicide Prevention Center) about that research—*Suicide: Inside and Out* and *Endangered Hope.* You can read them and decide for yourself whether I was *really* depressed or not.

At any rate the Constructive Living approach to coping with depression makes good sense to me on both a professional and a personal level. Some depressions are illnesses. The first thing you want to do is check out a depression with a physician who has some experience in these matters and is willing to spend some time with you. Some physicians are so busy that they often find it expedient simply to give out antidepressant or tranquilizing medication for almost any emotional problem that appears before them. If you are in and out of a doctor's office in five minutes or so with a prescription for some medication to treat your "depression," you might do well to get a second opinion. There is more to treating depression than medication alone.

Much of what gets called depression by ordinary folk is not an illness at all. It is the natural psychological state resulting from lack of exercise and lack of living sensibly, among other causes. Neither are alcoholism, laziness, bad penmanship, most obesity, drug abuse, nor crime illnesses, but that discussion belongs elsewhere. A good deal of depression, both clinical depression and shinky depression, can be affected by changing what you do.

Physical activity is important, even if you are not in the mood. The physical activity itself may actually change your mood. So put on the warm-up suit, the sports shoes, the swimming trunks, the riding outfit, whatever is appropriate. Preparing your outer wear will help prepare your mind for the activity. Then do it.

Stimulus input is important, too. When we are depressed, we sustain the depression by sitting or lying quietly in a darkened or dimly lit room. We avoid people and other stimuli from the world around us. We lose contact with part of ourselves by shutting ourselves off from the rest of the world.

So it is helpful to get up and out of the house. If you don't feel like it, do it anyway. Shopping malls are fine places for encountering a variety of strong stimuli. Public parks are somewhat gentler resources. If you have a shinky kind of depression, you will be tempted to run back to peaceful isolation in response to the initial discomfort. But stick it out for a while; you will eventually get accustomed to this flood of information banging on your senses. And the depression will evaporate in the moments when you are drawn into the movement around you.

Changing your environment will help you cope with depression. Your environment reminds you of who you are. On a more fundamental level it *is* who you are, but we'll leave that notion aside for the moment. The walls of your apartment, the bed, the sofa, your clothing, your dishes, and so forth keep stirring up memories of who you have been. So Constructive Living principles recommend that you repaint the walls of your living quarters, rearrange the furniture, repair your clothes or buy new, more colorful ones. Notice that these suggestions not only serve to change your surroundings, they also provide purposeful physical activities and new stimuli to help you emerge from depression.

Don't wait for someone to rescue you from the doldrums. Don't wait for medication to save you either. While taking your medication, get active. While undergoing counseling or instruction, increase the variety of contacts you have with other people and things. Get a pet; take a trip; go shopping. Don't let a shinky depression be the excuse for losing years from your life.

Stress

Stress is an overrated concept. There is no doubt that we find ourselves pushed and pulled by a variety of influencing factors in our lives. Leaving aside the specialized scientific definitions of stress, the folk concept includes some notion that outside forces cause unpleasant and even dangerous effects on our minds and bodies. Stress is thought to be bad; it should be reduced or eliminated. Let's examine in more detail some of the assumptions underlying this concept.

Stress isn't merely some external force. It is also an attitude. The concept of "stress" is much like the concept of "weed." There is no identifying characteristic of any group of plants that marks them as weeds. A plant becomes a weed because someone considers them misplaced, unwanted where they are. The same kinds of stimuli that push some to stressed-out despair may prompt others to achievement and satisfaction.

"When the going gets tough, the tough get going" is a common saying. It is a statement about response to stress, I suppose. What we do about these pressing stimuli is vitally important. We cannot merely see ourselves as passive recipients of pressures from the outside world, victims of stress, without ignoring the major element of our behavior, our rejoinder to the challenges imposed by change. Our environment and our response are of a piece. It is the whole set of circumstances and interpretation and response that determines our reality, no single item from that set.

If one's goal, then, is to reduce undesired stress, there are three areas where reduction is possible. Changing one's circumstances is a possible place to start. Get to work on projects early so that last-minute time pressures are lessened, organize your work space so that you can find important papers and tools readily, find work settings where people have a sensible perspective about work, use CL reciprocity principles to improve social relations at home and on the job, practice healthy behavior so that the stress of illness is minimized, and so forth. The above suggestions are common sense. They require no special insight, only some attention and effort.

Changing one's attitude toward stress is more difficult. Attitude change may come as a result of tackling the other two variables—circumstances and response. But just considering the possibility that what has been previously defined as absolutely terrible stress may contain positive aspects of stimulation and possibilities for change may be a useful initial step. When we make gross generalizations about anything, stress included, we may consider the matter closed and fail to look at the reality that prompted our abstract evaluation. Over and over again Constructive Living instructors invite their students to keep observing reality. The experience of tension and worry and pressure is unpleasant, but it is also a teacher. It contains information about what needs doing.

What needs doing includes our response to stress. I think most people are smarter than some so-called mental health experts seem to think. We ordinary folks know that if our response to stress is escape into alcohol or other drugs, or travel, or shopping, or promiscuity, or even reading about self-improvement and undergoing psychotherapy, the stressful circumstances aren't likely to remedy themselves. We may relish the temporary time-out, but sooner or later we have to face that unpleasant, stressful situation. And the problem may have been magnified by our escape behavior. We know all that. Yet we may have the hope that there is some smooth, easy way to solve our problems, eliminate those stressors. If we just had more knowledge, more insight, more time, more willpower, more character, more confidence, more faith, more something-that-might-save-us. We know better than that—particularly if we have lived long enough to seek the magical solutions and have found them to be beautifully wrapped but empty packages.

Feeling stressed? What do you need to do next? What is the sensible, practical, constructive response to your situation? What needs to be done about the circumstances that created the stressful situation? To do nothing about these circumstances is to do something about them.

Insecurity

If you don't feel insecure at times, you are being unrealistic. Insecurity is a sensible perspective at some moments in your life. We can die at any moment, loved ones can leave us or die, our possessions can be destroyed in a calamity, we can lose our jobs and our savings, we can come down with an untreatable disease—those are just a few of the disasters lurking on the horizon of the possible. Life is full of uncertainties. Anyone who feels secure and protected all the time just isn't looking at the real world.

There is no way to make life absolutely safe and secure. There is no way to look at life's possibilities and ignore the possibilities of tragedy. There is no way to avoid feelings of insecurity in those moments. Just like any other feeling, insecurity is natural, even helpful.

Insecurity invites us to work to make our world as safeguarded as possible. It prompts us to empathize with those whose lives appear to be even less protected than our own. It is part of the complex collage of being a mature human being. It doesn't need to be fixed, but it does need to be put into proper perspective.

Don't get the mistaken idea that insecurity prevents you from doing something. Be insecure and go right ahead with what needs doing. That's bottom-line Constructive Living.

Insecurity prompts us to find some meaning in life. Knowing that we shall all have illness, pain, aging problems (if we live that long), losses of loved ones, and ultimate death prods us to seek to make some sense of it all. There are many lifeways available to guide us in making life meaningful. We shall suffer; we shall feel insecure. But we need not add unnecessary suffering to our suffering. Finding significance in everyday life offers us some comfort. If you look deeply into Constructive Living, you will find one reasonable model for meaningful living.

Taking Risks

Beginnings can be both exciting and frightening. A new business venture may fill you with the excitement of fresh possibilities or the dread of the unknown, or both. Some people find the takeoff in an airplane exhilarating; I'm likely to be scared to death. A wedding day may bring on both delight and doubt. Public speaking opens new possibilities for communication as well as new opportunities to fail.

These occasions all provoke heightened awareness, consideration of a variety of angles and options, and a gamut of feelings. We are stimulated by the challenges and risks. We taste life's spices.

A bland diet may be safe, but it is uninteresting. To avoid spice altogether makes eating inconsequential. We end up empty, hollow. The more consistently we flee from what frightens us, the more we are bound by our fears and the greater the range of what frightens us. A contracted, bland, risk-free life may be relatively secure in one sense, but it feels frightening nevertheless because everything has been sacrificed to fear, and fear demands total attention.

To be sure, racing headlong toward anything and everything that frightens us is foolishness. Apprehension signals us to stay away from radioactivity and dark inner-city streets and cars with faulty brakes. But life's opportunities often come with risk and trepidation affixed firmly up front. Assessment of the situation should never exclude the fear, but the fear shouldn't be allowed to blanket the other factors either. Taking the good chance may be worth it, whatever the outcome.

Foolish gambling is quite another matter. It's not romantic; it's childish and stupid. There is no need to use words like *compulsive gambler*. There is no need to label it *addictive character disorder*. You don't need anyone else's help. The sensible way to deal with too much gambling is to stop. You will lose some of the excitement and thrill of the barely possible, but you will gain a more secure economic base, a more stable family life, and the chance to use your cleverness on genuinely rewarding pursuits. Grown-ups need not be pushed around by impulses. Grow up!

A Boring Job

Taking drugs seems to be the answer some young people have found to get through the day on a repetitious, low-paying job. The cost of such a means of handling boredom is very high. What alternatives are there? One alternative is to find a way to do the job better. Another is to prepare for a better job while enduring the one at hand. Another is to lose oneself in mastering the tiny intricacies of the routine job at hand.

A reminder: Work doesn't have to be fun. Writing isn't enjoyable for me. Even when work is exhausting and frustrating and tedious, it may still be rewarding. We make money, we help our customers and clients, we contribute to the world, we do our part to make the product or provide the service, we take the burden off fellow workers, we create meaning in our lives. People without work merit our sympathy. If there are no formal jobs appearing before your eyes, it is wise to find something constructive to do on your own.

Assignments

IN CONSTRUCTIVE LIVING the instruction often takes the form of assignments. For example a shy person may be assigned the task of greeting a stranger every day. Of course when making such a greeting assignment, we can expect that the responses from a variety of strangers will vary. Some may return the recognition with a smile, others may ignore the greeting, and so forth. Whatever the responses that come from the strangers, our CL student has accomplished the assignment by the act of contact itself. The doing of the assignment was important, whatever the result. This principle is generalized to any undertaking, assigned or not. The doing with full attention of any activity is in itself significant, whatever the outcome. We cannot control the results of our efforts. Outcomes may depend on the mood of others, weather conditions, consumer response, legislation, the economic picture, and the like. Outcomes may present us with information about what we need to do next. Then we are presented with another activity that needs to be done with full attention.

It is this movement from activity to activity with attention and receptivity to the information from consequences of previous activities that Constructive Living assignments are designed to cultivate. You may call what we offer "games," or "exercises," or "assignments," or "foolishness," but do them. Don't merely talk about them or analyze them or ponder them. It is in the doing that you discover the essence of Constructive Living.

There is no need for students to understand all about CL or all about themselves before beginning the assignments. We take an experimental approach, trying out as many assignments as necessary to achieve the desired results. Reality teaches us what is useful and what is not for a particular student.

The doing of the assignments per se is the work of Constructive Living. It is not the relationship with the instructor or the skill of the instructor that produces changes in a student's life. It is the student's action on the world that results in change. So CL instructors can take neither credit for improvement in a student's condition nor blame for lack of improvement.

For newcomers to Constructive Living it is quite all right to use these assignments or exercises as though they were tranquilizers. The next time you are anxious or bored or hopeless or upset in some way, and you can't come up with anything constructive to do in the moment, pick out a Constructive Living exercise and do it. When you finish one exercise and find you still have time on your hands, move on to another. You will find yourself distracted from your misery, at least temporarily. And you will learn something about constructive activity in the midst of discomfort.

Of course the exercises have a broader purpose and deeper meaning than mere tranquilizing distraction. But as a start they offer immediate relief from some of the unnecessary suffering that plagues all of us at times. There is no need to ready yourself psychologically to do an exercise; just do it. I expect my students to do their assignments. Sometimes they do, sometimes they don't. The traditional Western therapist expects that patients have been psychologically injured in some way, most likely during childhood. If I were a student, I would rather that others expected me to be competent than to be a victim. We tend to become what others expect of us.

Constructive Living Assignments

1. This exercise works to overcome procrastination. Write a letter at once to anyone; the letter may have any content whatsoever. Mail the letter immediately. Use the same approach to other life activities. For example overcome the reluctance to begin that sewing project by starting on it promptly. Deal with the resistance to cleaning the garage by cleaning it right away.

Of course! The solution to putting off things is to do them right away. Why do people seek some magical technique that will make all this effort easy? Please notice, however, that while painting the fence, the inner debate about getting around to doing it, as well as the discomfort associated with putting off this chore, has disappeared.

2. Carl Johnson suggests investing a day or more in responding to others with "Yes, thank you," "No, thank you," "Excuse me," or "Isn't that interesting." No other words are to be uttered. You may write whatever notes are necessary. Notice how your life proceeds with this particular focus.

3. Paul Jones recommends the following exercise: Use a cloth napkin at your meals. When you sit down to a meal, observe the napkin and consider your purpose in using it. Place it on your lap, noticing how it sits there. As you eat, take a moment now and again to notice where your napkin is. If you put it somewhere other than your lap, think back to why you did so. At the end of each meal recall a specific service your napkin performed for you during the meal. Thank your napkin for the service. Before you put your napkin away, notice whether there is anything related to it that needs doing.

4. Suppose you were permitted to create a new world after you died. Suppose you were asked to populate it with plants and animals and people drawn from your imagination and memory. How interesting and varied would your creation be? What details in form and color would your flowers show? What patterns would their leaves and stems take? What about people's faces, bodies, behavioral tendencies? Would your world have enough variety for you to live in it, among your creations, without your being bored?

Observe your surroundings as though you were preparing to create a new world. Note the tiniest details. When you forget to pay attention and then notice that you have forgotten, simply get back to noticing. To aid in your observation it may be helpful to draw some of the objects in your surroundings in great detail. Spend ten minutes each on drawing three leaves, for example. As you draw, notice how much you didn't notice before.

5. Begin correspondence with someone you never met. The recipient of your first letter could be a widow or widower recommended by a friend, a hospital patient, a nursing-home resident. Or the letter can be directed to a nursing home or hospital ward as a whole. The contents of your letter should include something about yourself, but its main emphasis should be on learning about the life of the recipient. You may or may not get a response. Repeat the exercise as needed.

6. Notice something new, Patricia Ryan Madson suggests. Keep alert for even small changes in your environment. Friendly quizzes to see if others have discovered the elements that are new to you makes this aspect of attention into a game. You may discover that what you just discovered has been around for a long time.

7. Whenever you have that troubling thought about your ex-boyfriend or ex-girlfriend or ex-spouse, get out the vacuum cleaner and clean house. Barbara Sarah gave this assignment to someone who seemed distracted by such thoughts during a training session.

8. There are many forms of silence assignments. Most of us talk much too much. We talk in order to distract ourselves from life, much as many people read newspapers to accomplish the same purpose. Periods of silence allow us more free attention to notice reality and discover what needs doing. Reflective silence (only words of thanks and apology are permitted) and tea-ceremony silence (only conversation related to the present, immediate surroundings) are often assigned by Gregg Krech and Gregory Willms.

    Other silence assignments include limiting the number of sentences permitted during a day (say, limiting speech to fifteen or twenty sentences) and counting to ten before speaking. Notes can be written at any time in these exercises.

However, it is more trouble to write than to speak, so notes tend to be written infrequently. Of course when you see a car backing into a tree, it is quite all right to go off silence to warn the driver. Sometimes we forget and speak automatically; for example, even though you are on silence you might call out, "Come in," when someone knocks on the door. When you notice your error, simply return to silence. As always, what needs to be done next? Assigning ourselves periods of silence is common in Constructive Living. See the chapter entitled "Taking in Life" for more information about the rationale for silence assignments.

9. "I may never be good at Constructive Living"—when such a negative prophecy arose in an individual session, the student was assigned the task of making up a Constructive Living maxim to be offered any other student who might speak such words of despair. It isn't necessary to be good at Constructive Living tomorrow. Right now will do just fine.

10. I recommend that the readers of this book take time out to write themselves a letter about what they have learned so far from Constructive Living and what they want to remember two or three weeks from now. Then give the letter in a stamped, self-addressed envelope to a friend or relative to mail in a couple of weeks. The letters can continue as often and for as long an interval between writing and delivery as you wish.

11. At Morita therapy meetings in Japan Dr. Noriaki Kohguchi reported on the use of a walking meter as an objective measure of how many paces a student takes each day. Especially if you suspect you are not getting sufficient exercise, buy or borrow such a device and keep a chart of the number of steps you take each day for a week. Set daily goals for the following week and "make strides" toward achieving your goals.

12. As you prepare your annual income tax forms, take some time out now and then to reflect on what you have received from specific representatives of the government during the past

year, what you have returned to these representatives, and what troubles you have caused them.

13. Attention comes clear, and it drifts. Such is the case for all of us. What can you do to remind yourself to return to awareness of your surroundings? One tactic is to put up happy-face stickers (or some other sign) around your house and car and work places to remind yourself to pay attention whenever you notice them. Another method is to draw or paint everyday objects, spending at least a half hour on the drawing of a hand or shoe, for example. Doing art forces us to look at the object for long periods, noticing details, improving attention. If sleepiness becomes a problem, stand up, move about, shake your arms and legs. Remember, behavior (e.g., bouncing up and down) can sometimes influence feelings (e.g., sleepiness).

14. The CL journal is a study aid for everyday life. The format may vary somewhat, but most common is a daily journal with each page divided into two large columns and a narrow column for time along the left edge. The two large columns are for feelings and behavior. At any convenient time during the day write down the time of a few minutes earlier, what you were feeling at that time, and what you were doing at that time. We recommend that you write about your experience a few minutes earlier so that you don't repeatedly write "Writing in the journal" in the behavior column. But too much earlier and we forget what we were doing and feeling. The journal should contain as much detailed information in the behavior column as in the feeling column. A page or two a day with any time intervals at all is sufficient. You might be finished with the day's journal by midmorning.

Notice in your journal that you have a written record showing that feelings fade over time, that there are times when you are not feeling anything at all (but no times when you are not doing anything at all), and that some behaviors seem unrelated or even contrary to what you are feeling at the time. Resist your temptation to load up the feelings column with long entries about thoughts and wishes while neglecting material in the behavior column. Both columns are important. Generally a week or two of journal work is sufficient, but some people prefer to continue with it for longer periods of time.

15. A related assignment is to report in great detail (to a CL instructor, a friend, a tape recorder) what you did during a two to three-hour period during the day. Report only your behavior. Which foot touched the floor first as you got out of bed? Which arm went into the sleeve of your sweater first? Exactly how did you prepare your breakfast, take a shower, make that phone call? You must pay attention to your actions in order to report them in exact detail. At first you are likely to find that your mind has drifted while you acted automatically. You may find gaps in your reports, details you just can't recall. Keep at it until you are skillful at noticing the details of your actions for at least a few hours at a time. Doing life well is what Constructive Living is about.

16. After a walk or a movie or any outside activity, quiz yourself on the details of what you noticed about your surroundings. What was the decor of the theater? What cars passed along the street? How are your neighbors' homes landscaped? How was your new business contact dressed? Become skillful at noticing your environment. It is a way of finding out about who you are.

17. Examine the maxims and stories and koans in this book and other Constructive Living books to discover obvious and hidden meanings. I write here not of some hidden, mystical meanings but of meanings that become apparent when you are paying attention to your life and understand Constructive Living principles better. It's helpful to go back to the maxims and stories from time to time to see if your interpretation of them has changed. They offer a way of measuring your development in this lifeway as well as being teaching tools.

18. Monitor your speech so that you don't talk in a sloppy fashion. The way we speak affects the way we think about our

world. To say "I feel that you don't want to go" when you mean "I discern (or believe or guess) you don't want to go" is imprecise. Furthermore such speech allows you to avoid looking at the clues that led you to your conclusion that the other person doesn't want to go. The word *feel* is overused and has inflated importance because of careless speech patterns in our society. Other words, too, are improperly or overly used. *I can't,* and *I like,* and *I'm excited about,* and *I'm not comfortable with,* and *I'm concerned about* are examples. A Constructive Living instructor will help you monitor your speech habits.

19. Practice your understanding of Constructive Living by considering what CL advice you would give to your friends or relatives or neighbors when they present problems of their daily lives to you. In your own life consider what advice an imaginary CL instructor might give you. If the advice is not practical and reality-grounded, it is not CL advice. It may not suggest activities that are easy or pleasant, however.

20. It is often helpful to have social support in your study of CL. Get together with a friend or small group and compare your understanding of the principles with theirs. Explore purposes and alternatives for achieving them. Suggest assignments to one another and report on your success or failure in carrying them out. Do support one another's study even when you don't feel like it.

Constructive Living Reflection Assignments

1. Thank someone ten times a day using ten different methods of expression—for example, "Thanks," "How kind of you," "I appreciate that," a note, a smile and nod, and so forth. Like many exercises in the list below, this exercise is most effective if used on someone with whom you are at odds. It is to be carried out whether you feel gratitude or not. You

214 • David K. Reynolds, Ph.D.

must look for acts performed in your behalf and acknowledge them by your thanks. Notice your reluctance to carry
out this assignment when you are upset. Do it despite your
reluctance.

2. Give a gift to someone every day. The gift need not be expensive or new; a token gift is sufficient. Give the gifts
whether the recipient thanks you or even acknowledges the
gift at all. In addition, give away a minimum of three smiles
each day.

3. Perform a secret service for someone else at least twice a week.
A secret service is one for which you get no social credit and
the activity doesn't benefit you directly. If anyone sees you
doing the service, it is not secret. The service need not involve
major time and effort. Polishing a pair of shoes and returning
them to their original place, folding a sweater and putting it
away, adding candies to a desktop candy jar, ordering a magazine subscription for someone else, and submitting an anonymous letter in praise of a fellow worker to the company
newsletter are examples of secret services.

4. Write a letter of thanks to your mother, citing at least three
specific things she did for you when you were in first or second grade of elementary school. Write another letter on the
same theme to your father. Mail the letters or not as you
wish. It is helpful to write the letters even if one or both
parents are dead. If appropriate, take the letter to the grave
and read it aloud.
    Write letters of thanks to each of your parents covering the
next three years of your life, and the next three years, and so
on up to the present. Again, you need not feel gratitude in
order to write these letters. Unpleasant memories and feelings
may emerge as you recall these periods in your life. They are
not to be ignored; the unpleasant happenings are part of reality too. However, for this exercise only the words of appreciation are to be included in these letters. Write additional
letters of thanks to others who have been important in your

life, such as teachers, grandparents, marriage partners, employers, children, and close friends.

5. Write a letter of apology to your mother citing at least three specific things you did to cause her trouble during junior high school. Write another letter on the same theme to your father. Again, it is not necessary to mail the letters. As in the previous assignment write the letters even if one or both parents have died.

   Write other letters of apology to your parents covering other three-year periods of your life. Write additional letters of apology to others who have been important in your life. You need not feel remorse or repentance for the deeds you recall. Merely point out what you did that caused them inconvenience, and apologize. Beware the danger of writing in general terms. "I know I caused you a lot of trouble in junior high school" is unacceptable. Be specific, concrete, detailed. Try to envision your parents' faces when you came home drunk or wrecked the car or caused them some other misery.

6. Clean a drawer or handbag or suitcase or closet or garage. As you clean the contents one by one and put them back in their proper places, thank them aloud for some specific service they performed for you in the past. For example, thank the rake for helping you gather autumn leaves last November, and thank the soup ladle for helping you serve the bean soup at the party on Thursday. It's a good idea to tell others in your family what you are about to do so that they aren't shocked to find you talking to the kitchen utensils or garden tools.

7. Take an old bag and tongs or gloves and pick up trash on your next walk. Use the paper towel with which you dried your hands in a public restroom to pick up papers off the floor or wipe the drops of water from the counter.

8. Arrive early at the office and bow to your typewriter or word processor and thank your stapler and stamp pad and calculator for the services they have provided recently. Office

equipment assists you in getting your tasks accomplished. Treat these coworkers with care.

9. At the end of each day spend fifteen minutes reflecting over the day in a structured way. Reflect on what other people did for you that day, what you did for other people that day (not necessarily the same people), and what troubles you caused other people that day. Be concrete and specific. It may be helpful to write a page of notes using the above three headings as a daily reflection journal.

10. Reflect on what you have received from your shoes, your belt, your car, electricity, your carpet, your wallet, your stove, soap, and water today. Reflect on what you have returned to these features of your world and the troubles you have caused them. Remember that it has only been relatively recently in human history that we began to see human beings as separated from and superior to the rest of the world. Such a perspective has produced loneliness and isolation, anomie. Such a perspective fostered mass production without attention to or investment in individual products. Do what you need to do in order to make amends to these nonliving partners.

11. Consider detailed ways you can repay those who have died. Hint: give to a charity in their name, tell positive stories about their lives to their grandchildren, complete a project they began, take good care of something they treasured. Do what needs to be done.

12. Compute the amount of money your parents (or corresponding adults who had responsibility for your childhood years) spent out of pocket for you from the time you were born until you reached age twenty-one. Calculate your share of the rent, your share of the gas on vacations, dental fees, clothes, books, school supplies, holiday and birthday gifts, food, and so forth. Calculate in as much detail at the dollar amounts of the time. An electronic calculator will be useful for this exercise.

Next calculate the amount of money you spent on your

parents during the same period, from birth until you reached age twenty one. Include birthday gifts, holiday gifts, and the like. Compare the amount they spent on you with the amount you spent on them. Of course you can expect some discrepancy. Is it greater than you expected?

Next do the same computations for the period since you reached age twenty-one. Calculate for the years of your adulthood up to the present or until your parents died. In your adult years how much did your parents spend on you? Perhaps they contributed to your wedding, your buying a house, your children's education, your purchase of a car. How much did you spend on your parents since you became an adult? One might expect that, since mature adult equals are involved, there would be no discrepancy between the two amounts. Does that expectation match the reality?

Related exercises involve calculating the height of the stack of sheets your mother (or mother surrogate) washed for you during childhood, the height of the stack of dishes she washed for you, and the amount of time your parents invested in your homework, sporting, and scouting activities.

These reflection exercises are designed to present a more objective picture of past reality. It is difficult to measure intangibles such as love and attention. It is easier to measure money spent, dishes washed, and time invested in school projects or sewing clothes. The exercises are not designed to invoke some sort of feeling. Whatever feelings emerge are natural and appropriate to the person you are at the moment. Most important is to see reality. Don't let faddish fictions cause you to ignore this reality of support and service. You received these benefits whether you noticed them or not, whether you appreciated them or not.

A Note for Instructors

When students experience success following an assignment, their desires for even greater advances soon appear. In fact they may criticize themselves in their improved situations, wishing for ever-increasing gains. It may be necessary to remind them of the objective improvements that have resulted from their efforts thus far.

If a student comes complaining of weak will or an inability to make decisions, then it is helpful to give a variety of assignments. The student either does the assignments or doesn't do them, either way demonstrating an ability to make decisions. If the student complains of lacking patience, it is helpful to delay, making the student wait at each step of the assignment course. The student may demonstrate the ability to wait even when impatient. Similarly, well-chosen assignments can help students discover their ability to accomplish their goals even when angry or frustrated or lacking in confidence.

Of course it is best when the students can devise their own assignments and come to their own Constructive Living understandings. It is also most natural and transfers best to other situations when this self-discovery takes place at the students' own pace.

Further Assignments

Other assignments and exercises can be found in Constructive Living books. For example, assignments can be found in *Playing Ball on Running Water* (pp. 105–116), *Even in Summer the Ice Doesn't Melt* (pp. 151–158), *Pools of Lodging for the Moon* (pp. 103–106), *A Thousand Waves* (pp. 125–127), *Thirsty, Swimming in the Lake* (pp. 107–111), *Rainbow Rising from a Stream* (pp. 131–138), and *Plunging Through the Clouds* (pp. 25–26).

Remote World

PLUG YOUR EARS with cotton for a day, wear dark sunglasses at home on a day with dim light, tape your legs or fingers together for a period of time. Needless to say, don't endanger your or others' health and safety by these exercises. Use them long enough to get a sense of the detail of the services your body provides. Is there something that needs to be done for your body?

I had an ear problem that caused a temporary impairment of hearing. The world backed off. Many taken-for-granted cues that my world was operating smoothly and routinely were either absent or muted. I sometimes failed to hear the ringing of the telephone. The fan and key click of my computer were barely audible. I seemed to live more within my mind than before.

My hearing deficit caused trouble to others. The volume on the television and stereo was uncomfortably high for them. They sometimes needed to repeat themselves to be understood. They couldn't count on my responding immediately to a call or a doorbell or the sound of brakes.

I began to realize what great service my ears had performed over the years. Of course the same applies to my eyes and nose and tongue and fingers and legs and other body parts. It is commonplace to say that when we lose something, we begin to appreciate its value. Even before my hearing deficit I would have vaguely generalized that my ears are important. But only with the loss of hearing did I begin to recognize the detail and degree of their importance. It is that detail that we find it useful to examine in Constructive Living.

We are provided with a variety of natural opportunities to recognize the considerations provided us by our bodies. A recent cold sent my senses of smell and taste to bed for a few days. My nose wouldn't have been able to warn me of smoke in the house or spoiled food. On the positive side, because everything tasted about the same, it was relatively painless to avoid sweets and to eat certain healthy foods that wouldn't ordinarily appear on my plate. Responding to circumstances is what Constructive Living teaches. Recognition of the specific services your body provides may prompt more appreciation of it and better care of it too.

The Practice of Constructive Living

Introduction

THIS SECTION IS written for Constructive Living instructors. I hope that everyone peeks in on the advice I offer instructors. You see, my goal is to make everyone a CL instructor. The distinction between instructor and student is temporary and artificial. Anyone who lives sensibly accumulates experiences that can be usefully passed on to others. Constructive Living merely offers a format, vocabulary, and structure for passing along information about realistic living.

Students who come for Constructive Living instruction often expect that something will be done to or for them. They are seldom prepared to carry out the assignments that comprise the core of Constructive Living training. Students usually come with the expectation that they will spend long periods talking about their feelings and their personal histories, with particular emphasis on the negative qualities of significant others in their pasts.

Methods

Getting some information about personal history is useful in Constructive Living instruction, because a history provides information for both reflection assignments and action assignments. However, Constructive Living instructors don't spend time routinely inquiring about distant past history. Asking the questions "What do you wish to start?," "What do you wish to stop?," and "What do you wish to continue?" is one way to elicit focused information during the beginning session and again periodically during the training.

Listening is an important part of Constructive Living instruction. The information gained from listening helps flesh out material for verbal instruction and assignments. Furthermore it allows the student the opportunity to unload some of the things on his or her mind. Until that process is complete, some students are unready to listen to any instruction.

Furthermore the instructor's listening provides a model of listening for the student. While treasuring the student's words the instructor provides an example for the student to follow when the instructor speaks in turn.

Attention to detail is a value fundamental to Constructive Living. Reality comes only in detail, never in abstraction. The instructor attends to the details of the sessions and uncovers details of the student's life. The student is encouraged to attend to the details of everyday life, including the assignments.

A skillful CL instructor pays close attention to the hooks, cues, and patterns displayed by the student in speech and other behavior. Hooks are the student's desires, which make assignments appealing (e.g., "I want to fly to Rio," "I yearn to be asked out on dates like the other girls," "If I could only graduate from college," "I'd like to give a public speech").

Cues are brief bits of information that tell the instructor some important detail about the student's situation. Cues may appear only once during a series of instruction sessions (e.g., the name of one boy in class may be mentioned, a complaint about the mother may pop up only once and indirectly, a hobby may be included in a list of daily activities). Experience brings with it an ear tuned to pick up the cues that will be helpful in making assignments.

Patterns are recurring segments of information that tell the CL guide about the student's situation (e.g., a negative attitude may keep appearing in conversation, or the instructor's words may be cut off again and again by the student). Skills (such as highly developed verbal skills) are acknowledged, and the student is encouraged to work in other areas that are not so well developed. The instructor and student are likely to pick up relatively quickly on patterns in others that are similar to patterns within themselves. We instructors get hints about areas for work on ourselves when we find ourselves particularly sensitive to certain problem areas in others. Our students are our teachers.

Assignments are most effectively made on the basis of these hooks, cues, and patterns. Assignments are weighed in terms of both the short-term effect on the student and the long-term effect. An immediate crisis situation naturally requires assignments with immediate effects. By *effects* here I don't mean the outcomes of the assignments (which is outside of anyone's control) but the impact on the student of the process of doing the assignment.

Exercises are assigned and presented in a manner that increases the likelihood that the student will actually carry them out. For example, for an athletic, competitive man who is in danger of dying from heart disease, a Constructive Living strategy would be to tell him that he is not competitive enough, that his competitive nature needs development in even more areas. We might have him do yoga and meditation very well, better than others, as a step toward turning his activities in a more healthy direction. We use what the students bring us.

Obviously when the students come up with their own assignments and carry them out, there is special benefit for them. They won't be meeting with an instructor forever. A rapidly achieved independent stance is our goal. The reader might wish to refer to the chapter entitled "Assignments" for further details of this aspect of Constructive Living instruction.

Instructors offer information in terms of realistic observations and outcomes. An instructor might point out that the student is weeping while saying her life is perfect, or that if the student drops out of school he would lose this opportunity to get his diploma. Note that these observations stay close to the observed reality. There is no attempt to invent some underlying hidden motivation for the weeping or to convince the student of some undiscovered resentment that is causing resistance to continuing school. We work with what is straightforward and obvious, not some untestable theory of the unconscious. Nevertheless students may discover new interpretations and possibilities for action within long-standing circumstances.

Some students exhibit unrealistic perceptions of the social world. When they tell us that they are already excessively thanking others and serving them, that their problem lies not at all within themselves but in the others who don't appreciate them or do anything for them, we simply point out that in that case the reflection/reciprocity assignments should be easy and natural for them, given their natural inclination to carry out these exercises anyway. And we ask them to tell us some of the specific words of thanks they offered others today. The trend of communication within a session is often from the student's generalization and abstraction to the instructor's query for concrete, specific detail.

Getting Life Lived Until We Die

Few people in youth and middle age have seriously considered the likely consequences of old age and death in any detail. They have lived as though their parents and other loved ones will live forever. They have failed to plan hobbies and pastimes that can be carried out when they have limited physical resources in old age. They have put off telling older loved ones important messages or sharing activities with them, as though their elders would be alive indefinitely. They may not have created a will or any specific instructions for giving away personal mementos in case of their own death.

A number of exercises in Constructive Living guide students to deal with these situations. They may be asked to interview elderly relatives, write their own wills and memorial services, and begin hobbies that can be continued in spite of certain physical limitations, for example.

Individual Sessions During Certification Training

The ten-day intensive certification training involves a number of teaching formats, including examinations, lectures, and excursions. During the training each trainee or intern meets with at least one instructor for an individual teaching session for each of the ten days, except for exam days. The trainees can select areas of their lives for discussion and assignments during these office hours. They can learn the teaching styles of a variety of instructors as those styles are modeled in individual sessions. In this section are suggestions for guidance of trainees during these individual sessions.

As much as possible the rooms for individual sessions should be simple and neat so that the trainee isn't distracted by a lot of random visual stimuli. Chairs should be selected and placed so that the intern is not seated lower or in a less comfortable chair than the instructor. There should be nothing in the seating arrangements that indicate higher status for the instructor.

The first session should include time for introductions, exchanging background information, and the invitation to work on whatever the interns wish to improve or develop during their period of intensive training. Naturally some trainees wish to conceal what they consider to be their weak areas in this social situation. The instructor should encourage self-revelation by modeling it. During this session the interns may be asked to close their eyes and report on what they have noticed about the contents of the room.

Assignments encouraging attention to visual, auditory, olfactory, taste, and tactile stimuli will be given during the training. We usually begin with assigning a visual audit of the trainee's surroundings. One variation is to take a "reality walk" with the trainees while they name aloud what they are seeing.

Sessions regularly begin with questions about how the trainees are eating, sleeping, and exercising. If the trainees perceive problems in any of these basic areas, appropriate assignments are suggested. The trainees are then asked for suggestions that might improve their educational experience during the training. Open-ended questions such as "What's on your mind?" and "How are you doing today?" are offered periodically. Then the trainees are asked to report on their activities, including their completed assignments from the previous sessions or from the morning seminar period. A Constructive Living journal may be assigned to help keep track of activities and concomitant thoughts and feelings. Assignments to draw maps of the kitchen or bedroom or to sketch some common objects also assist in the development of observation and attention skills. Attention alone, however, is insufficient. Exercises involving finding something that needs fixing and then fixing it carry the trainees to the next step of action based on observation. Taking a bag along on a walk for picking up trash is one such exercise.

If trainees report on specific areas of their lives that need developing, assignments are offered toward those particular ends. For example the trainees may be asked to write a resume, to send out job applications, to change their hairstyle, to interview another trainee, to go dancing, to get up in the morning at a particular time in a particular way, to write their assumptions about others in the group and check out those assumptions (perhaps with an apology and secret service to those they misread), to carry out three admirable behaviors, or to thank their self-criticism and annoying tears.

Individuals come for intensive training with a variety of backgrounds. Some of them have read many Constructive Living books and have practiced the exercises for years. Some have lived CL-like lives naturally, without having known about this practice. Some come with little previous knowledge or experience. These latter newcomers to CL may be assigned the task of assisting, or shadowing, or observing more experienced trainees. They may be placed together with advanced trainees as roommates. Observing the everyday lives of others during certification training is an important part of the teaching.

Individual sessions provide the opportunity for monitoring the trainee's speech and correcting imprecision and non-CL speech patterns. Common habits of speech such as *I feel like* (for *I intend to* or *I want to*), *I feel that* (for *I believe that* or *I suspect that*), *I can't* (for *I haven't* or *I don't want to* or *I won't*), *Don't worry* (for *I don't worry about it* or *Worry, but do what needs doing*), *We're excited by* (for *We look forward to*), and *How are you feeling?* (for *How are you doing?*) are corrected when they come up naturally during the session.

During the training period all trainees and instructors will have some period (at least one day) of silence. Individual trainees may be asked to go on silence or to put themselves on silence at other times. During periods of silence the writing of notes is permitted, and of course breaking of silence is permitted during emergencies. Writing takes more effort than speaking, so even with the writing option word-based communication is minimal. Variations on total silence include limiting the number of sentences permitted during a day (typically ten or fifteen, each sentence defined as an utterance made with a single breath), or limiting the topics or manner of speech in some way (for example, only *thank you* and *I'm sorry* allowed; or no self-references allowed, only questions).

These silence assignments are particularly useful for verbally skillful people. Such trainees may discover that much talking has interfered with their attention to surrounding reality. During the morning seminar and in individual sessions trainees are encouraged to report on what they noticed while on silence, when the silence was difficult, when it was beneficial, what reactions they encountered when shopping, and so forth.

During individual sessions trainees may be asked to write letters of thanks and letters of apology to significant others in their lives for actions during particular periods in their past. The letters may be written to living or dead parents, for example. They may be asked to compute the amount of money their parents spent on them up to age twenty-one and compare that amount with the money they spent on their parents during that same period. Then they may be assigned the same comparative computations for the period since they turned twenty-one. When doing these computations, it may be helpful to keep the following figures in mind: According to the journal *American Demographics* (August 1991, p. 59), the amount of money a family will likely spend on a child born in 1990 until the child reaches age seventeen years will be $151,170 for low-income families, $210,070 for middle-income families, and $293,400 for high-income families. In 1990 to raise a child aged fifteen to seventeen years cost low-income families $5,490, middle-income families $7,490, and high-income families $10,270 per year.

Related assignments include computing the amount spent on alcohol and alcohol-related subjects, the amount spent on tobacco, the height of the stack of dishes washed by their mothers for them in childhood, the height of the stack of sheets laundered for them by their mothers, and similar objective measures of services in their behalf. It may be useful to have a sufficient number of calculating devices available so that the counts can be as detailed as possible.

Secret-service assignments build group spirit and offer the opportunity to pay back others for their support. A secret service is something done for someone else in secret. It may be something as simple as slipping a tablet on the bed of someone who has run out of paper. If anyone at all sees the service while it is being performed, it is not secret; another must be done. Secret services should not be performed for the instructors but for other trainees. Secret services are not reported during individual sessions so that no social credit is earned for them. Once secret services have been assigned, it is not unusual to find trainees doing unassigned secret services on their own, and they look around for the services being carried out for their benefit too.

Another type of assignment is to become trackless. As much as possible the trainees are assigned the task of leaving no sign of their presence in a room after they leave it. Books and mugs and articles of clothing may not be left lying around; wrinkles should be smoothed from cushions; dishes must be carried to the kitchen after eating. This gamelike assignment sensitizes the trainees to habits that may cause others to have to straighten up after them. Another step is involved in recognizing that the dishes *deserve* to be washed, the jacket *deserves* to be hung up, and so forth.

Trainees, like advanced students outside of certification training, are assigned the task of creating their own assignments for themselves and carrying out those assignments. The training instructor may use these exercises to check on the trainee's understanding of the distinction between reflection and action aspects of Constructive Living.

Some of the assignments during certification training will be different from those given to ordinary students, however, because one of the objectives of the trainees is to learn about the theory and practice of Constructive Living. Many students outside of this training setting come seeking assistance with some immediate problem or set of problems. Eventually they may become interested in the broader theoretical picture after they have a handle on solving their present difficulties. Koans, for example, are available to anyone in many of the books about CL, but they are rarely emphasized in individual sessions outside of certification training. Constructive Living koan study involves being able to give right and wrong answers and to know why an answer is right or wrong. CL koans usually have follow-up queries to check on the trainee's understanding. These follow-up queries as such aren't offered in the books.

Near the end of the ten-day training period, two sorts of assignments are customarily made. The first is to prepare a short presentation about CL directed toward a particular audience of the trainee's choice. For example, how would one explain Constructive Living to one's family in five to ten minutes? To a civic group in a ten-minute speech? To a psychotherapist who asks about CL? These prepared talks are presented before the group of trainees, in role-playing fashion if necessary. Like the midterm and final examinations, these verbal presentations give the trainees the opportunity to put CL concepts into their own words. Explaining to others causes us to discover our areas of conceptual fuzziness and strength. Teaching causes us to learn.

The second assignment given to trainees at the end of training is to write letters to themselves. These letters are mailed to the trainees about a month after the training ends. Each trainee writes to himself or herself whatever message it would be useful to read a month later—advice, encouragement, things to remember, things to do, a checklist, or CL principles. The trainees place the letters into stamped envelopes, seal them, and address them to themselves. The sponsor of the certification training then mails the letters about a month later. This reinforcement of what was learned during training has proved quite helpful to a number of trainees.

Constructive Living Reflection

The practice of Constructive Living reflection is spelled out in *Plunging Through the Clouds*. Subtle differences between Constructive Living reflection and the original Naikan introspection practiced in Japan may be found. In Constructive Living reciprocity/reflection there is more emphasis on discovering reality's support and less emphasis on recollection of personal misdeeds. The reflection process itself is cooler in CL and less likely to shade into religious or reality-transcending experience.

We don't assign the instructor as the student's topic of CL reflection. If the student requests to reflect on the instructor, the report should be made to someone else.

The instructors, too, should be doing daily reflection on what is received from the student, what is returned to the student, and what troubles the instructor is causing the student. For instructors to think of themselves as teachers of Constructive Living reflection is like taking one piece from a jigsaw puzzle and thinking that piece is the whole puzzle. Instructors are no more than reality's representatives here, at this moment, just as the students are.

The Bottom-Line Queries

When students come to me, the bottom-line questions I present to them are: Are you satisfied with your life as it is? To what degree have the methods you tried so far been effective for you?

If they are satisfied with their lives, then I see no reason why I should take their money and instruct them in Constructive Living. It's not my responsibility or my right to change them. If they aren't satisfied and have come to study with me, we must get on with exercises and assignments to change what they decide needs changing. There's no time for listening to long lists of complaints.

If I give assignments and they don't do them, then I point out that wall of reality again. If you are dissatisfied with your life and come to me for advice about change, all I have to offer are assignments. Therapeutic talking has been ineffective for you in the past. I don't intend to talk in our sessions. If you want to talk to someone go to a therapist, a friend, or a clergyperson.

Some CL instructors offer discounts to those who do the assigned exercises. Such a practice may be useful at the beginning. In the long run, however, we expect our students to catch on that doing a constructive task well is reward in itself and that it increases the likelihood that reality will bring other rewards as well.

Maximum Benefits

Research in Japan indicates that, on the average, maximum benefits from Morita therapy begin about two years after beginning therapy.

The basics of Constructive Living can be learned in a handful of sessions or even merely by reading the literature. However, it takes a period of months or years to put the practice into everyday life on a fairly consistent basis. Students learn quickly that CL is easy to talk about and difficult to practice at times. It is thanks to the student's effort that progress can be seen. It is relatively easy to offer assignments to students; doing the assignments is what brings the benefits.

Constructive Living Communications

From Susan Kahn, on parenting:

Henry [Susan's husband] and I sometimes call Alex [their new baby] our "master's level" Constructive Living teacher. There is truly no time-out. These many months are golden opportunities for controlling our behavior and doing what needs to be done. I have a new answer for your question about how you know whether something is a whim or something that needs to be done: Become a parent!

Alex also gives me a whole new perspective on Naikan. . . . I had no idea that so many people do so much when a baby is born—both for the baby and for the parents. There are people who did things for me and made me things and bought me gifts before I was even born—and I don't even know who they are. Add them to those on our Naikan list of people whose names we don't know.

Even though I had "made a decision to become a parent" (whatever that means), it certainly is different from *doing* parenthood. I had no idea how all-encompassing being a parent truly is. These things are now revealed for me in the doing. They are uncovered by experience rather than by formal Constructive Living reflection. But I don't think I would reflect on them without having sat formal Naikan. I think Naikan was something I didn't understand until after the intensive sitting. I thought there was some "thing," some principle or "Aha!" that I would "get" and then "have"—forever of course. But I needed the intensive sitting and some time after to realize that Naikan is Naikan, just Naikan. And that it is not separate from anything; it is life, if that is how you live. It's not a bad way to live.

From a high school student, on her own shinky nature:

I am a high school senior with a packed schedule—with homework, sports, and a boyfriend being major time- and thought-consumers. In other words *Lots* of stress and worrying. I take everything I do very seriously, and it would not be a far guess if you said I was a perfectionist. I have to have *everything* perfect, including my feelings. If I'm not completely happy, I stop everything, panic, become overanxious, and start to analyze. As it turns out, this constant analyzing of my feelings has a detrimental rather than a helpful effect on my happiness. Analyzing too much causes me more anxiety and stress. It's bad, too, because it doesn't affect only me but those around me as well.

In my relationship with my boyfriend (a relationship I care a lot about), my analyzing of him and of our relationship prevents us from being truly in love—I am just so caught up in making sure that everything is going "fine" that it distracts us from enjoying being together, from having fun.

Up until now I've never thought that my constant analyzing was hurtful. I realize now, though, that I have definitely been living in the past and the future, and not enough in the *now*.

From an underachiever, on letter writing:

Long ago I got bogged down in self-examination and became almost paralyzed from taking action by too much self-analysis. This was the model that psychology presented to me. I have had years of therapy from many different kinds of therapists, and at almost fifty years old I am still a blatant underachiever. . . . I have wanted to find the "secret" for more effective living—or constructive living, if you will—and when I did, to use what I learned for the benefit of others. I am almost as hopeless as they come, and I feel that what works for me would work for just about anyone. . . . I used your technique to get this letter written rather than putting it off until I forgot about it.

From a social worker, on just doing it:

For the past month I have been absorbing your ideas, deeply impressed by them. For years I have been telling my clients to adopt the Nike slogan "Just Do It!" and had been unaware that this slogan is an integral part of CL until I began reading your books. I have become increasingly aware of how the tapes and slide shows in our heads chain us to inaction. I have urged my clients to turn off the tapes and asked them to do some meditating in order to focus and center themselves. But the CL concepts are marvelous, and I would like to learn more about them as a professional, as I have so many people who are stuck, so many marriages that are mired in passivity and hopelessness.

From a college student, on isolation:

I am a twenty-three-year-old single female finishing my last year in college. In the past two years I feel I have experienced many personal changes and have spent a great deal of time analyzing why I feel the way I feel. At this point in my life my introspection has solved none of my problems, nor has it led to any healthy conclusions. Instead I have so isolated myself that I have become an extremely lonely person who cannot interact with other people. Needless to say, I am tired of my own self-serving attitude but feel powerless to change it.

From a widow, on digging up the past:

A dear friend is a clinical psychologist and is constantly after her sister and me to go back and take a microscope to every aspect of our lives— dig, dig, dig! We tell her that what is done is done. We have lives to live now.

"No, no, no, your husband did blah, blah, blah. Bring your anger up and deal with it," she tells us.

But I'm not bothered any more by something that happened eleven or twelve years ago. I don't wish to continue beating the proverbial dead horse!

I digress. How does one become eligible for CL training?

From a college student, on self-analysis:

I am a twenty-one-year-old college student who has been taught to work through and analyze every aspect of my life, including the past, even questions I have about my future. In return I have always felt like "today" never existed for me. I hardly ever feel as if I'm in the present, and I know that because of this I often feel desperate and I feel like I don't have any control over my life. If I dwell on and continually try to work through and answer questions about my past and future that are unanswerable, I'm afraid I'll never get anywhere in life.

From a woman with depressed moments, on therapy:

I've been trying to overcome depression and bulimia for ten years. I never last more than a month or two with a psychologist because I can't stand rehashing the past and basically paying someone to listen to me complain. Those sessions always make me feel worse. Those shrinks just love to dwell on things and make a mountain out of a molehill. I hope I can find one of your books because my M.D. is pushing me to see another shrink. I'd really like to find an alternative to all the psychobabble. Thanks for your help.

From a woman with agoraphobic moments, on therapy:

I am agoraphobic and can attest that getting into my feelings through traditional psychotherapy only made things worse—*much* worse.

From a recovering alcoholic, on being stuck:

I'm a forty-seven-year-old recovering alcoholic of six years, happy to be alive and sober. However, I struggle with dwelling on the past and the future. I know this keeps me stuck in my recovery. Support groups are depressing me also. I'm grateful every new day, and I want to stop focusing just on myself. Constructive Living is what I could use.

From an adopted child, on relief:

After years of seeing a potpourri of psychologists and others, I became even more depressed. Constantly I was made to believe that my parents did not love me unconditionally or that because I was adopted and therefore do not know my natural mother, I have a mental block, and so on and so forth. After reading about CL I feel like twenty years of guilt has been lifted from me!

From an overeater, on not eating:

I read an article about Constructive Living in a magazine, and the concepts were a breath of fresh air. One of the sentences in the article that caught my eye mentioned helping bulimics realize that "you can be hungry and not eat." Considering that I've fought an eating disorder for ten years and have spent a lot of time sitting in therapy analyzing my inner child, these concepts really appeal to me. Lately I've been feeling like I'm not making much progress toward happiness and sanity by dwelling on my unhappiness and insanity.

From a Prozac failure, on exploring the past:

I am able to find it very amusing that after years of regression types of therapy, a treatment center for codependency, several attempts with antidepressants (the latest of which took place this weekend when two days of Prozac made me realize once again that medication was probably not the answer for me) and various twelve-step programs, that the simplicity of the CL approach makes so much sense. Thirty-eight years of my life have been spent either in the problem or trying to figure the problem out, and it has been an exhausting and expensive search. Having accepted sometime ago that my childhood was horrendous, filled with varying types of abuse, I proceeded to ask one of my many therapists if going back through the sludge was an absolute necessity. She looked at me as if she had not been prepared for such a question and told me it was not necessary. I remember thinking the pain of going back seemed more dreadful than any present pain I was feeling. I am truly relieved to hear that there are other options besides the traditional. I can now go on without harboring guilt for not uncovering every morsel of pain from my past. It has made me tired.

From DKR to a CL reflection correspondent:

Your postcards seem stretched to demonstrate that you are causing trouble to others (e.g., troubling a peaceful yard by warming up a car). You are causing trouble all the time, of course; so am I. But the focus has shifted away from that detailed search of others' contributions to yourself even as you are one-who-troubles. I'm not sure that your current focus is what Constructive Living reflection or Naikan best aims for. I believe that the major benefit of CL reflection comes from a sort of losing yourself, rather like that of Zen.

Now I'm reading Ippen, a famous Shinshu teacher-monk of medieval Japan. His writings reflect the coming together of *jiriki* (essentially, salvation by one's own works) and *tariki* (essentially, salvation by grace), a key area of Buddhist philosophy. I didn't see the founder of Naikan as a sad, guilty, self-punitive human. He humbly recognized his proper and realistic role in this great reality. He smiled and laughed a lot. Naikan is about how we fit into this grand reality. It is about writing clearly on the postcard and thanking it as it goes off to do its work for us. It is about recognizing that even as we are causing trouble, we are also giving in return to others. Look for the detail there, too, and you will find it (your stamps support postal workers' families, for example).

I guess what I'm saying is that your postcards look skewed toward Catholic-confession reflection. That's no big surprise, considering your background. One danger of some of the trends in American Naikan is moving people away from objectivity toward a sort of lowlier-than-thou subjectivity. I'll fight that tendency because it isn't "realistic" in the larger sense, and runs the danger of raising demagogues, priests, and charismatic con artists.

Again, this material reflects no more than my bias. Anyone with his or her eyes open knows I'm blind and wrong and stupid and evil sometimes. But those aspects of the momentary me aren't all I want to focus on, even when doing Constructive Living reflection. Does this meandering make sense?

From DKR to a distraught husband:

Thank you for your letter. Unfortunately your experiences are not all that rare. I hear about such tragedies much too often. You seem to be responding better than most. I applaud your efforts in difficult circumstances. Please keep doing the best you can.

Here are some bottom-line reminders about reality. You cannot control your wife, no matter what foolishness she chooses to believe . . . you have responsibility for you alone, not for her. If she is worth the wait, wait—meanwhile do the best you can for the children, her, yourself, and others in your world. Consider the high cost to her of recognizing how her self-centeredness has caused trouble and pain to you and the children. She has a harder path ahead than you. Keep looking at reality and responding realistically.

Here is difficult but worthy work for you: I recommend that you do Naikan reflection on what you received from your wife, what you did for your wife in return, and the troubles you caused her during each of the years from your courtship until the present. In the times when you feel heavily burdened by the troubles she is currently causing you, it is good to reflect on the good she has done for you and the troubles you caused her in the past. There is more of a balance there than you may have discerned lately. Perhaps thirty minutes a day, each day recalling details of one year that you knew her, and writing notes about your recollections would be helpful.

From a puzzled young man, on unrecognized debts:

I don't understand why I should feel grateful to my mother for giving birth to me. I didn't ask to be born.

A CL reply: You didn't ask the farmer to grow the food you ate for lunch today or the cook at the restaurant to buy and prepare the food you ate. But you had an obligation to pay for that food. Your payment was a kind of recognition of their service in your behalf. I wouldn't ask you to try to create some feeling of gratitude. Feelings are uncontrollable directly by your will. But I would ask you to recognize your debts. One of those debts is to your parents for giving you life—

whether you asked for it or not, whether they were perfect parents or not, whether you deserved what they gave you or not.

From a beginning student, on practicality:

I have just finished reading a few of your books on Constructive Living and Morita's psychotherapeutic methods, and I want to thank you for writing them. They make more sense to me than any "self-help" material I have read in quite some time.

Over the past several years I've also read various books about Zen Buddhism, which I enjoyed very much, but understanding the practical application of such ideas has been difficult. I've known for a long time that deciding to do something and trying to do it are not the same as *doing it*, but knowing that's true and acting on the knowledge are very different things.

My direct experience with psychotherapy has been limited to a few sessions with a therapist, which I did not find very helpful. It's nice to have someone listen to one's problems, I suppose, but the therapist did not have much to offer in the way of practical advice. One twelve-step meeting was all I could bear; the self-blaming religious overtones were pretty offensive, and I didn't really believe I was powerless to control my actions unless I surrendered to a "Higher Power."

I've also read many so-called self-help books, most of which advised reliving the pain of the past to a great degree, while concentrating on "inner child" and "adult child" problems. I don't want to be an adult child forever, or stuck with one label after another, a survivor of this or a victim of that. Constantly redefining the source of my troubles has not helped me cope with life any better, nor has rehashing my unhappy childhood.

Trying to decipher the practical value of books like *A Course in Miracles* has not been very productive for me either—I could swear there are more emotions to be felt than just love and fear, and wading through volumes of repetitive religious psychobabble is not a rewarding pastime.

But alas, here I am, still neurotic (isn't everyone?), and still spending too much time imagining disastrous outcomes and intellectualizing my excuses for not doing what needs to be done. At forty I fear my life may be more than half over and I know I don't want to spend the rest of it worrying and obsessing, but not *doing* all the things I say I want to do.

So I'm writing to you because I would like to know if there are any Constructive Living group programs in my area in which I could participate. My financial resources are somewhat limited (finding a new job is one of those things that needs doing), so a group would probably be more practical for me right now. I believe I'm ready to learn to accept my feelings, define my purpose, and do what needs to be done, and having some direct guidance would be most welcome.

From an audience member, on positive thinking:

(*Interrupting*) "You say that in CL theory only actions affect reality directly. How do you know that thoughts don't directly affect reality? How do you know that?"

"Because I'm thinking that I wish you would be quiet so that I can get on with this presentation."

(*Persisting*) "Yes, but how do you know—"

"It doesn't seem to be working."

"I don't think you are answering my question."

"Yes, I am. Or perhaps you are."

From a newcomer, on her first week using CL:

I've begun thanking and appreciating everything that serves me, provides for my needs—air to breathe, food to eat, water to shower with, the mirror, the blinds that provide privacy, my muscles, and on and on. . . . I'm finding that in this process of thanking things an unexpected but natural outcome is that I want to give back, to show my appreciation, and make sure those things are being valued properly. . . . They are the end result of incredibly complex resources being converted by a variety of people's labors and designs. They deserve to be valued. From that vantage point what needs doing is to make sure the earth is cared for, that my desk is kept clean and in top shape along with every other item in my environment. In fact it looks like an endless exchange of give-and-take, honoring and appreciating what provides for my needs. There is plenty to care for and to tend. It's like being a gardener in every aspect of life. It's a wonderful honeymoon. Will it last?

Taking In Life

CONSTRUCTIVE LIVING EVOLVED out of learning and experience. Morita and Yoshimoto and others throughout history and human culture gave us clues about how to live fully. And those clues were tested and refined with our own experience. The result is digested and formatted in written form in books and articles and letters; it is spoken out in lectures and workshops and individual sessions. The result is not as important as the process.

You can memorize CL principles and quote CL wisdom and cite CL references. Such achievements are incidental compared with daily demonstrating the openness to life upon which CL is based. That learning process is crucial, not the conclusions. Morita and Yoshimoto and others came across these principles of living by doing life with attention to the whole of it. They benefited most from their own discoveries.

So much of what reality sends us gets missed because we are attending only to the feeling component, or we are attending only to the part that reflects on our own convenience, or we are intentionally ignoring and rejecting some portion of it. Accepting reality as it is doesn't mean trying to like or understand it all. Acceptance has nothing to do with enjoyment or technical knowledge. It is a kind of blurring of the boundaries between us and the rest of reality, outgrowing ourselves so that we can take more in, exchanging that exclusive self-focus for a broader perception. In the process we discover more to see and touch and taste and smell, and we discover more to hear.

Did I Hear You Correctly?

Listening is an important aspect of Constructive Living guidance. People need to know that they have been heard. Often we are so distracted by our own concerns or by our mental preparations to respond that we fail to hear what is being said. How often have you missed the last words spoken to you because you were busy preparing a reply? How often have you interrupted someone even before the other person could finish speaking?

Of course listening is not the whole of it. In our tendency to oversimplify, complete psychotherapies have been built around just listening or listening and reflecting back to the speaker what was heard. Other therapies center on increasing communications among couples. Listening is an important first step in finding out what's on someone's mind, but (like insight or understanding) it must be followed by purposeful, constructive action in order to reap maximum benefits.

Listening is a gift we can offer others. It is a resource we can offer even when we are poor or bedridden or institutionalized. Offering our ears to a child, to an ill or dying person, may be a gift beyond measure, more prized even than comforting words.

We want so much to have others listen to us. We want them to understand and sympathize with our problems and worries. We may forget that they have such needs too. Seventy-five years ago Morita wrote that patients don't come to hear what doctors have to say; they come to talk.

As recommended above, try observing periods of silence so that you can listen more fully. In Constructive Living we sometimes assign total silence. We're not rule-bound in CL. So if you see a vehicle about to run down your friend, it is appropriate to yell out "Watch out for that truck!" even though you are on silence. Even during total silence we allow writing notes. It is more troublesome to write than to speak, so note writing is usually minimal. Gestures and nodding and smiling and the like are permitted without limit; they don't count as speech for this exercise.

A less severe assignment is to assign yourself a quota of ten sentences a day. For our purposes a sentence is something you can say in one breath. See whether you can make do with even fewer sentences than the maximum ten. Silence gives us the opportunity to become more skillful at listening. Silence usually results in more attention to all sorts of information from reality. As you walk down a hall, you might notice desktop flowers through an open door if you're not busy chattering at the time.

Quality Time

QUALITY TIME TOGETHER usually implies infrequent time, limited time. But it isn't necessarily so. What about the situations in which couples (retired couples, for example) spend a great deal of time together? Can that be quality time too? How can such quality time be fostered? Suggestions about what to do follow. These suggestions are based on life experience and common sense. You already know our Constructive Living advice for testing the applicability of these suggestions for your own circumstances. You already suspect that I will offer no magical, single solutions to your interpersonal difficulties here. A proper garden takes some thoughtful care, not just once a year or two.

Courtesy and Politeness

Whether you feel like it or not, whether he or she ought to know without your saying it, whether you are exhausted, or grouchy, or drunk, or sick, or irritated, or unhappy, or depressed, or despairing, or not, your partner deserves courteous and polite speech and behavior. To fail to present such civility communicates how little you value your partner and how deeply self-centered you are. Each day a minimum of ten words of thanks and an equal number of apologies are recommended.

Planning and Working Toward a Common Goal

Having a common purpose or objective does much to pull people together and keep them behaving in a cooperative fashion. For some couples that common goal is the well-being of their children. There are many other possibilities as well. For example planning trips and traveling, working on home improvements, jointly participating in a business, writing memoirs and family histories, community activities, studying together, church activities, and such are enterprises of shared purpose.

Protection of Privacy and Personal Space

However much we like to be with others, we also need alone time and space. The length of time and degree of privacy varies from person to person and time to time. Some people with a lot of shinky moments may need more periods of quiet isolation to settle their minds and bodies. Others may need a lot of activity in order to avoid excessive rumination. Where space is limited, staggered bedtimes may provide the necessary privacy during late evening and early morning hours.

Praise and Thanks Rather Than Criticism and Demands

Positive reinforcers are more effective than punishment for influencing people's behavior; they are also more pleasant to give and to receive than punishment. Assertiveness may be necessary at times; however, it may mask impatience and other flaws, including a lack of sensitivity to others' perspectives. When we build our interactions with others on rights and legal measures, there is some measure of protection, but the joys of warm trust and gift giving are imperiled.

Your partner's behavior can be shaped by smiling and praising as it approaches the ideal you desire. You may make your desires known straightforwardly or by hinting. But if your orientation is weighted toward offering these social rewards in order to get what you need from your partner, you miss the satisfaction of praising and thanking for your partner's sake. Partners deserve our public recognition of the services they perform.

Physical Activities Together

Tennis, walking, a workout at the gym, croquet, making love—all these occasions provide opportunities for developing closeness. Some people who are impatient with chatting find they are better able to communicate while rowing a boat or hiking or clearing out the garage.

Sharing Chores

Household tasks should be shared within the physical limits of the household members. Cooking, washing dishes, laundry, vacuuming, and so forth are of importance to all. We develop appreciation for others' efforts and take more care in reducing the creation of disorder when we share in responsibility for maintaining the household.

Flexible Routines

Routines allow smoothness and predictability in life. Quality time is fostered by a certain degree of flexibility within the large patterns of everyday life. Be prepared to sacrifice your own orderly convenience sometimes for the convenience of someone else. I do not recommend discarding useful habits and routine observances altogether, however. A life without order is unlikely to be constructive for any individual or for those living nearby.

Develop New Interests

Our partners get boring if they (and we) don't keep learning and growing. New interests put new information into our interactions. Our talk becomes worth listening to again because it carries less redundancy. We want to make ourselves worthy of the investment of our associates' time. So take a course, read a book (you are doing that now), attend a lecture, take a guided trip, interview a public official, develop a hobby, discover something new and interesting about the world to share with your partner.

Engage in Physical Contact

Touch communicates and stimulates. The physical contact need not be sexual. Massaging, patting, kissing, snuggling together at a ball game, hugging, hair grooming, holding hands, and so forth are possible at any age with any partner depending on your cultural values. Touch makes other people more real somehow. They cease to become merely concepts or symbols distanced by some mental template.

Participate in Outside Social Activities Together

Such social engagements need not be frequent. Yet there seems to be something important about presenting a joint social face to the world at times. Some couples attending parties purposely drift into conversations with different people so that they have new information to share with each other on the drive home. At funerals, awards ceremonies, graduations, birthday parties, grand openings, and other celebrations of joy and sorrow and remembrance and progress we want others to see us lined up with those who share our lives at home or work or school, wherever and whomever we wish to present to the social world as "one of us."

Find Problems Together and Fix Them

I'm not thinking here of "working on a relationship." I don't know what a "relationship" might be; I certainly don't know how to work on one. We recommend finding problems at home, or at the workplace, or at church, or at civic organizations, or in volunteer settings, wherever it is that you can work jointly to repair something. Customize your environments so that you and those you care about can operate comfortably and gracefully within them.

Conflicts Are Puzzles Seeking Satisfying Solutions

Good communications don't solve all interpersonal problems. Sometimes we have different, mutually exclusive, objectives. No matter how skillful I am at communicating my needs, and no matter how skillful you are at communicating your needs, the problem cannot be resolved without some additional effort. Work at developing a track record of effort toward finding solutions to conflicts that are (at least to some degree) satisfying to all parties concerned. See conflicts as puzzles demanding the resources of all interested parties in producing a workable solution. Refuse to be polarized into opposing camps. Keep working for a cooperative push toward discovering the best course of action for all concerned.

All solutions are temporary. Circumstances keep changing, so we keep changing too.

Take Care of Living Things

Find living things to take care of together. Living things include garden plants, wild birds, pets, grandchildren, people who need volunteer care. Give your time and energy in the service of these living creatures. See what it does for them, for you, for your partner.

Maintain Your Appearance

Staying trim and well groomed are not only good for your health and mental state, they are ways of telling others that you value them and that you care about what they have to look at regularly. They are worth the effort.

Of course it isn't sensible to starve yourself into bulimic narrowness. For your partner's sake you need to keep yourself healthy and energetic. You need not buy into foolish advertisements offering instant beauty through cosmetics and perfumes and shampoos either. Those around you deserve to deal with a reasonable you.

Avoid Complaining and Nagging

Complaining and nagging share the characteristic of being unconstructive verbal behaviors aimed more at relieving unpleasant feelings than at solving problems. A habit of complaining annoys people, and it doesn't fix the predicament. Moreover complaining tends to bind up one's thinking about a particular subject into a ball of moaning. Be still and do what you can to solve the problem. If you must unload verbally, do it in a notebook, during a period of solitude or with a therapist. That's what therapists have to listen to a lot—and they get paid for it. Constructive Living instructors are not therapists, so they won't let you get away with repetitive complaining.

Similarly nagging annoys people, and it doesn't solve problems directly. It is based on the hope that many reminders will prompt others to solve some problem we have. If you can't solve this problem on your own and a single reminder to your partner doesn't work, use your imagination to discover some alternate course of action. Remember that other people are not controllable directly by your will. Your own behavior is all that you can control directly. What you perceive to be a problem may not look like one to others.

Quality time won't grow when fertilized with quantities of complaints, nagging, criticism, scolding, and harangues. Who wants to live in such unpleasant circumstances?

Principles of Constructive Living—An Examination

BECAUSE CONSTRUCTIVE LIVING is based on an educational model, it is appropriate for there to be an examination to test your intellectual understanding of CL principles. More important, however, is the moment-by-moment examination presented to you in everyday life.

PART 1

(Part 1 was prepared by Patricia Ryan Madson, Ron Madson, and Gregory Willms.)

A. Objective Questions

For the following questions, please circle the letter or letters of the best Constructive Living answers:

1. T or F   Feelings can be controlled directly by the will.
2. T or F   Feelings are to be accepted as they are.
3. T or F   Every feeling has its uses.
4. T or F   Feelings remain inside us unless we work them through.
5. T or F   Feelings fade in time unless they are restimulated.
6. T or F   Feelings can be indirectly influenced by behavior.
7. T or F   The central purpose of CL reflection is to produce feelings of gratitude.
8. T or F   Feelings must be ignored.

9. T or F   Constructive Living helps you know your feelings and accept what you do.

10. T or F   The cure for neurosis lies not in reducing negative symptoms but in adding character.

11. Which of the following is directly controllable?
    a. Your feelings
    b. Your behavior
    c. Your thinking
    d. All of the above

12. Which of these questions belong to Naikan?
    a. What did I give to others?
    b. What did others give to me?
    c. What trouble did others cause me?
    d. What trouble did I cause others?
    e. How can I forgive my parents?
    f. How can I forgive my inner child?

13. Which of the following are Constructive Living principles?
    a. Know your purpose
    b. Accept your feelings
    c. Do what needs to be done
    d. All of the above
    e. None of the above

14. It is important to pay attention to reality because
    a. Reality is inherently interesting
    b. Reality shows us what needs to be done
    c. Reality is truth
    d. All of the above
    e. None of the above

15. Constructive Living builds
    a. Self-esteem
    b. Self-confidence
    c. Reality-esteem

d. Reality-confidence
e. All of the above
f. None of the above

16. Naikan is
    a. A perspective on reality
    b. A meditation form
    c. A psychotherapy
    d. All of the above
    e. None of the above

17. The principles behind Constructive Living are
    a. Japanese
    b. Part of perennial wisdom
    c. Both
    d. Neither

18. Some goals of Constructive Living are to
    a. Reduce suffering
    b. Build character
    c. Act purposefully
    d. Keep feelings under control
    e. Keep your neurotic moments under control
    f. Learn to be proud of your doing
    g. Be true to your feelings
    h. Follow your purpose
    i. Pay attention to reality
    j. Accept your depressing moments
    k. Live your life sensibly
    l. Feel more gratitude toward others
    m. Always be doing

19. Contributors to Constructive Living were
    a. T or F   Ishin Yoshimoto, the founder of Naikan
    b. T or F   Masatake Morita, the founder of Morita
                 Therapy

B. Essay Questions

20. Who is (are) your teacher(s) in Constructive Living?
21. What is the central practice of Constructive Living?
22. What does it mean that you don't have to fix your feelings?
23. What is the usefulness of Naikan?
24. Briefly explain: "There is meaning in the smallest task."
25. Describe three specific examples of how you have used Constructive Living in your life.

PART 2

These additional essay questions include trick questions. Be very careful with your answers.

1. What is the difference between someone who walks over and sits on a lemon meringue pie and someone who first says "I know I'm about to do this disagreeable thing again" and then walks over and sits on a lemon meringue pie?

2. How are the two people in the above question different from someone who gets up off a lemon meringue pie and says "I learned a lot from the experience of sitting on that pie" and then proceeds to sit on another one? How are they different from the person who can explain in great detail about the causes and motivations for sitting on pies while continuing to do so?

3. Was the first taste of wine or exotic cheese or sushi or a pipe or beer delicious? What, if anything, changed over time? (The chemical composition of the substance tasted probably didn't change appreciably.)

4. What is controllable other than behavior? Why do you do what you do?

5. How do we discover necessary behavior?

6. What is suffering? What is the cure for neurotic suffering? How does one become cured?

7. What is an ideal mind? Where is your mind located?

8. Mind, time, society, culture—all these are examples of concepts. Is it necessary to fix concepts? Is it possible to fix concepts? If so, how does one fix a concept?

9. In Constructive Living we advise our students to "accept reality (including any feeling) as it is." Does the word *accept* mean "to appreciate"? "to forgive"? "to embrace"? "to cherish"? "to acknowledge"? Put the meaning of the word *accept* into your own words.

10. Why go to the trouble to clean up a dirty room? Give a CL action answer and a CL reflection/reciprocity answer.

11. Feelings of guilt about cheating will fade over time, but the profits from cheating may remain much longer. Why shouldn't you cheat?

12. How is CL reflection different from nostalgia? How is it different from thinking that everything occurs for the best? How is it different from looking on the bright side?

13. Given that we would like to introduce both CL action and CL reflection/reciprocity to all our students, how do we decide which to teach first? Consider which you would offer first to a student who has (a) fights with her mother; (b) a term paper due on Friday; (c) a strong fear of germs; (d) no meaning in life; (e) worries about his future in his corporation.

PART 3

Another way to test your understanding of Constructive Living ideas is through interpretation of what may be found in the literature. Below are quotes from a number of CL books. Do the quotes make sense to you? Could you write a short essay on each of them? If not, you may wish to go to the source for clarification of those that are unclear. You may wish to ponder what meaning those quotes might have specifically from a Constructive Living perspective.

A. From David K. Reynolds, *Playing Ball on Running Water* (New York: Morrow, 1984).

No one can heal a mind (p. 13).

To hold one of us responsible for another's behavior is meaningless for the one and demeaning for the other (p. 20).

I mistrust anyone who offers constant happiness, endless success, instant confidence, or effortless self-growth (p. 64).

Talk, talk, talk. How often it is used to back away from reality (p. 73).

B. From David K. Reynolds, *Even in Summer the Ice Doesn't Melt* (New York: Morrow, 1986).

The myth of the self-made person is bankrupt (p. 14).

What is certain is that I am sometimes this, sometimes that (p. 22).

We are what we do (p. 37).

Even the most unpleasant feelings are the natural result of our wanting to live and to live fully (p. 41).

This attitude is part of the treasuring of all things because all things are borrowed. There is nothing that is truly mine (p. 98).

C. From David K. Reynolds, *Water Bears No Scars* (New York: Morrow, 1987).

Unpleasant feelings and sensory experiences such as anxiety, fear, pain, and discomfort are disturbing but indispensable to our existence (p. 22).

There's no need to get yourself to do it. Just do it (p. 41).

Living constructively right now is cure (p. 42).

Don't work in the hope of becoming cured (p. 78).

For the graduate of this lifeway, summer is hot and winter is cold (p. 84).

It is not only that trying to cure oneself doesn't lead to cure, but also that trying to cure oneself *is* neurosis at that very moment (p. 93).

D. From David K. Reynolds, *Pools of Lodging for the Moon* (New York: Morrow, 1989).

Neurotic suffering grows from self-centeredness (p. 22).

We are just another means of achieving reality's purposes (p. 28).

It's quite all right to be the fool who lives life well (p. 39).

When carried out properly, drinking a cup of coffee is no small thing (p. 55).

We cannot generate gratitude simply by telling ourselves to be grateful (p. 71).

E. From David K. Reynolds, *A Thousand Waves* (New York: Morrow, 1990).

Constructive Living is a way to become nothing special (p. 41).

The danger of mental crutches is that sometimes they work. . . . Then we run the risk of becoming feeling-centered again (p. 69).

There are lots of hangers in the closets of our pasts . . . no single event or experience determines who we are (p. 75).

F. From David K. Reynolds, *Thirsty, Swimming in the Lake* (New York: Morrow, 1991).

To label something "an eating disorder" makes it no more medical than to label jealousy "an emotional disorder" or to label filth "a bathing disorder" or to label smoking or drinking alcohol "an addictive disorder" or to label poor manners "an etiquette disorder" (p. 34).

Recognizing and understanding our tendencies doesn't excuse them (p. 44).

Morita suggested that his students might give up but keep on climbing the mountain (p. 67).

One result of understanding these writings is the realization that the proper use of ourselves *is* the proper use of our surroundings and vice versa. The two are not different (p. 73).

"Food won't make you fat"—Mary Ann Thomas (p. 113).

G. From David K. Reynolds, *Rainbow Rising from a Stream* (New York: Morrow, 1992).

You have been taught that feelings are the most important thing in your life. It isn't so. At the root of many problems in our country is this feeling-focus. . . . You have been taught that you can "work on" your unpleasant feelings. It can't be done. Not only is it impossible to "work on" your depressed or anxious feelings; moreover, you have no need to "work on" them (pp. 16–17).

It is all right to dwell on past mistakes, to give up hope, to think negatively—while doing mindfully what is right in front of one's nose that needs doing (p. 26).

In more recent times some people believe that salvation lies in discovering past childhood sexual abuse and allowing rage to emerge and be expressed. Salvation doesn't come that cheaply or that simply or that suddenly. Salvation, if such there be, must find itself worked out over and over moment by moment in life's eternal present (p. 28).

Every feeling is a new feeling, just as every moment is a fresh one, emerging from and into reality (p. 31).

Feelings send us important messages about what needs to be done in our lives. Don't forget that they are *not* the *only* messages; they should not be the only determinants of our behavior. So working to "fix" feelings, instead of working to notice them and understand their messages, is a mistake (p. 37).

Where do the fresh moments we experience come from? Where do our thoughts come from? Where do the words we speak come from? Where does the rich variety of reality come from? (p. 46).

We label the events in our lives "tragedies," "successes," "nightmares," "triumphs," "challenges," "defeats," and so forth. Reality doesn't mind, it just keeps on presenting us with information that deserves our attention and action. What we do about what reality brings us is up to us (p. 63).

Getting caught up in an obsession with perfecting the mind is itself a sort of narrow-mindedness (p. 72).

A life philosophy is the product of one's life, not the other way around. We don't choose a lifeway and then live by it. We grow a life philosophy over years of living one (p. 74).

We all have scrapes on our knees. Scrapes, too, are nothing special (p. 85).

Pride in oneself is a pale cousin to the much more solid *confidence in reality* (p. 87).

Giving yourself away out of habit or timidity is merely inefficient and exhausting (p. 88).

Constructive Living is not merely another language; Constructive Living is your *native* language (p. 125).

There is reality's work only *you* can do (p. 126).

PART 4

Members of the audience asked the following questions following a lecture in Japan in 1992. The questions are not significantly different from those asked after my lectures in the United States, although they were submitted originally in Japanese. We humans are all so alike.

This set of questions tests your ability to give responses to natural queries from nonspecialists. The preferred response to some of the questions is to point out the misunderstandings underlying their structure or content. What do your answers tell us about you?

How can I help someone else to progress in CL?

What CL can I do right now?

What should I do with my mind to allow more humor in my life and be able to make others laugh?

When I sleep and wake with anxiety, what should I do?

Please give me advice about motivation and changing my thinking and my lifestyle. I feel stress, then become depressed, then drink alcohol. I understand the need to quit, but I can't.

Please discuss the best method for controlling feelings.

Does this perspective on reality supporting us apply to starving people in Third World countries?

PART 5

Here are some real-life problems that might present themselves to you. A friend or neighbor or client or business associate might come to you with the following problems. As a test of your understanding of CL, what advice would you give someone with such complaints? Remember to take the presenting problems as givens. Don't try to figure out deep, underlying psychological causes, and don't try to give a complete explanation of CL theory and practice during the interaction. What other information do you need to know? Keep your interpretations and suggestions specific to the problem at hand.

1. A college student faces an upcoming exam, but as she reads the pages of her textbook, the contents don't stick in her mind. So she has stopped studying, skips classes, and feels increasingly anxious about the exam.

2. A middle-aged former engineer fears he has stomach cancer. His father died of stomach cancer. No physician has been able

to find any cancer in this man. He stays home and takes care of the house while his wife works in an office. He naps a lot and fights with his wife because dinner isn't ready for her when she returns home after work.

3. A macho truck driver complains of sexual impotence with his wife but not with other women.

4. A saleswoman fears heights but faces a meeting with prospective buyers in their office in the twenty-fifth floor. She states that she is unable to get in the elevator and that her briefcase is too heavy for her to climb all those stairs.

5. An elderly man has been told by his physician this morning that he has a heart condition and that he must restrict his intake of salt. He complains that he can't eat food without a liberal dash of salt.

6. A middle-aged divorcee is lonely but fears the hassle of dating.

7. A writer complains that she is getting older and has trouble getting ideas for stories and getting freelance work. She has no major financial problems even without working, but she wants to continue writing.

8. A young adult male complains of headaches, stomach problems, cold hands and feet, dizziness, and ringing in the ears. The only medication prescribed by any of the many physicians he has seen is tranquilizers.

9. A teenager worries that he might be a latent homosexual. He has had no sexual contacts with either sex. He states that his fears stem from once seeing a surfer walk across the beach in tight trunks and thinking how beautiful the surfer's body looked.

10. A husband complains that his wife provokes him to hit her. He must control his tendency toward violence or go to jail.

A Brief History of
Constructive Living

THE FUNDAMENTAL IDEAS for Constructive Living (CL) can be traced to the psychological foundations of ancient Buddhism, Sufism, the Judeo-Christian tradition, and related pursuits. Some of these ideas were codified by Masatake Morita (or Shoma Morita, an alternative reading of his given name) and Ishin Yoshimoto in twentieth-century Japan. Both of these innovative geniuses tried to make their insights known to the West, but failed primarily because of language difficulties. Some of their students' students also worked to introduce these ideas into the West: Akira Ishii had success establishing Naikan centers in Europe based on Yoshimoto's methods, and F. Ishu Ishiyama brought Morita therapy to clinical psychology in Canada. Related principles of mental health can be found in the writings of Milton Erickson, Fritz Perls, Ram Dass, Robert Heinlein, and many others.

Those who gave me most of the basic building blocks for Constructive Living were Japanese. Morita and Naikan psychotherapies are more narrowly practiced in Japan than in the West, but they provided theoretical and practical guidelines around which Constructive Living was put together. I began studying Morita therapy and Yoshimoto's Naikan in Japan in the 1960s. My doctoral dissertation in the Department of Anthropology at UCLA was based on fieldwork in these methods. The doctorate was awarded in 1969. The dissertation was rewritten as *Morita Psychotherapy* (1976). It was followed shortly by *The Quiet Therapies* (1980) and *Naikan Psychotherapy* (1983). With these books, chapters in academic edited works, and journal articles (see Bibliography) I aimed to found a scholarly literature on the subject. Many popular books followed in both the United States and Japan.

In the early 1970s I was teaching at the University of Southern California School of Medicine in the Department of Human Behavior. There were a few opportunities to formally teach material about Morita psychotherapy and more opportunities to use Morita's ideas during individual counseling of medical students and others who had come across this approach in popular-magazine articles. By the end of the 1970s the need for a combination of Morita's and Yoshimoto's systems was clear to me.

In the early 1980s I had begun teaching certification courses with both Morita and Naikan elements outside the formal academic setting. Because the courses emphasized Moritist thought, the certifications were in "Morita Guidance." I wanted to avoid the medical and psychotherapeutic implications of calling what I did Morita psychotherapy. Certainly the lifeways Morita and Yoshimoto taught were not useful solely to those who carried the clinical diagnosis of neurosis. I sought to avoid the restrictions that would follow from installing within the mental health field what was coming to be called Constructive Living. Using the English term *Constructive Living*, I could avoid both potential anti-Japanese prejudices in the West and criticisms from conservative Morita therapists in Japan that I was not practicing classic Morita therapy. The book entitled *Constructive Living* (1984) marked the formal beginning of the Western extensions and adaptations of these Eastern ideas, but it was not until 1991 that "Constructive Living" became a registered trademark in the United States. The name itself emerged following a discussion with Dr. N. Shinfuku about the merits and limitations of using Japanese names when introducing these ideas into the West. The exotic East attracted attention but distanced Westerners, who might consider the principles inapplicable to their own lives.

By 1995 Constructive Living certification training courses had been held in Los Angeles; Hawaii; Florida; New York; San Francisco; Washington, D.C.; Chicago; Cleveland; Vermont; Denver; New Zealand; Canada; and Japan. About 250 individuals were trained during these courses, with more than 130 of them certified as instructors.

I was very interested in quality control. Certification involved an intensive ten-day course during which I was able to observe the everyday lives of the trainees. Certification was awarded to those who demonstrated an intellectual and experiential understanding of CL principles. Certified instructors can now be found in Canada, England, Germany, Japan, New Zealand, and Mexico as well as in most sections of the United States.

Beginning in 1988 annual meetings of the International Association for Constructive Living were held alternating on the East and West coasts. Only certified instructors were invited to attend. Those very active in the CL movement could keep up with the latest methods and ideas during these meetings. In addition to reports from participants and a chance to exchange information and conduct business, an advanced training course was offered at each meeting. About a third of those certified at the time attended any given meeting. A newsletter of Constructive Living was begun in the 1980s entitled *Rolling Mist*, under the editorship of Mel Clark, and renamed *nothing special* when the editorship passed to Robert Addleton for a few years. In 1993 Gregg Krech and Linda Anderson took over editorship of the newsletter at the TôDô Institute in Middlebury, Vermont. They renamed it *Constructive Living Quarterly*.

Throughout the late 1980s and early 1990s a stream of articles about Constructive Living appeared in the media. There was wide exposure of CL ideas in the May 1990 Silver Anniversary issue of *Cosmopolitan*. That article about Constructive Living prompted more than five thousand readers from every state and a number of foreign countries to write to our Constructive Living Center in Coos Bay asking for more information. The November 1992 issue of *Self* magazine led to another eruption of more than 2,500 inquiries. Articles also appeared in *Vogue* (December 1984 and April 1988), *The New York Times* (June 3, 1986), *Psychology Today* (February 1987), *The Los Angeles Times* (September 21, 1987), *East West* (June 1988), *Yoga Journal* (May–June 1988), *Today's Man* (Fall 1989), *USA Today* (August 23, 1990), *Bottom Line* (December 11, 1990), *Your Personal Best* (charter issue), *New Dimensions* (May–June 1990), *New Woman* (November 1991), *American Health* (March 1991), and *Fitness* (October 1992).

Beginning in the late 1960s I was spending at least the spring and fall each year in Japan. My contacts continued there with the groups who practiced Morita therapy and Naikan therapy separately. I presented papers at their annual meetings and helped to organize the American delegations to the first and second international congresses of Morita therapy (1990, 1993), Naikan (1991, 1994), and Meaningful Life Therapy (1990, 1993). Meaningful Life Therapy (MLT) applied Moritist principles to the lives of cancer patients and others suffering from long-term diseases. Through CL contacts and CL books and articles MLT was first introduced to a wide audience in the West. It can fairly be said that the recognition and success of Constructive Living was an important factor in the decision by the Japanese to sponsor initial international congresses in these fields. In the late 1980s the Mental Health Okamoto Memorial Foundation began supporting cross-cultural activities within and outside of Japan. *The International Bulletin of Morita Therapy* (*IBMT*) made available information about a professionalized, clinical style of Morita therapy to English-language readers, but CL authors had difficulty getting articles published in that journal. After initially supporting and promoting *IBMT*, I found it necessary to resign from an editorial position with the journal.

In 1988 I was invited by the World Health Organization to conduct a National Training Course in Constructive Living for the People's Republic of China. Psychiatrists from throughout that country attended and expressed enthusiasm for CL methods. In some respects I was reintroducing Chinese thought back into China. Within a few years, thanks to the work of the Okamoto Foundation, Seikatsu no Hakkenkai, and Professor Kenshiro Ohara, Morita therapy was firmly fixed as a subspecialty in Chinese psychiatric practice.

In the United States instructors used CL in their daily lives, offered lectures and workshops, provided individual instruction, and sponsored trainings of various sorts. By the early 1990s certification training and/or IACL meetings had been sponsored by Linda Anderson; Perri Ardman; Trudy Boyle; Crilly Butler, Jr.; Richard Casavant; Said Hassanzadeh; Susan and Henry Kahn; Gregg Krech; Ron and Patricia Madson; Gottfried Mitteregger; Marilyn Murray; Haruyo Ogi; Diana Peterson; Mary J. Puckett; Philip and Sheila Saperstein; Barbara

Sarah; Rami Shapiro; Mary Ann Thomas; Mihoko Tohma; Gregory Willms; Yen Lu Wong; Joan Woodward; and a New Zealand group. Other workshops, Naikan, and group instruction had been offered by many of the above individuals as well as Cindy and Ron Green, Juliet Guroff, Daniel Hoppe, David Hudson, Annette Moy, Frederic Paterno, Daniel Rybold, Patricia Stewart, Ed Summer, and Jesus Zamora.

Gregg Krech became codirector of the TôDô Institute (TDI) when it moved from Los Angeles to Virginia, right outside of Washington, D.C., in 1991. For many years he was the central resource for ordering books and tapes about CL. He also recorded and produced CL audiotapes. In 1991 he traveled to New Zealand to conduct certification training there. His efforts led to the introduction of Constructive Living into Southeast Asia, beginning with Thailand. In 1992 TDI incorporated with nonprofit status and relocated to Middlebury, Vermont, where Gregg Krech and his wife, Linda Anderson, formed the initial core staff.

By early 1993 our updated mailing list of people interested in Constructive Living contained more than ten thousand names. A large number of those who wrote or telephoned us reported Constructive Living principles useful in their lives and in the lives of those with whom they lived and worked. Even without face-to-face instruction, correspondence instruction, or telephone instruction, readers could get enough information from books and articles to begin living more constructively. CL groups were operating in Los Angeles, San Francisco, Chicago, New York, and Washington, D.C.

The 1980s and 1990s saw a blossoming of Constructive Living ideas in the West. Constructive Living books sold over 100,000 copies. Millions of readers were exposed to CL ideas through magazine and newspaper articles. With notable exceptions members of the professional community were slower to pick up these methods, probably because of CL's inherent challenges to traditional Western psychodynamic approaches to the treatment of behavior disorders. The broad-based educational approach of our methods to what had previously been seen as medical-clinical problems disputed the authority and expertise of established interests. But the trend was unstoppable and the effectiveness indisputable.

Formal criticism of Constructive Living began in the early 1990s. Much of it came from the Seattle-Vancouver area. Concerns were expressed about deviation from Moritist theory, training nonprofessionals as instructors, the limited supervised practice, and resistance to adopting a traditional Western professional-therapy image. It was difficult to criticize my credentials—in 1992, representing Constructive Living, I received one of the first Kora Prizes awarded by Japan's Morita Therapy Society to individuals and groups who had successfully promoted the extension of Morita therapy—so the criticism was directed at my methods and the instructors I had trained. Despite the criticism, the academic SUNY Press published a second volume of edited contributions by CL instructors on the breadth of Constructive Living practice in the West.

The writing of this handbook began in 1990 and was completed in 1993. Despite ongoing dynamic change, the theory and practice of Constructive Living had coalesced sufficiently during this period to present a snapshot in handbook form. The leadership and activities of Constructive Living have passed largely to the second generation of CL instructors. I am delighted and grateful to see their increasing contributions to the theory, practice, and literature.

—

Conclusion

—

Endings

I AM ABOUT to conclude my writing of this manuscript for *A Handbook for Constructive Living*. There is a directory on my hard disk called "Nextbook" with some entries already in it.

Of course, there are no clear endings. Like the artificial chapters and scenes we impose on the flow of our lives, endings are arbitrary points we attach to transition. Our minds are engaged in structuring the world through oppositional concepts such as beginning-ending, neurosis-wellness, good-bad. When, for example, does a vacation trip end? There is no single point in time when we become cured of our neurotic tendencies, when we become psychologically mature, when we die. The conceptual systems called law and medicine and finance may require artificial ending points in order to conduct business. But the natural world slopes into endings and subsequent or simultaneous beginnings in no clear-cut fashion, even on the atomic level.

The conceptual ending we fear most is death. Morita saw that fear as the basis for all our fears. I doubt that Yoshimoto would have disagreed. I don't fear flying in airplanes; I fear the death that may result from my flying in airplanes. We disguise the face of death with cosmetic applications to the corpse at funerals. The Japanese avoid offering four of anything to a guest because the word *four* is pronounced *shi* in Japanese—a homophone for the word for death. Most religions deny or redefine death so that it isn't so fearful. Hospitals hide it. The military invests it.

We can use death as a benchmark, a ruler to measure our lives. Compared with death, our foolish neurotic suffering is nothing. Compared with death, the social distinctions we draw among people are insignificant. Compared with death, yesterday's failures and triumphs are trivial. Thus we compare concept with concept.

What we really "have" is now and here. This now and here we can call an ending—to a book, to a way of life, to outmoded ideas, to absurdity. Or we can call this now and here a beginning—new perceptions, new acceptance, new objectives, new deeds, new acknowledgment. Just this here now.

If you board a train in Chicago and the train is headed for New York, no matter how long you ride, you'll never arrive in Los Angeles. Even if the train is quite modern and fast and the engineer is exceedingly famous and all your friends are on that train—you'll never arrive in Los Angeles. At every station along the way you are in transit. You have a chance to change trains. Don't dally around the station. Board a train that is headed in the direction you want to go.

Appendix: Intensive Naikan Guidance

BECAUSE CONSTRUCTIVE LIVING reflection/reciprocity exercises are derived from the practice of Naikan, a Japanese educational process developed by Ishin Yoshimoto, I have included some detailed advice on how to practice intensive Naikan in its original form.

The beginning material in this section comes from my translation of a pamphlet entitled *The Naikan Forum (Number 1)*, published in Japanese by the Naikan Konwa Kai in 1991. Because the reflection aspect of Constructive Living is closely linked to the practice called Naikan in Japan, the valuable advice from the founder of Naikan and current Naikan leaders in Japan is offered with our appreciation. Detailed information about the practice of Naikan and Constructive Living reflection may be found in *Plunging Through the Clouds* and *Flowing Bridges, Quiet Waters*.

Yoshimoto's Advice

Ishin Yoshimoto, Naikan's founder, considered the examination of self to be Naikan, whatever the student's purpose. He defined "bad" as having no earnest desire to know oneself. He held that the purpose for which each of us is born is to examine ourselves.

Naikansha (people who come to do Naikan reflection or Constructive Living reciprocity/reflection) should never be forced to do without food, drink, or sleep during Naikan. If, however, their Naikan leads them to request such deprivations, they are permitted to do so. A very few people find themselves distracted from their reflection by the serving and eating of meals. Eating is one of the limited pleasures for most Naikansha during Naikan, so it is important to have tasty and healthful meals. Mrs. Yoshimoto tries to fit food to the season (hot food in winter) and to the person (more food for big eaters). After three or four days of little exercise some appetites drop; others retain normal appetites right up to the end of the week.

The Naikansha doesn't come to do Naikan because of a guide's skill or fame. Strictly speaking, the Naikan guide ceases to be an instructor after the methods of Naikan are initially explained. While conducting the *mensetsu* interviews (the reporting of Naikan recollections), the guide's primary task is to listen. When the guide speaks, the Naikansha's repentance-filled voice stops. When the guide speaks too much and then stops, the Naikansha waits, and the guide feels some pressure to talk more in order to fill the silence. So the guide should take pains not to interrupt the flow of the interview with excess talking.

Nevertheless when the Naikansha strays from Naikan, the guide has some responsibility to redirect the thinking back along Naikan lines. For example, if the Naikansha begins a lengthy criticism of the mother, the guide's duty is to remind the Naikansha that Naikan is reflection on the self in regard to the mother. There is no need for the guide to become angry or upset about these lapses; a simple reminder is sufficient.

It's all right to query but not to preach. Don't expect newcomers to do as well on the first few days as those who have been doing Naikan for six or seven. If the Naikansha is not too good at first, just move on to the next theme. Once in every two or three interviews the guide may ask the Naikansha if there are any questions. This prompting gives the Naikansha the chance to ask anything that might be disturbing or interfering with the Naikan. It also gives the Naikansha the chance to continue some previous reporting that may have been cut off or interrupted during an earlier *mensetsu* interview.

While listening to Naikan reports, the guide should sit properly on the same level as the Naikansha. The Naikansha sees the guide's posture and responds with trust. The guide should put the hands together in greeting and respect for Naikansha. The *gassho* is not necessarily a religious hand position. One can hit a person effectively with one hand but not with both hands together in *gassho*. *Mensetsu* interviews should begin and end with courtesy. As the guide models the proper attitude, the Naikansha follows naturally.

Yoshimoto considered the Naikansha's voice to be that of the Buddha. Naikansha are the Buddha's representatives cautioning the guides and reminding us of our errors. The guide is not a moral judge. Yoshimoto remarked that when we see bad in other people, there are three general responses possible. We can (a) be angry; (b) have nothing to do with the transgressor; or (c) cry. The repentance of a Naikansha reminds guides that they, too, have done such things or even worse.

Tapes of classic Naikan reports may be played at mealtimes in order to provide models for Naikansha who are restrained or are having difficulty remembering. After hearing these tapes they may be asked how their Naikan compares with those they heard. Yoshimoto believed that such comparison promotes deeper Naikan.

Tears have no relation to Naikan depth. You can see students crying during their graduation ceremony, then laughing as they go out the school gate.

Yoshimoto asked Naikansha to continue Naikan on the train home, or while playing volleyball, or while watching television. The formal relationship with the Naikan guide, however, ends when the intensive Naikan ends. In extreme cases, wrote Yoshimoto, even when passing on the street the pair should ignore each other.

There is no need to know the details of the background or personal history of the Naikansha; his or her name and address are useful perhaps for follow-up. As you listen to the Naikansha, you will know what kind of people they are.

It is best to have one or at most two Naikan guides. Using a separate room where the guide waits for the Naikansha's report has the advantage that others can't hear, but has the disadvantages that the Naikansha's movement from the *byobu* to the reporting room may disturb the concentration of other Naikansha. Yoshimoto preferred that the guide make the effort to go to the *byobu* of the Naikansha, who represents the Buddha. Yoshimoto called the Naikan *byobu* the *hoza,* the holy place under the Bodhi tree where the Buddha attained enlightenment.

If someone talks and disturbs the others, he is asked to leave, his money is returned, and he is invited to come back in a few years if he is ready to do Naikan. A person who laughs and takes Naikan lightly isn't scolded directly. It is more effective to draw him into Naikan thinking with questions and comparisons with models on audio tapes. Some wish to leave Naikan during the week. The two main reasons for wanting to leave Naikan are not getting into it and wanting to begin repaying others immediately. For people who wish to leave Naikan early, a special tape is played of a Naikansha who stuck it out and went on to do fine Naikan. Another technique employed to delay early departure at Yoshimoto's Nara center is to postpone departure until night, when no transportation is available, and then suggest that the Naikansha stay and reconsider overnight. The hope is that perhaps during the night such a person will recall the faces of those who encouraged him or her to do Naikan and won't be able to leave. If these techniques fail, it is necessary to return the money and send the Naikansha home—the Naikansha must want to do Naikan.

Tobacco is allowed if doing without it interferes with Naikan, but the ideal is for the Naikansha to become so engrossed in Naikan that tobacco is given up voluntarily. If forced to do without smoking, the Naikansha might keep thinking about it and fail to do Naikan. Clearly, every detail of setting and procedure is designed to facilitate Naikan.

Written memo lists are allowed only for those who need them; when doing deep Naikan there is no time for writing, Yoshimoto believed.

Modern Naikan Leaders

Yoshihiko Miki and his wife, Junko, run the Nara Naikan Center. They offer the following: Turn responsibility for doing Naikan back to the Naikansha so that there is no dependency on the guide. No guide ever says that a Naikansha's Naikan is deep enough. The Nai-kansha's reporting gives hints to the guide about his or her own Nai-kan. Don't criticize or give up on any Naikansha. The guide sets up the maximal conditions for Naikan to occur with optimal food, bath, facilities, and so on. The Naikan guide is a model of the service and care provided by our surroundings all the time. As the Naikansha observe the service of the Naikan guide, they may be encouraged to do deeper Naikan.

Akira Ishii is an Aoyama Gakuin University professor who intro-duced and developed the practice of Naikan in Europe. His method of initiating Naikan in a group setting has been adapted for Construc-tive Living practice. A detailed account of his method may be found in *Rainbow Rising from a Stream*. He also extended Naikan practice in the area of journal Naikan—writing one's reflections in a journal to be read at some later date by a guide. Professor Ishii sometimes does Naikan interviews by telephone, at least once by telephone from an airplane.

A Naikan Calendar

This thirty-day calendar of Naikan sayings is translated from the Jap-anese. It is composed of quotes from the founder of Naikan, Ishin Yoshimoto. You may substitute the terms *self-reflection* or *self-examination* for *Naikan* in this collection of sayings if you prefer.

1. Intensive Naikan is basic preparation, but everyday Naikan is the real thing.

2. In life do Naikan and develop a thankful heart in order to prepare for death.

3. Please reflect on what you have received, what you have re-turned, and the troubles you have caused others.

4. Naikan was founded by the Buddha and Shinran; I'm just a small-time missionary.

5. You might die tonight.

6. Naikan looks at death.

7. The insect that is born and dies in summer doesn't know about spring and fall.

8. No one changes by hearing preaching.

9. Now how are you doing Naikan? What are you investigating?

10. If you died now, where would you go?

11. The most important work for a new bride is Naikan.

12. Intensive Naikan is like power poles, and daily Naikan is like power lines.

13. Faith or not is displayed in your everyday life.

14. Wholehearted commitment is better than waffling.

15. It is important to live each day with Naikan.

16. This evil, terrible me belongs in hell, so I'm grateful that now I can breathe so easily.

17. In order to build a big building, you must dig a deep foundation. Naikan is building a deep foundation for human life.

18. You are fooled by your mind into believing there is tomorrow, so you may waste today.

19. For what purpose were you born? Are you living facing that purpose?

20. The words we live with today become part of our lives tomorrow.

21. Wholeheartedly investigate yourself without holding back, for the purpose of enlightenment and peace of mind.

22. If you died now, your future life is a continuation of this one.

23. Naikan is the biggest and most final purpose for which you were born into human life.

24. If you are prompted to do Naikan, even if you're in the middle of rice planting or any other busy activity, come quickly.

25. Naikan is the great art of the human spirit.

26. Naikan is the entrance ceremony, not the graduation. It provides you with hearing ears and seeing eyes.

27. The purpose of Naikan is that no matter what the setbacks, you can live with gratitude and obligation, realigning the heart.

28. You can see whether you are creating deeds leading to heaven or hell.

29. The day you were born was the day your mother suffered.

30. Please, somehow just now turn your heart to Naikan.

Intensive Naikan Pitfalls

I am about to offer some criticisms of intensive Naikan. I do so recognizing and respecting the potency and utility of this method for both Easterners and Westerners. Naikan moves people, in many senses of the word *moves*.

Shinky people may like to do intensive Naikan because it allows them to escape from present reality. Their lives are pared down to what happens behind the screen of meditation. Constructive Living reflection exercises require some attention to present reality in order to accomplish them. For example in order to carry out a secret service, a student must pay attention to the habits of the recipient of the service. Similarly the Ten Thank-yous assignment requires that the student pay attention to the services of others in order to respond appropriately with a word of thanks.

In intensive Naikan there is a clear distinction between when one is doing it and when one is not. The time and place for intensive Naikan are set aside. Roles are identified. Even the formal procedure for the practice is spelled out in terms of the format for reporting Naikan, eating, and so forth. Constructive Living emphasizes that there is no time-out from this life.

Some CL instructors may believe that it is easier to determine when a student is doing intensive Naikan "properly" than to evaluate when a student is doing action CL properly. The narrow, ritualized frame for reporting intensive Naikan progress allows for a more circumscribed set of activities than everyday life. Yet the depth of Naikan was so difficult for even the founder of Naikan to determine that he eventually gave up on the attempt.

Another disadvantage of intensive Naikan is the image it conveys of the mystical East. Such a mystique may attract some to Naikan, but it will deflect many others from serious consideration of the practice for Western participants. In Constructive Living we have adapted the ideas and methods borrowed from many times and places to be useful and appealing to the widest possible population. Reflection exercises in CL may puzzle and even irritate some students, but they are straightforward and easy to understand in Eastern and Western contexts.

A trap of intensive Naikan that is peculiar to the Constructive Living context is its occasional encroachment on the time that would otherwise be spent in teaching specific CL principles and techniques. New students may be intrigued and eager to learn this powerful and perspective-altering method. They may then lose the opportunity to learn other useful tactics for dealing with everyday life.

These pitfalls notwithstanding, Naikan remains a powerful tool to change the minds of humans so that we become more realistic. I am not concerned with producing gratitude, a feeling that comes and goes, but with helping people see reality as it is. That is the purpose of both the reciprocity/reflection and the action aspects of Constructive Living, and of science as well.

Bibliography

Books

HOFFMAN, YOEL.
  Every End Exposed. Brookline, MA: Autumn Press, 1977.
MERTON, THOMAS.
  The Springs of Contemplation. New York: Farrar, Straus & Giroux, 1992.
REYNOLDS, DAVID K.
  Morita Psychotherapy. (English, Japanese, and Spanish editions.) Berkeley: University of California Press, 1976.
  ———. *The Quiet Therapies.* Honolulu: University of Hawaii Press, 1980.
  ———. *The Heart of the Japanese People.* Tokyo: Nichieisha, 1980.
  ———. *Naikan Psychotherapy: Meditation for Self-development.* Chicago: University of Chicago Press, 1983.
  ———. *Constructive Living.* Honolulu: University of Hawaii Press, 1984.
  ———. *Living Lessons.* Tokyo: Asahi Shuppansha, 1984.
  ———. *Modern Aesop's Fables.* Tokyo: Nichieisha, 1984.
  ———. *Playing Ball on Running Water.* New York: Morrow, 1984.
  ———. *Even in Summer the Ice Doesn't Melt.* New York: Morrow, 1986.

———. *Water Bears No Scars.* New York: Morrow, 1987.

———. *Constructive Living for Young People.* Tokyo: Asahi, 1988.

———. *Winning the Game of Life.* Tokyo: Asahi, 1988.

———. *Pools of Lodging for the Moon.* New York: Morrow, 1989.

———. *A Thousand Waves.* New York: Morrow, 1990.

———. *Thirsty, Swimming in the Lake.* New York: Morrow, 1991.

———. *Rainbow Rising from a Stream.* New York: Morrow, 1992.

———. *Reflections on the Tao Te Ching.* New York: Morrow, 1993.

REYNOLDS, DAVID K., ED.

Flowing Bridges, Quiet Waters. Albany: SUNY Press, 1989.

———. *Plunging Through the Clouds.* Albany: SUNY Press, 1993.

REYNOLDS, DAVID K., AND FARBEROW, NORMAN L.

Suicide: Inside and Out. Berkeley: University of California Press, 1976.

———. *Endangered Hope.* Berkeley: University of California Press, 1977.

Book Chapters

REYNOLDS, DAVID K.

"Morita Therapy in America." In Kora, T., and Ohara, K., eds. *Modern Morita Therapy.* Tokyo: Hakuyosha, 1977.

———. "Morita Psychotherapy." In Corsini, R., ed. *Handbook of Innovative Psychotherapies.* New York: Wiley, 1981.

———. "Naikan Therapy." In Corsini, R., ed. *Handbook of Innovative Psychotherapies.* New York: Wiley, 1981.

———. "Psychocultural Perspectives on Death." In Ahmed, P., ed. *Living and Dying with Cancer.* New York: Elsevier, 1981.

———. "Japanese Models of Psychotherapy." In Norbeck, E., and Lock, M., eds. *Health, Illness, and Medical Care in Japan.* Honolulu: University of Hawaii Press, 1987.

———. "Morita Therapy in America." In Ohara, K., ed. *Morita Therapy: Theory and Practice.* Tokyo: Kongen, 1987. (In Japanese.)

————. "On Being Natural: Two Japanese Approaches to Healing." In Sheikh, A. A., and Sheikh, K. S., eds. *Eastern and Western Approaches to Healing*. New York: Wiley, 1989.

REYNOLDS, DAVID K., AND YAMAMOTO, JOE.
"Morita Psychotherapy in Japan." In Masserman, Jules, ed. *Current Psychiatric Therapies* 13 (1973): 219–227.

Articles

————. "Naikan Therapy: An Experiential View." *International Journal of Social Psychiatry* 23, no. 4 (1977): 252–264.

————. "Psychodynamic Insight and Morita Psychotherapy." *Japanese Journal of Psychotherapy Research* 5, no. 4 (1979): 58–60.

————. "Morita Therapy and Reality-Centered Living." *International Bulletin of Morita Therapy* 1, no. 1 (1988): 35.

————. "Meaningful Life Therapy." *Culture, Medicine and Psychiatry* 13 (1989): 457–463.

REYNOLDS, DAVID K., AND KIEFER, C. W.
"Cultural Adaptability as an Attribute of Therapies: The Case of Morita Psychotherapy." *Culture, Medicine, and Psychiatry* 1 (1977): 395–412.

REYNOLDS, DAVID K., AND MOACANIN, RADMILA.
"Eastern Therapy: Western Patient." *Japanese Journal of Psychotherapy Research* 3 (1976): 305–316.

Tapes

KRECH, GREGG.
Doing a Good Job. Arlington, Va.: TôDô Institute, 1989.
————. *Naikan*. Arlington, Va.: TôDô Institute, 1990.

REYNOLDS, DAVID K.
The Sound of Rippling Water. Arlington, Va.: TôDô Institute, 1987.

———. *The Mountain Flows; The River Sits.* Arlington, Va.: TôDô Institute, 1989.

———. *Doing What Needs to Be Done.* San Francisco: New Dimensions Foundation, 1990.

Contact Information

For information about the nearest Constructive Living instruction and Constructive Living group programs, call:

New York	(914) 339-9637
New York City	(212) 348-4990
Washington, D.C.	(301) 530-5356
San Francisco	(415) 584-0626
Los Angeles	(213) 389-4088
Chicago	(708) 848-6238
Cleveland	(216) 321-0442
New England	(802) 352-9018
Kansas City	(913) 362-2119
Jacksonville	(904) 389-3015
British Columbia	(604) 247-2032
Japan	(0473) 33-5830
England	(0884) 254-101

or contact Dr. Reynolds:

Constructive Living
P.O. Box 85
Coos Bay, Oregon 97420

Telephone: (541) or (503) 269-5591

Index

A

acceptance, 60, 77, 78
actors, 17
addictions, 182–186
Addleton, Robert, 264
Anderson, Linda, 264–266
anxiety, 179–182
apology letter, 215, 227
Ardman, Perri, 141, 265
assignments, 206–218, 221–224, 228
attention, 211
attention exercise, 9

B

behavior-centered, 13
boundaries, 90
Boyle, Trudy, 265
Burke, Howard, 141
Bush, Simon, 140
Butler, Crilly, Jr., 265

C

candidates for CL, 6
Casavant, Richard, 265
Clark, Mel, 264
codependency, 172
comparison of Morita therapy and CL, 95–98
compulsions, 182–186
computations, 216–217, 227
confidence, 3–4

D

daily reflection, 216
death, 271–272
depression, 199–201
desires, 126–127
distraction, 14–16, 181
Dogen, 121
dying, 27–28

E

ecstatic feelings, 82

F

fear, 179–182
feeling-centered, 4, 13, 33, 58
freedom in behavior, 10
Freeman, Victoria Register, 160

G

gambling, 204–205
gratitude, 39–40
Green, Cindy, 266
Green, Ron, 266
grief, 194–196
Guroff, Juliet, 266

H

Hassanzadeh, Said, 265
Hindery, Twila, 141
Hometchko, Kay, 140
Hoppe, Daniel, 266
Hudson, David, 266

I

impatience, 187–189
influencing feelings, 17–19
Inoue, Noriaki, 121
insecurity, 203–204
intensive Naikan, 42–44, 66, 273–280
International Bulletin of Morita Therapy (IBMT), 265
interpersonal relations, 192–194, 245–250
Ippen, 237
Ishii, Akira, 262, 277
Ishiyama, F. Ishu, 262

J

jiriki, 36–37, 51, 55, 237
job interview, 17–18
Johnson, Carl R., 139

Jones, Paul, 139, 141
journal, 211

K

Kahn, Henry, 265
Kahn, Susan, 232–233, 265
kernel of good, 61
Klohr, Kathy, 141
koans, 228–229
Krech, Gregg, 209, 264–266

L

Larsen, Lynn, 140
letters to self, 229
listening, 243–244

M

Madson, Patricia Ryan, 140, 251, 265
Madson, Ron, 251, 265
maxims, 139–142, 212
Meaningful Life Therapy (MLT), 265
meditation, 84
Mental Health Okamoto Memorial Foundation, 265
mental health professionals, xiii, 5, 12, 25, 33, 102, 130, 182
Merton, Thomas, 110
Miki, Junko, 276–277
Miki, Yoshihiko, 276–277
Mitomo, Shonosuke, 97, 110
Mitteregger, Gottfried, 265
Miyamoto, Musashi, 121
Mizutani, Keiji, 97, 109
Morita, Masatake, ix, 52, 53, 55, 94, 96, 117, 121, 134, 243, 262, 271

Moy, Annette, 266
Mullen, Peter, 141
Murphy, Gary, 141
Murray, Marilyn, 265
myths about feelings, 20

N

no-self, 54

O

Ogi, Haruyo, 265
Ogle, Peggy, 141
Ohara, Kenshiro, 97, 265

P

pain, 194–197
paralysis by feelings, 83
Paterno, Frederic, 266
peace of mind, 58–59
Peterson, Diana, 265
practice, 98
procrastination, 189–192
proper speech, 212–213, 226
psychotherapy, 79–81, 95, 99–108, 115, 116
Puckett, Mary J., 265
purpose, 21

R

reality, 25–27
risk, 204–205

Roberts, Jim, 141
Rybold, Daniel, 266

S

sabotage, 71–72
Saperstein, Philip, 265
Saperstein, Sheila, 265
Sarah, Barbara, 139, 265–266
scheduling, 184–185
secret service, 214
self-esteem, 172
Shapiro, Rami, 266
Shinfuku, Dr. N., 263
shinkeishitsu, 6, 96, 97, 111–114, 115, 132
shyness, 186–187
silence, 208, 209
stages of development, 22–25
Stewart, Patricia, 266
stress, 201–203
suicide, 19
Summer, Ed, 266
Suzuki, Tomonori, 94, 95

T

taiken, 62
tales, 148–165, 212
tariki, 36–37, 51, 55, 237
temper, 187–189
thank-you letters, 214–215, 227
themes of CL action, 20–22
Thomas, Mary Ann, 258, 266
TôDô Institute, 264
Tohma, Mihoko, 266

toraware, 97, 132
trackless assignment, 228

W

waiting, 16–17, 120–121, 181
waves, reality's, 52
Willms, Gregory, 209, 251, 266
Wong, Yen Lu, 266
Woodward, Joan, 266
workaholics, 63

Y

Yoshimoto, Ishin, ix, 35, 52, 53, 55, 66, 69, 262, 271, 273–279

Z

Zamora, Jesus, 266
Zen, 78, 121, 123